What people are saying about …

COLD-CASE CHRISTIANITY

"My friend J. Warner Wallace is one of the most thoughtful and winsome apologists for the gospel I know. *Cold-Case Christianity* is literally packed with insights to share with the skeptics in your life, and this book will give you the confidence to share it!"

Dr. Rick Warren, author of *The Purpose-Driven Life* and pastor of Saddleback Church

"*Cold-Case Christianity* is a fantastic book. I wish I had this resource when I first examined the Christian faith. It would have answered many of my questions and helped set me on the track to truth."

Josh McDowell, speaker and author of *Evidence That Demands a Verdict*

"What happens when an atheist cop takes the same forensic skills he uses to solve the toughest crimes—homicides with a trail that's been cold for decades—and applies them to the eyewitness testimony and circumstantial evidence for the life of Jesus of Nazareth? A fascinating new approach to the question of gospel credibility, that's what. *Cold-Case Christianity* is simply the most clever and compelling defense I've ever read for the reliability of the New Testament record. Case closed."

Gregory Koukl, president of Stand to Reason and author of *Tactics: A Game Plan for Discussing Your Christian Convictions*

"*Cold-Case Christianity* offers a fresh approach to biblical fact-finding that actually makes apologetics fun! I highly recommend it to anyone interested in the evidence that backs up the Christian faith, whether you're a skeptic, a spiritual seeker, or a committed believer. Everyone will benefit from reading J. Warner Wallace's powerful new book."

Mark Mittelberg, author of *The Questions Christians Hope No One Will Ask (with answers)* and coauthor of *Becoming a Contagious Christian*

"The moment I heard of J. Warner Wallace's idea for a book, I thought it was one of the freshest ideas I'd heard in a long time. And now seeing the book in hand, he totally delivers. This is one of the most fun and clever ways to learn just how strong and enduring the case for Christianity is. I've always maintained that if we apply standard tools of investigation in an unbiased way that Christian truth claims would be vindicated. Jim's 'cold-case' detective work shows this idea to be right on the money."

Craig J. Hazen, PhD, founder and director of the Christian Apologetics Program, Biola University, and author of *Five Sacred Crossings*

"Today Americans are searching for truth. The most fundamental truth is the reality of a sovereign God. During his journey from agnosticism to apologetics, J. Warner Wallace uses his 'cold-case' investigative techniques to prove the reality of the divine. READ his book. You will not regret it."

William G. Boykin, LTG(R) US Army, executive vice president of Family Research Council, former deputy undersecretary of Defense for Intelligence, and founding member of US Army Delta Force

"*Cold-Case Christianity* reads like the fast-paced detective drama it actually is. The book is chock full of interesting evidence and arguments, and it is unique among the literature in exhibiting a legal-reasoning approach to the evidence for and against historic Christianity. I enthusiastically endorse this great book and thank J. Warner Wallace for his excellent work."

J.P. Moreland, Distinguished Professor of Philosophy, Biola University, and author of *The God Question*

"*Cold-Case Christianity* is one of the most insightful, interesting, and helpful books in defending the faith I have read in a long time. Whether you are a Christian or a skeptic, J. Warner Wallace will challenge you to consider the evidence through fresh eyes. I have been studying the evidence for the faith for many years, and yet Jim helped me look at the historical, scientific, and philosophical facts in a new way. I could not recommend it more highly."

Sean McDowell, educator, speaker, and author of *Is God Just a Human Invention?*

"J. Warner Wallace's *Cold-Case Christianity* offers a fascinating angle on the evidence for the resurrection of Jesus. While Wallace does have experience as a former atheist—a bonus feature—he brings his expertise as a cold-case detective to bear on the forensic aspects of the events surrounding the first Easter. This book is a unique contribution to the growing literature on Jesus's resurrection."

Paul Copan, professor and Pledger Family Chair of
Philosophy and Ethics, Palm Beach Atlantic University

"As a longtime prosecutor, I have come to appreciate the persuasive power of a circumstantial case. J. Warner Wallace has made a career investigating 'cold-case' homicides. He now brings that dogged pursuit of truth and hard-nosed judgment to the world of ancient documents, witness statements, and changed lives. From forensic statement analysis to assessment of motives to an in-depth analysis of what makes conspiracies tick, Jim presents the material in a way that is both readily accessible but also sufficiently in-depth to carry the 'burden of proof.'"

Al Serrato, assistant district attorney, State of California

"Detective J. Warner Wallace is as creative telling a story as he is solving a crime. This is his ultimate case, where he investigates his own personal transformation by applying many lessons he learned on the job."

Robert Dean, producer of *Dateline NBC*

"J. Warner Wallace, my colleague in the fraternity of law enforcement, has made a valuable contribution to this generation and those to come. His book has the potential of becoming a classic for those seeking truth. Jim does a superb job of using the discipline and logic of a police detective as a matrix through which to examine the evidence for God, Jesus, the reliability of Scripture, and the message of the gospel. Skeptics, seekers, and committed believers will all find his analysis interesting and compelling. Armchair detectives and scholars alike will treasure this work. This book will be an important resource in my personal library."

Robert L. Vernon, assistant chief of police (ret.) LAPD,
and founder of Pointman Leadership Institute

"WARNING: Do not start reading this book unless you have time set aside. You will NOT be able to put it down. This is a one-of-a-kind, groundbreaking book that everyone should read. J. Warner is in a unique position to investigate the claims of Christianity. He is quickly becoming my favorite apologist. Twelve stars out of a possible ten!"

Don Stewart, host of *Pastor's Perspective* and author of over seventy books

"Cold-Case Christianity reads like an exciting detective novel and a textbook at the same time. Using his seasoned detective skills, J. Warner Wallace builds an incredible case that Christianity must be true. I'd love to bring him to every college campus in America to present his case and let the students be the jury."

Rick Schenker, president of Ratio Christi, the
University Student Apologetics Alliance

"With his background as a detective, J. Warner Wallace is qualified to sift through evidence and reach well-reasoned conclusions. Warner's *Cold-Case Christianity* is therefore unique among apologetics resources available today: The historical facts and related evidence are examined via the same protocols that a professional investigator would follow in handling a case. Wherever one falls on the faith spectrum—Christian, skeptic, or somewhere in-between—Warner's application of investigative principles in his examination of Christianity makes for a must-read contribution to the realm of apologetics."

Alex McFarland, author of the best-selling *10 Most Common Objections to Christianity*, and apologetics director, North Greenville University

"I am fortunate to be both J. Warner Wallace's friend and former chief and thoroughly enjoyed reading *Cold-Case Christianity.* Jim is a seasoned and incredibly skillful investigator who has a real talent for uncovering the important pieces of evidence and logically linking them together to arrive at the truth. This book is a compelling investigative work paralleling the steps Jim takes while investigating a crime with the steps he has taken to reveal the truth about Christ. *Cold-Case Christianity* is a bright light that illuminates the truth in a persuasive and convicting style."

Jim Herren, chief of police, UCLA Police Department

"I have had the pleasure of working with J. Warner Wallace for the past twenty-five years, and it is what I have learned from him that I cherish the most. His brilliant work, *Cold-Case Christianity*, provides readers with an opportunity to learn from Jim's experiences as a cold-case detective and discover his true passion—a passion that is equally matched by his character, knowledge, and wisdom. *Cold-Case Christianity* has opened a new resource for all to see and displays the endless contributions Jim has made to Christianity."

John J. Neu, chief of police, Torrance Police Department

"The work of an investigator requires an eye for observation and a mind to recognize its relevance. God has blessed Jim Wallace with such gifts. Those gifts have been sharpened by years of use and proved in such works as this. In the tradition of the great Sir Robert Anderson of Scotland Yard, Wallace digs for the facts and presents them reasonably."

Ken Graves, speaker and pastor of Calvary Chapel, Bangor, Maine

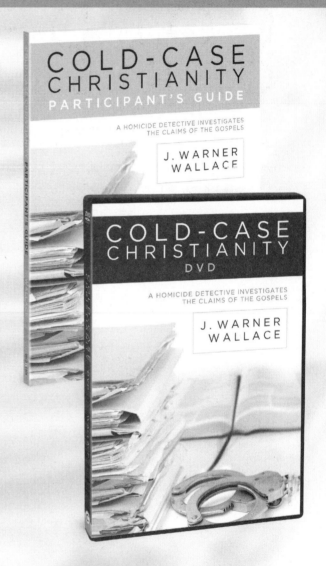

COLD-CASE
CHRISTIANITY

A HOMICIDE DETECTIVE INVESTIGATES
THE CLAIMS OF THE GOSPELS

J. WARNER
WALLACE

David C Cook®
transforming lives together

COLD-CASE CHRISTIANITY
Published by David C Cook
4050 Lee Vance Drive
Colorado Springs, CO 80918 U.S.A.

Integrity Music Limited, a Division of David C Cook
Brighton, East Sussex BN1 2RE, England

LCCN 2012951458
ISBN 978-1-4347-0469-6
eISBN 978-1-4347-0546-4

© 2013 J. Warner Wallace
Published in association with the literary agency of Mark Sweeney and Associates,
28540 Altessa Way, Apt. 201, Bonita Springs, FL 34135.

The Team: Don Pape, John Blase, Amy Konyndyk, Renada Arens, Karen Athen
Cover Design: Nick Lee
Cover Photos: Shutterstock, stock.xchng
Illustrations: J. Warner Wallace

Printed in the United States of America
First Edition 2013

19 20 21 22 23 24 25 26 27

022819

CONTENTS

SPECIAL THANKS:

My deepest thanks to Sean McDowell for motivating me to write this book and for being a true brother in the faith, to Craig Hazen for being the most enthusiastic encourager and connecting me to the people who made the book a reality, to Lee Strobel for having the heart and desire to support this work, and to my literary agent, Mark Sweeney, for answering every phone call and taking a chance with a cold-case detective.

This book is dedicated to my best friend, most trusted partner, and smartest critic—my wife and inspiration, Susie. Thanks for being the first person to read every word and for helping me to be the kind of man who would even dream about writing a book.

LEE STROBEL

I loved hanging out with homicide detectives.

I started my journalism career as a general assignment reporter on the overnight shift at the *Chicago Tribune*, and that meant covering the frequent murders committed around the city—crime-syndicate hits, gang-related violence, domestic disputes gone awry, robberies that got out of hand. Later I was assigned to the criminal courts, where I reported on the major homicide trials from around Cook County.

All of which meant that I spent a lot of time interviewing and socializing with homicide detectives. I liked them because they were no-nonsense, get-to-the-point people, with an uncanny ability to cut through the fog of deception that defendants used to cover their tracks. These street-toughened investigators were seldom fooled by a phony alibi or a flimsy excuse as they systematically unraveled the mysteries that confounded everyone else. They were evidence driven—"just the facts, ma'am," as the old Jack Webb character in *Dragnet* used to say—and so was I, constantly checking and rechecking my information before publishing my reports for the city to see.

Back then, I was an atheist. I thought that faith in God was based on conjecture, wishful thinking, and emotions; in fact, the idea that there might be evidence supporting the existence of God was totally alien to me. And I wasn't alone.

J. Warner Wallace is a cold-case homicide investigator who also started out as an outspoken spiritual skeptic. He began with the assumption that the supernatural was impossible. Yet when he diligently applied his skills as a detective—allowing the evidence to take him wherever it would lead—he came to a far different conclusion. Assessing the evidence with razor-like precision, he solved the most important mystery of all time—whether Jesus of Nazareth is the unique Son of God.

In his savvy and captivating book, Jim will introduce you to the kinds of tools and techniques that he routinely uses to crack unsolved murders that have long baffled other cops. He will show you how this same analytical thinking can be used to crack the case of a long-ago killing on a cross—and the incredible resurrection that followed. It's a fascinating process, with Jim drawing on his quarter century of police experience to explain how and why the evidence of history decisively tips the scales in favor of Christianity.

If you're a spiritual skeptic like Jim and I were for many years, then you'll find this investigative adventure to be an irresistible, eye-opening, and potentially life-changing journey, full of helpful insights and wisdom. Like a good cop, I hope you'll pursue the evidence to the conclusion it ultimately supports. That verdict, in the end, will be yours to reach.

If you're a follower of Jesus, then Jim's account will not only bolster your own faith, but also sharpen your skills in explaining to others why so many incisive thinkers throughout history have concluded that Christianity is uniquely credible and trustworthy.

Undoubtedly, you've seen media stories that have traced how cold-case detectives have pieced together an evidential puzzle in order to solve the most perplexing of homicides. Perhaps one of those accounts was based on a case that Jim actually helped crack. But as important as these investigations are, none of them approach the significance of the case that this book tackles.

So get ready to shadow Jim as he probes the evidence for faith. You'll find his approach to be compelling, his logic to be sound, and his conclusions to be amply supported. Unravel with him the historical case for Jesus—and discover its eternal implications for you and all the people you know.

Lee Strobel, author of The Case for Christ *and* The Case for Faith; *www.LeeStrobel.com*

RICE BROOCKS

Over one hundred years ago, the German philosopher Friedrich Nietzsche boldly proclaimed that God is dead. This would become an anthem, of sorts, for atheists and skeptics of the time period who predicted that the scientific revolution of the twentieth century would eventually bury not only God but all religious faith and bothersome morality.

What they didn't foresee were inquisitive individuals such as cold-case detective J. Warner Wallace investigating this alleged death of God to determine the validity of the claim. At the time of his own personal inquiry, Wallace was an atheist with a vested interest in confirming that this "death" was indeed real. Utilizing his skills as a homicide detective, he began to diligently sift through the evidence. It wasn't long before he had come to the completely opposite conclusion from that of Nietzsche. Indeed, God was and is alive and well, in spite of the loud pronouncements to the contrary from the ranks of the unbelieving.

This book, *Cold-Case Christianity*, is the chronicle of Wallace's journey from atheism to faith as well as a reliable road map out of the darkness of unbelief for all who are sincerely searching for the truth. Like countless others before him, Wallace discovered that the truth of Christian faith rests on the credible testimony recorded in the New Testament Gospels. Far from the distorted caricatures presented by skeptics, the portraits of Jesus's life, death and resurrection from the dead bear the marks of genuine eyewitness testimony.

The results of these findings not only transformed Wallace's personal life but his professional career as well. After twenty-five years of working as a detective helping solve the most mysterious of murder cases, he has since become a renowned spokesperson for the Christian faith, touching the lives of millions of people around the world. His unique background as a detective has made him the spiritual version of Sherlock Holmes, helping shed light on the evidence for God's existence as well as uncovering and exposing the malevolent schemes of the forces of darkness spoken about in Scripture.

Working at an exhausting pace as he writes and speaks, Wallace challenges thousands each month to become Christian "case makers" by becoming reliable guides to others needing to hear a credible presentation about the truth of Christianity. His voice is one of the most unique and inspiring you will ever hear. He has injected a fresh approach—as well as tenacity and contagious enthusiasm—into the world of Christian apologetics. His relentless passion for truth will inspire you to cast aside any vestiges of apathy or ignorance and immediately get involved in the great challenge of reaching this generation for Christ.

For someone like me, a Christian minister reaching out to university students around the world, Wallace's work has been a source of tremendous encouragement. The number of young people abandoning the Christian faith after leaving home is of great concern to me. In fact, it is what led me to write the book *God's Not Dead*, which inspired a movie by the same name and helped millions know that there is, indeed, substantive evidence for God's existence. The movie was so successful that I was approached about helping with the script for a sequel. One of the first things I mentioned to the screenwriters was the story of Jim Wallace and his journey as a detective from skepticism to faith. I arranged a meeting with Jim and the writers, and after spending a short time with him, they looked at me and said, "Wow—he's amazing." I couldn't agree more, and you are about to find that out for yourself as you read this fantastic book.

The filmmakers were so impressed with Jim that they wrote a section in the script that features a court room drama—a very familiar environment for him through the years. In a tense and dramatic exchange with an antagonistic attorney attempting to discredit a high-school teacher for daring to mention Jesus Christ in a public classroom, Jim defends the fact that Jesus indeed lived and that the four Gospels are reliable records of His words, and therefore, quoting Jesus is not just an expression of religious faith but a matter of history.

Whether or not you see the movie *God's Not Dead 2*, carefully reading and studying this book will turn you into a catalyst for change in a world desperately in need of faith. Though Jim is definitely one of a kind, the lessons taught in *Cold-Case Christianity* can be grasped and retold by anyone desiring to bring the truth of the gospel of Jesus Christ to others.

Rice Broocks, author of God's Not Dead: Evidence for God in an Age of Uncertainty

THE DETECTIVE WAY

I got the call at about 1:00 a.m. Detectives who are assigned to the homicide unit also investigate officer-involved shootings (OISs), and all of us on the OIS team were called out for this one. When I arrived at the scene, Officer Mark Walker was standing by his patrol car, talking with a sergeant, and waiting for our arrival. I shook his hand, made sure he was ready to talk about the shooting, and began to walk through the events that precipitated our "callout."

Mark told me that he was working patrol when he saw a man driving down the street, swerving from lane to lane as though he was drunk. He pulled the driver over and approached his car. When he leaned in to talk to the man, he could smell the alcohol on his breath. Mark asked the man to step out from the car, and the driver reluctantly complied. As the man stood outside his car, Mark could see that he was angry and defiant. Mark decided to conduct a quick "pat-down" search to make sure the irritated driver wasn't carrying any weapons. Mark had no idea that the driver was Jacob Stevens, a parolee with a long arrest record in an adjacent city. Jacob had just been released from state prison. He was on parole for an assault charge, and tonight he was carrying a loaded Colt .45-caliber pistol hidden in his waistband. Jacob knew that he would go back to jail if the gun was discovered, and he was determined to stay out of jail.

When Mark asked Jacob Stevens to turn around so he could conduct the pat-down search, Jacob turned away for a moment, pulled his gun, and then turned back toward Mark, pointing the gun at Mark's chest.

"I knew that he had the drop on me," Mark told me as he recalled the events. "His gun was already drawn and pointed at me before I could even get my hand on mine."

Jacob had no intention of discussing the situation with Mark. He'd already decided that he wasn't going back to jail, even if it meant killing this police officer. Jacob pointed his gun at Mark and started to squeeze the trigger. Mark was about to enter the fight of his life, and he was starting off with a distinct disadvantage; he was already seconds behind his opponent.

All of us who work in law enforcement understand the importance of wearing our bullet-proof vests. When we first became officers, we were trained with these vests, and at some point most of us were shown how the vests performed in *live-fire* tests. We knew that they could stop a bullet, including a .45 round. On this night, Mark was going to put his vest to the test.

"I just tensed my stomach muscles and prepared to take the shot as I pulled my gun out of the holster. I knew he was going to get the first round off."

While Mark knew *that* his vest could sustain the impact of a .45-caliber round, tonight he trusted *in* the vest for the very first time. In that singular moment, Mark went from "belief that" to "belief in." It's one thing to believe that the vest can save a life; it's another thing to trust it to save your own life. Mark obviously survived the shooting and lived to describe it for us. The lesson I learned from Mark, however, had far more impact on my life than he would ever know.

FROM "BELIEF THAT" TO "BELIEF IN"

I was thirty-five years old before I first paid attention to a pastor's sermon. A fellow officer had been inviting me to church for many months, and while I was able to put him off for some time, I eventually acquiesced and attended a Sunday-morning service with my family. I managed to ignore most of what the pastor talked about until he began to paint a picture of Jesus that caught my attention. He characterized Jesus as a really smart guy who had some remarkably wise things to say about life, family, relationships, and work. I began to believe *that* this might be true. While I was uninterested in bowing my knee to Jesus as God, I was at least willing to listen to Jesus as a teacher. A week later I purchased my first Bible.

My friends knew me as an angry atheist, a skeptic who thoughtfully dissected Christians and the Christian worldview, yet I suddenly found myself reading the Gospels to hear what Jesus had to say. Something about the Gospels caught my attention, more as an investigator than as someone interested in the ancient philosophy of an imaginary sage. By this time in my life, I had already served as a patrol officer and a member of the Gang Detail, the Metro

Team (investigating street narcotics), the SWAT Team, and the Crime Impact Team (investigating career criminals). I had interviewed hundreds (if not thousands) of eyewitnesses and suspects. I had become familiar with the nature of eyewitness statements, and I understood how testimony was evaluated in a court of law. Something about the Gospels struck me as more than mythological storytelling. The Gospels actually appeared to be ancient eyewitness accounts.

I conducted so many interviews and had such success getting suspects to "cop-out" that my department sent me to a number of investigative schools to refine my skills; I was eventually trained in Forensic Statement Analysis (FSA). By carefully employing this methodology and scrutinizing a suspect's choice of pronouns, use of tensed language, compression or expansion of time (along with many other linguistic tendencies), I was typically able to determine if he or she committed the crime, and I could often establish the time of day when the crime actually occurred! If this technique could provide me with such incredible insight into the statements of suspects and witnesses, why couldn't it be used to investigate the claims of the Gospels? I began to use FSA as I studied the gospel of Mark. Within a month, and in spite of my deep skepticism and hesitation, I concluded that Mark's gospel was the eyewitness account of the apostle Peter. I was beginning to move from a belief *that* Jesus was a wise teacher to a belief *in* what He said about Himself. I began a journey from casual assent to committed trust, from *belief that* to *belief in*.

In my current assignment, I investigate cold-case murders. Unlike other lesser crimes, an unsolved homicide is never closed; time doesn't *run out* on a murder investigation. My particular agency has dozens of unsolved murders that remain open, waiting for someone to take the time to reexamine them. There are many similarities between investigating cold cases and investigating the claims of Christianity. Cold-case homicides are events from the distant past for which there is often little or no forensic evidence. These kinds of cases are sometimes solved on the basis of eyewitness testimony, even though many years have passed between the point of the crime and the point of the investigation. While there may not be any surviving eyewitnesses to the actual murder, there are often witnesses available who can help puzzle together the events leading up to the crime or the behavior of a suspect following the crime. These witnesses can be evaluated in a number of ways to confirm their reliability. In the end, a strong "circumstantial" case can usually be made by collecting witness statements and verifying these observations with what little forensic evidence is available. By taking this approach, I have arrested and successfully prosecuted a number of cold-case suspects who thought they had gotten away with murder.

Christianity makes a claim about an event from the distant past for which there is little or no forensic evidence. Like cold cases, the truth about what happened can be discovered by examining the statements of eyewitnesses and comparing them with what little additional evidence is accessible to us. If the eyewitnesses can be evaluated (and their statements can be verified by what we have available), an equally strong circumstantial case can be made for the claims of the New Testament. But are there any reliable eyewitness statements in existence to corroborate in the first place? This became the most important question I had to answer in my personal investigation of Christianity. Were the gospel narratives *eyewitness accounts,* or were they only *moralistic mythologies?* Were the Gospels reliable, or were they filled with untrustworthy, supernatural absurdities? The most important questions I could ask about Christianity just so happened to fall within my area of expertise.

I hope to share some of that expertise with you in this book. Somewhere on my journey from "belief that" to "belief in," a friend told me about C. S. Lewis. After reading *Mere Christianity*, I purchased everything Lewis had written. One quote from *God in the Dock* stuck with me through the years. Lewis correctly noted, "Christianity is a statement which, if false, is of no importance, and, if true, is of infinite importance. The one thing it cannot be is moderately important."[1] Christianity, if it is true, is worthy of our investigation. Over the years I've retained my skepticism and my desperate need to examine the facts, even as I've journeyed from "belief that" to "belief in." I am still a detective, after all. I think I've learned a few things that may help you investigate the truth claims of the Bible.

I will tell you up front that I am going to provide you with a number of examples from my career as a homicide and cold-case detective as I share what I've learned over the years; I will be telling some *cop stories.* I've carefully edited these examples, however, changing the names of those who were involved and modifying the details of each case slightly to protect the officers and victims. I've had the privilege of working some of the most important and well-publicized cases our city has encountered in the past twenty years. While I want you to learn from what we did right and what we did wrong, I want to respect the privacy of the detectives (and victims' families) along the way.

If you're a skeptic who rejects the Bible like I did, my experiences and insights might help you assess the gospel writers in a new light. If you're someone who has encountered Christians who were unprepared to defend what they believe, I'd like to encourage you to be patient with us because the Christian tradition is actually intellectually robust and satisfying, even if we believers are occasionally unable to respond to your challenges. The answers are available; you don't have to turn off your brain to be a believer. Yes, it is possible to become a Christian *because* of the evidence rather than *in spite* of the evidence. Many of us have done just that.

If you're already a believer, my experiences might provide you with a few tools that can help you defend your faith in a more vigorous and informed way. You may learn something new about the history of Christianity or the nature and power of evidence. I want to encourage you to become an informed Christian, to worship God with your mind, and to prepare yourself as a Christian *case maker*. Let's start by examining ten simple principles of evidence that may change the way you look at Christianity forever.

LEARN TO BE A DETECTIVE

Ten important principles every aspiring detective needs to master

Chapter 1
Principle #1:

DON'T BE A "KNOW-IT-ALL"

"Jeffries and Wallace," Alan barked impatiently as the young officer scrambled to write our names on the crime-scene entry log. Alan lifted the yellow tape and passed beneath it, crouching painfully from the stress he had to place on his bad knee. "I'm getting too old for this," he said as he unbuttoned the coat of his suit. "The middle of the night gets later every time they call us out."

This was my first homicide scene, and I didn't want to make a fool of myself. I had been working robberies for many years, but I had never been involved in a suspicious death investigation before. I was worried that my movements in the crime scene might contaminate it in some way. I took small, measured steps and followed Detective Alan Jeffries around like a puppy. Alan had been working in this detail for over fifteen years; he was only a few years short of retirement. He was knowledgeable, opinionated, confident, and grumpy. I liked him a lot.

We stood there for a moment and looked at the victim's body. She was lying partially naked on her bed, strangled. There was no sign of a struggle and no sign of forced entry into her condominium, just a forty-six-year-old woman lying dead in a very unflattering position. My mind was racing as I tried to recall everything I had learned in the two-week homicide school I recently attended. I knew there were important pieces of evidence that needed to be preserved and collected. My mind struggled to assess the quantity of "data" that presented itself at the scene. What was the relationship between the evidence and the killer? Could the scene be reconstructed to reveal his or her identity?

"Hey, wake up!" Alan's tone shattered my thoughts. "We got a killer to catch here. Go find me her husband; he's the guy we're lookin' for."

What? Alan already had this figured out? He stood there, looking at me with a sense of impatience and disdain. He pointed to a framed picture toppled over on the nightstand. Our victim was in the loving embrace of a man who appeared to be her age. He then pointed to some men's clothing hanging in the right side of her closet. Several items appeared to be missing.

"I've been doing this for a long time, kid," Alan said as he opened his notebook. "'Stranger' murders are pretty rare. That guy's probably her husband, and in my experience, spouses kill each other." Alan systematically pointed to a number of pieces of evidence and interpreted them in light of his proclamation. There was no forced entry; the victim didn't appear to have put up much of a fight; the picture had been knocked over on the nightstand; men's clothing appeared to be missing from the closet—Alan saw all of this as confirmation of his theory. "No reason to make it complicated, newbie; most of the time it's real simple. Find me the husband, and I'll show you the killer."

As it turned out, it was a little more difficult than that. We didn't identify the suspect for another three months, and it turned out to be the victim's twenty-five-year-old neighbor. He barely knew her but managed to trick the victim into opening her door on the night he raped and killed her. She turned out to be single; the man in the photograph was her brother (he visited occasionally from overseas and kept some of his clothing in her closet). All of Alan's presuppositions were wrong, and his assumptions colored the way we were seeing the evidence. Alan's philosophy was hurting his methodology. We weren't following the evidence to see where it led; we had already decided where the evidence would lead and were simply looking for affirmation. Luckily, the truth prevailed.

All of us hold presuppositions that can impact the way we see the world around us. I've learned to do my best to enter every investigation with my eyes and mind open to all the reasonable possibilities. I try not to *bite* on any particular philosophy or theory until one emerges as the most rational, given the evidence. I've learned this the hard way; I've made more than my share of mistakes. There's one thing I know for sure (having worked both fresh and cold homicides): you simply cannot enter into an investigation with a philosophy that dictates the outcome. Objectivity is paramount; this is the first principle of *detective work* that each of us must learn. It sounds simple, but our presuppositions are sometimes hidden in a way that makes them hard to uncover and recognize.

SPIRITUAL PRESUPPOSITIONS

When I was an atheist, I held many presuppositions that tainted the way I investigated the claims of Christianity. I was raised in the *Star Trek* generation (the original cast, mind you) by an atheist father who was a cop and detective for nearly thirty years before I got hired as a police officer. I was convinced by the growing secular culture that all of life's mysteries would eventually be explained by science, and I was committed to the notion that we would ultimately find a *natural* answer for everything we once thought to be *supernatural*.

My early years as a homicide detective only amplified these presuppositions. After all, what would my partners think if I examined all the evidence in a difficult case and (after failing to identify a suspect) concluded that a ghost or demon committed the murder? They would surely think I was crazy. All homicide investigators presume that supernatural beings are not reasonable suspects, and many detectives also happen to reject the supernatural altogether. Detectives have to work in the real world, the "natural world" of material cause and effect. We presuppose a particular philosophy as we begin to investigate our cases. This philosophy is called "philosophical naturalism" (or "philosophical materialism").

Most of us in the *Star Trek* generation understand this philosophy, even if we can't articulate it perfectly. Philosophical naturalism rejects the existence of supernatural agents, powers, beings, or realities. It begins with the foundational premise that natural laws and forces alone can account for every phenomenon under examination. If there is an answer to be discovered, philosophical naturalism dictates that we must find it by examining the relationship between material objects and natural forces; that's it, nothing more. Supernatural forces are excluded by definition. Most scientists begin with this presupposition and fail to consider any answer that is not strictly physical, material, or natural. Even when a particular phenomenon cannot be explained by any natural, material process or set of forces, the vast majority of scientists will refuse to consider a supernatural explanation. Richard Lewontin (an evolutionary biologist and geneticist) once famously wrote a review of a book written by Carl Sagan and admitted that science is skewed to ignore

Philosophical Naturalism

The presuppositional belief that only natural laws and forces (as opposed to supernatural forces) operate in the world. Philosophical naturalists believe that nothing exists beyond the natural realm.

any supernatural explanation, even when the evidence might indicate that natural, material explanations are lacking.

> We take the side of science in spite of the patent absurdity of some of its constructs, in spite of its failure to fulfill many of its extravagant promises of health and life, in spite of the tolerance of the scientific community for unsubstantiated just-so stories, because we have a prior commitment, a commitment to materialism. It is not that the methods and institutions of science somehow compel us to accept a material explanation of the phenomenal world, but, on the contrary, that we are forced by our *a priori* adherence to material causes to create an apparatus of investigation and a set of concepts that produce material explanations, no matter how counterintuitive, no matter how mystifying to the uninitiated. Moreover, that materialism is an absolute, for we cannot allow a Divine Foot in the door.[2]

Scientists aren't alone; many historians are also committed to a naturalistic presupposition. The majority of historical scholars, for example, accept the historicity of the New Testament Gospels, in so far as they describe the life and teaching of Jesus and the condition of the first-century environment in which Jesus lived and ministered. But many of these same historians simultaneously reject the historicity of any of the miracles described in the New Testament, in spite of the fact that these miracles are described alongside the events that scholars accept as historical. Why do they accept some events and reject others? Because they have a presuppositional bias against the supernatural.

Bart Ehrman (the famous agnostic professor of religious studies at the University of North Carolina at Chapel Hill) was once in a radio debate with Michael Licona (research professor of New Testament at Southern Evangelical Seminary) on the British radio program *Unbelievable?*[3] While debating the evidence for the resurrection, Ehrman revealed a naturalistic presupposition that is common to many historians. He said, "The bottom line I think is one we haven't even talked about, which is whether there can be such a thing as historical evidence for a miracle, and, I think, the answer is a clear 'no,' and I think virtually all historians agree with me on that." Ehrman rejects the idea that any historical evidence could demonstrate a miracle because, in his words, "it's invoking something outside of our natural experience to explain what happened in the past." It shouldn't surprise us that Ehrman rejects the resurrection given this presupposition; he arrived at a particular natural conclusion because he would not allow himself any other option, even though the evidence might be better explained by the very thing he rejects.

MENTAL ROADBLOCKS

I began to understand the hazard of philosophical presuppositions while working as a homicide detective. Alan and I stood at that crime scene, doing our best to answer the question "Who murdered this woman?" One of us already had an answer. Spouses or lovers typically commit murders like this; case closed. We simply needed to find this woman's husband or lover. It was as if we were asking the question "Did her husband kill her?" after first excluding any suspect other than her husband. It's not surprising that Alan came to his conclusion; he started with it as his premise.

When I was an atheist, I did the very same thing. I stood in front of the evidence for God, interested in answering the question "Does God exist?" But I began the investigation as a natural-

Begging the Question

When we smuggle our conclusions into our investigation by beginning with them as an initial premise, we are likely to beg the question and end up with conclusions that match our presuppositions rather than reflect the truth of the matter.

ist with the presupposition that nothing exists beyond natural laws, forces, and material objects. I was asking the question "Does a supernatural being exist?" after first excluding the possibility of anything supernatural. Like Alan, I came to a particular conclusion because I started with it as my premise. This is the truest definition of bias, isn't it? Starting off with your mind already made up.

ENTER WITH EMPTY HANDS

Christians are often accused of being "biased" simply because they believe in the supernatural. This accusation has power in our current pluralistic culture. Biased people are seen as prejudicial and unfair, arrogant and overly confident of their position. Nobody wants to be identified as someone who is biased or opinionated. But make no mistake about it, all of us have a point of view; all of us hold opinions and ideas that color the way we see the world. Anyone who tells you that he (or she) is completely objective and devoid of presuppositions has another more important problem: that person is either astonishingly naive or a liar.

The question is not whether or not we have ideas, opinions, or preexisting points of view; the question is whether or not we will allow these perspectives to prevent us from examining the evidence objectively. It's possible to have a prior opinion yet leave this presupposition at the door in order to examine the evidence fairly. We ask jurors to do this all the time. In the state of California, jurors are repeatedly instructed to "keep an open mind throughout the trial" and not to "let bias, sympathy, prejudice, or public opinion influence your decision."[4] The courts assume that people have biases, hold sympathies and prejudices, and are aware of public opinion. In spite of this, jurors are required to "keep an open mind." Jurors have to enter the courtroom with empty hands; they must leave all their *baggage* in the hall. Everyone begins with a collection of biases. We must (to the best of our ability) resist the temptation to allow our biases to eliminate certain forms of evidence (and therefore certain conclusions) before we even begin the investigation.

Dangerous Presuppositions
for Jurors

Dangerous Presuppositions
for Truth Seekers

As a skeptic, I was slow to accept even the slightest possibility that miracles were possible. My commitment to naturalism prevented me from considering such nonsense. But after my experience with presuppositions at the crime scene, I decided that I needed to be fair with my naturalistic inclinations. I couldn't begin with my conclusion, and if the evidence pointed to the reasonable existence of God, this certainly opened up the possibility of the miraculous. If God did exist, He was the creator of everything we see in the universe. He, therefore, created matter from nonmatter, life from nonlife; He created all time and space. God's creation of the universe would certainly be nothing short of … miraculous. If there was a God who could account for the beginning of the universe, lesser miracles (say, walking on water or healing the blind) might not even be all that impressive. If I was going to learn the truth about the existence of a miraculous God, I needed to at least lay down my presuppositions about the miraculous. My experience at crime scenes has helped me to do just that. This doesn't mean that I now rush to supernatural explanations every time I fail to find an easy or quick natural explanation. It simply means that I am open to following the evidence wherever it leads, even if it points to the existence of a miraculous designer.

A TOOL FOR THE CALLOUT BAG, A TIP FOR THE CHECKLIST

I keep a leather bag packed beside my bed. It contains all the gear I need when I'm called to a homicide scene in the middle of the night. My *callout bag* typically includes a flashlight, blank notepads, plastic gloves, a digital recorder, camera, and (of course) my gun and badge. My bag also contains an investigative *checklist* I created many years ago when I was a new detective. While I seldom need to refer to it anymore, it represents years of wisdom gleaned from partners, classes, training seminars, successful investigations, and failed efforts. You might be interested in assembling your own callout bag and checklist. If so, you may want to include this first principle related to presuppositions; it will serve you well as you investigate the Gospels.

When I was an atheist, I allowed the presupposition of naturalism to unfairly taint the way I looked at the evidence for God's existence. I failed to differentiate between *science* (the systematic, rational examination of phenomena) and *scientism* (the refusal to consider anything other than natural causes). I was thirty-five before I recognized how unreasonable it was for me to reject the possibility of anything supernatural *before* I even began to investigate the supernatural claims of Christianity. In those days, when I encountered phenomena that could not be explained *naturally*, I simply *dug in* and continued to reject the possibility that something *extranatural* might be operating. I refused to begin the journey with empty hands or an open mind.

Even though I'm a Christian today, I understand that much of the phenomena we observe can be explained satisfactorily by simple relationships between matter and the laws of nature. For this reason, I try to be careful not to jump to supernatural explanations when natural causes are supported evidentially. Not all of God's activity is overtly miraculous. God is still at work even in the interaction between the matter He created and the natural laws that reflect His nature (this is, in fact, miraculous enough). As a result, I try to encourage my skeptical friends to reexamine their natural presuppositions, but I'm careful to respect the claims of naturalists when they are evidentially supported.

Chapter 2
Principle #2:

LEARN HOW TO "INFER"

"I hate these kinds of cases," Mark muttered as he carefully pulled back the sheet on the bed. Detective Mark Richardson had a child of his own about the same age as the victim. Nothing is more disturbing than the homicide of a small infant, and it was Mark's turn to handle this murder. Three of us stood there and examined the scene while we waited for the coroner's investigator to arrive. Two of us were glad it wasn't our turn.

"How do parents do this kind of thing to their own kids?" Mark posed the question rhetorically, as if he didn't know the kind of response he was going to get from our senior partner.

"Don't call this dirtbag a 'parent,'" Al responded, casting a look of disgust in the direction of the disheveled parolee sitting on the couch down the hall. "If he did this, he's nothing more than the sperm donor for this kid."

I often get called out to assist members of our homicide unit at suspicious death scenes such as these when the manner of death is not immediately obvious. Better safe than sorry; these scenes have to be worked as homicides (until we determine otherwise), or

Cold-Case Homicides

While most felonious crime investigations are limited by a *statute of limitations* (a legislated period of time, beyond which the case cannot be legally prosecuted), homicides have no such restriction. This means that *fresh* homicides, should they go unsolved, can be investigated many years after they were committed. Investigators who have experience with cold cases can sometimes recognize the investigative pitfalls that cause cases to go cold in the first place.

they may become cold cases that I will eventually have to add to my list. The situation surrounding this death was suspicious, so I got called to lend a hand. The baby appeared to have asphyxiated as he was lying in his father's bed, just feet away from an unused crib located in the same room. Mom and dad had recently separated, and the baby's father had a history of violence against his wife going back several years. The baby's mother was no longer living at the house, and she often worried about the safety of her child. Her husband refused to release the baby to her, and she was afraid to seek legal help to retrieve the infant, based on her husband's violent nature. To make matters worse, her husband made several threats about strangling the boy in an effort to terrorize her.

We observed that the house was generally filthy and unkempt, and there were signs of drug use in the living room. When we first contacted the victim's father, he seemed nonresponsive and hostile. He initially refused to answer simple questions and displayed a general distrust of law enforcement personnel. He was a parolee with a history of drug use, domestic violence, and felonious behavior. At first glance, one might suspect that this man was capable of doing the unthinkable.

We called the coroner as we began to collect evidence and photograph everything in sight, and we didn't touch the body until the coroner's investigator arrived. Only then were we able to get a clear picture of the baby's condition. As we removed the bedding around the body and examined the child more closely, we discovered that he was surprisingly clean and tidy. He looked healthy and well fed. He was lying next to a bottle of fresh formula, cleanly dressed in a new diaper and pajama suit. His hair was washed, and he was lying next to a long pillow that had been propped up against one side of his torso. A second long pillow appeared to have been propped against the other side of the baby, but this pillow was now lying on the floor. The baby was lying, facedown, on the bed, a short distance from the first pillow. There were no signs of neglect or abuse on the child, not a single bruise or suspicious mark.

In our follow-up interview of the baby's father, Al came to learn that the child was his greatest treasure. In spite of his many admitted failures and his emotionless, hardened exterior, the man's one joy was the baby. He carefully slept with the infant every night and was so concerned about sudden infant death syndrome that he placed the child, faceup, between two large pillows next to him on the bed so he could monitor his breathing. On this particular night, one of the two pillows rolled off the bed, and the baby managed to roll over on his stomach. Given everything we saw at the scene and the condition of the baby, we ruled his asphyxiation an accidental death. Al agreed that this was not a homicide.

THINKING LIKE A DETECTIVE

As investigators, we just employed a methodology known as *abductive reasoning* (also known as "inferring to the most reasonable explanation") in order to determine what we had at this scene. We collected all the evidential data and made a mental list of the raw facts. We then developed a list of the possible explanations that might account for the scene in general. Finally, we compared the evidence to the potential explanations and determined which explanation was, in fact, the most reasonable inference in light of the evidence.

As it turns out, detectives aren't the only people who use abductive reasoning in an effort to figure out what really happened. Historians, scientists, and all the rest of us (regardless of vocation or avocation) have experience as detectives. In fact, most of us have become accomplished investigators as a matter of necessity and practice, and we've been employing abductive reasoning without giving it much thought. I had a partner once who gave me a bit of parental advice. Dave was a few years older than I was, and he had been working patrol for many years. He was a seasoned and salty officer, streetwise, cynical, and infinitely practical. He had two children who were already married when mine were still in high school. He was full of sage advice (along with some other stuff).

Inferences and Reasonable Inferences

To *infer* means "to gather in." In logic, inference refers to the process of collecting data from numerous sources, and then drawing conclusions on the basis of this evidence. In legal terms, an inference is a "deduction of fact that may logically and reasonably be drawn from another fact or group of facts found or otherwise established" (Cal Evid Code § 600 [b]).

In addition, courts across the land instruct jurors to draw "reasonable inferences." These are described as "conclusions which are regarded as logical by reasonable people in the light of their experience in life." *Lannon v. Hogan*, 719 F.2d 518, 521, (1st Cir. Mass. 1983).

"Jim, let me tell ya something about kids. I love my two boys. I remember when they were in high school and used to go out with their friends on the weekends. I would stay up late and wait for them to come home. As soon as they walked in the door, I would get up off the couch and give them a big hug."

This struck me as a bit odd, given what I knew about Dave. He seldom exposed a sensitive side. "Wow, Dave, I have to tell you that I don't usually think of you as a touchy-feely kind of guy."

"I'm not, you moron," Dave said, returning to form. "I hug them as tightly as possible so I can get close enough to smell them. I'm not a fool. I can tell if they've been smoking dope or drinking within seconds."

You see, Dave was an evidentialist, and he applied his reasoning skills to his experience as a parent. The smell of alcohol or marijuana would serve as evidence that he would later take into consideration as he was evaluating the possible activities of his children. Dave was thinking *abductively*. I bet you've done something similar in your role as a parent, a spouse, a son, or a daughter.

DISTINGUISHING BETWEEN *POSSIBLE* AND *REASONABLE*

All of us have learned the intuitive difference between *possible* and *reasonable*. When it comes right down to it, just about anything is *possible*. You may not even be reading this book right now, even though you think that you are. It's *possible* that aliens covertly kidnapped you last night and have induced a dreamlike, out-of-body, extraterrestrial hallucination. While you think this experience of reading is real, you may actually wake up tomorrow morning to discover yourself in an alien spaceship. But let's face it, that's not reasonable, is it?

While it's interesting to imagine the *possibilities*, it's important to return eventually to what's *reasonable*, especially when the truth is at stake. That's why judges across the land carefully instruct juries to

 Speculation

Speculation is dangerously nonevidential by its very definition:

"Reasoning based on inconclusive evidence; conjecture or supposition" (*The American Heritage Dictionary of the English Language*, Fourth Edition, 2003).

"A hypothesis that has been formed by speculating or conjecturing, usually with little hard evidence" (*Collins Thesaurus of the English Language—Complete and Unabridged* 2nd Edition, 1995, 2002).

refrain from what is known as "speculation" when considering the explanations for what has occurred in a case. Jurors are told that they "must use only the evidence that is presented"[5] during the trial. They are told to resist the temptation to consider the attorney's opinions about unsupported possibilities and to ignore unsupported speculation wherever they may hear it.

We also tell jurors to resist the impulse to stray from the evidence offered and ask questions like "What if …?" or "Isn't it possible that …?" when these questions are driven by evidentially unsupported speculation. They must instead limit themselves to what's reasonable in light of the evidence that has been presented to them.

In the end, our criminal courts place a high standard on *reasonableness*, and that's important as we think about the process of abductive reasoning. This rational approach to determining truth will help us come to the most reasonable conclusion in light of the evidence. It can be applied to more than criminal cases; we can apply the process of *abduction* to our spiritual investigations as well. But first, let's examine the concept with a real-life example from the world of homicide investigations.

ABDUCTIVE REASONING AND DEAD GUYS

Let's use the example of another death scene to fully illustrate the process. You and I have been called out to a "dead-body scene"—a location where a deceased person has been discovered and the circumstances seem rather suspicious. While scenes like this are sometimes homicides, they are often less sinister; there are a few other explanations. Deaths fall into one of four categories: natural deaths, accidental deaths, suicides, or homicides. It's our job to figure out which of the four explanations is the most reasonable in the following scenario.

We have been called to the scene of a DBR (a "Dead Body Report") to assist patrol officers who have already arrived and secured the location. Here are the facts we are given when we enter the room: A young man was discovered on the floor of his apartment when his roommate returned from work. The man was lying facedown. The man was cold to the touch, nonresponsive, and stiff. Okay, given these minimal facts, it is clear that we actually do have a dead guy, but which of the four potential explanations is most reasonable given the facts? Is this death a natural death, an accident, a suicide, or a homicide?

Given the minimal facts so far, all four of the potential explanations are still in play, aren't they? Unless we have something more to add evidentially, it will be difficult to decide if this case should be worked as a homicide or simply documented as something other than criminal.

Let's change the scenario slightly and add a new piece of evidence to see if it will help. Imagine that we entered the room and observed that the man was lying in a pool of his own blood and that this blood seemed to be coming from the area of his abdomen (under his body). These are the new minimal facts: (1) a man is dead, (2) lying facedown on the floor, (3) in a pool of blood that seems to be coming from the front of the man's lower abdomen. Given this new set of facts, is there any direction our investigation might take? Are any of our four explanations more or less reasonable?

Given the new evidence, we may be comfortable in removing the *natural death* explanation from our consideration. After all, what kind of natural event in the human body would cause someone to bleed from his lower abdomen? Without an orifice from which to bleed naturally, this does seem to be an unfounded conclusion to draw; a natural death might be *possible*, but it isn't *reasonable*.

What about the other three explanations? Could this still be an accidental death? Sure, the man could have tripped and fallen on something (we wouldn't know this until we turned him over). What about a suicide or a homicide? It seems that these three remaining explanations are still reasonable in light of what limited evidence we have about this case. Until we learn a bit more, it will be difficult to decide which of these final three options is the most reasonable.

Let's add a new dimension to the case. Imagine that we enter the room and see the man lying on the floor in a pool of his own blood, but now we observe a large knife stuck in his lower back. This presents us with a new set of facts: (1) the man is dead, (2) lying facedown on the floor, (3) in a pool of blood, and (4) there is a knife stuck in the man's lower back.

The presence of a knife in the victim's back seems to eliminate as unreasonable the conclusion that he died accidentally. It's hard to imagine an accident that would account for this fact; an accidental death might be *possible,* but it's not *reasonable.* If nothing else, the presence of the knife most certainly affirms the unreasonable nature of a natural death, doesn't it? The most reasonable remaining explanations are either suicide or homicide, and suicide seems less and less likely, given the fact that the victim's wound is located on his back. But since the wound is located in the lower portion of his back (within his reach), let's leave this option on the table for now.

Imagine, however, that a new fact has entered into our scenario. Imagine that we discover three extra wounds on the victim's upper back, in addition to the one we observed earlier. Our fact list now includes (1) a man who is dead, (2) lying facedown on the floor, (3) in a pool of blood, (4) with multiple knife wounds on his back. Our reasonable explanations are dwindling, aren't they?

In this situation, natural death, accidental death, and suicide seem out of the question. While someone may argue that they are still *possible*, few would recognize them as *reasonable*. The most reasonable conclusion in light of the evidence is simply that this man was murdered. As responsible detectives, you and I would have no choice but to initiate a homicide investigation.

Dead Man
Lying Facedown
Pool of Blood
Knife in Back
Multiple Stab Wounds

~~natural death~~
~~accidental death~~
~~suicide~~
homicide

MAKING MORE DIFFICULT DISTINCTIONS

We just used abductive reasoning to determine which explanation most reasonably explained what happened at this scene. It was simple, right? But what if the scenario is more ambiguous than our dead-body scene? What if two competing explanations seem similarly reasonable? Are there any rules or principles that might help us distinguish between the most reasonable explanation and a close contender? Well, over the years, I've given this a lot of thought as I've investigated potential homicide suspects in cold-case murders. When considering two or more closely competing explanations for a particular event (or suspects in a murder), I now assess the following factors (keep in mind that these terms are mine and may not reflect the language of other philosophers or thinkers in the area of abductive reasoning):

THE TRUTH MUST BE FEASIBLE

(The explanation has explanatory viability)

Before I even begin to think about the evidence related to a particular murder suspect, I need to make sure that he or she was available to commit the crime in the first place. I investigate the *alibis* of potential suspects, eliminating those who are simply impossibilities based on confirmed alibis.

THE TRUTH WILL USUALLY BE STRAIGHTFORWARD

(The explanation demonstrates explanatory simplicity)

When considering a number of suspects, I look for the man or woman who most simply accounts for the evidence. If one person can account for the evidence (rather than some theory that requires three or four different potential suspects to account for the same evidence), he or she is most likely the killer.

THE TRUTH SHOULD BE EXHAUSTIVE

(The explanation displays explanatory depth)

I also consider the suspect who most exhaustively explains the evidence that I have in a case. While a particular suspect may explain one, two, or three pieces of evidence, the suspect who accounts for most (or all) of the evidence is typically the killer.

THE TRUTH MUST BE LOGICAL

(The explanation possesses explanatory consistency)

The truth is rational; for this reason the truth about the identity of my killer must also *make sense*. Suspects commit murders for reasons of one kind or another, even if these reasons seem insufficient to you and me. The true killer will *make sense* to the members of the jury once they understand his or her misguided motivation. Conversely, some candidates will appear logically inconsistent because they lack motive altogether.

THE TRUTH WILL BE SUPERIOR
(The explanation achieves explanatory superiority)

Finally, I recognize that one of my suspects is unique in the superior way that he or she accounts for the evidence. In essence, this particular suspect is a far better choice when compared to other candidates who are offered. The quality of his or her connection to the evidence is better. When I see this characteristic of *explanatory superiority*, I know I have my killer.

When a suspect meets these five criteria, I am confident that I have reached the most reasonable conclusion; I know I have identified the killer.

AN ANCIENT DEATH-SCENE INVESTIGATION

Now it's time to apply this form of reasoning to a death scene that has been the topic of discussion for over two thousand years. What happened to Jesus of Nazareth? How can we explain His empty tomb? Did His disciples steal His body? Was He only injured on the cross and later recovered? Did He actually die and resurrect from the dead? We can approach these questions as detectives, using abductive reasoning.

The question of Jesus's fate might be compared to our dead-body investigation. We examined our death scene by first identifying the characteristics of the scene (the facts and pieces of evidence). We next acknowledged a number of potential explanations that might account for what we observed. Let's apply that same approach to the issue of the alleged death and resurrection of Jesus.

Dr. Gary Habermas[6] and Professor Mike Licona[7] have taken the time to identify the "minimal facts" (or evidences) related to the resurrection. While there are many claims in the New Testament related to this important event, not all are accepted by skeptics and wary investigators. Habermas and Licona surveyed the most respected and well-established historical scholars and identified a number of facts that *are* accepted by the vast majority of researchers in the field.

They limited their list to those facts that were strongly supported (using the criteria of textual critics) and to those facts that were granted by virtually all scholars (from skeptics to conservative Christians). Habermas and Licona eventually wrote about their findings in *The Case for the Resurrection of Jesus.*[8]

As a skeptic myself, I formed a list of New Testament claims as I first investigated the resurrection. When I was an unbeliever, I found four of Habermas and Licona's minimal facts to be the most substantiated by both friends and foes of Christianity:

1. Jesus died on the cross and was buried.
2. Jesus's tomb was empty and no one ever produced His body.
3. Jesus's disciples believed that they saw Jesus resurrected from the dead.
4. Jesus's disciples were transformed following their alleged resurrection observations.

You'll notice that none of these "minimal evidences" necessitates that Jesus truly rose from the dead. There may be any number of explanations that account for these facts (we'll get to those in a moment). This is simply a list of evidences that most scholars (believers and unbelievers alike) would accept, and all of us (believers and unbelievers alike) must explain. As I examined these *bare-bones* claims related to the resurrection, I assembled the possible explanations that have been historically offered to account for them (employing the process of abductive reasoning). I quickly recognized that every one of these explanations had its own deficiencies and liabilities (including the classic Christian account). Let's take a look at the potential explanations and list their associated difficulties:

The *Minimal-Facts* Approach

Gary Habermas (distinguished research professor at Liberty Baptist Theological Seminary) has popularized the minimal-facts approach to examining the resurrection by identifying those aspects of the resurrection story that are accepted by the vast majority of scholars and experts (from Christians to nonbelievers). This list of accepted "minimal facts" can then be used as the basis for our process of abductive reasoning.

THE DISCIPLES WERE WRONG ABOUT JESUS'S DEATH

Some skeptics have offered the possibility that the disciples were mistaken about Jesus's death on the cross. They propose that Jesus survived the beating (and the crucifixion) and simply appeared to the disciples after He recovered.

THE PROBLEMS:

While this proposal seeks to explain the empty tomb, the resurrection observations, and the transformation that occurred in the lives of the apostles, it fails to satisfactorily explain what the disciples observed and experienced when they pulled Jesus from the cross. It's been my experience that witnesses who first come upon the dead body of someone they care about quickly check for the most obvious sign of life. Is the person who was injured still breathing? This test is simple and effective; everyone is capable of performing it, and even those who know nothing about human biology instinctively resort to it. It's also been my experience that three conditions become apparent in the bodies of dead people: temperature loss, rigidity, and lividity. Dead people lose warmth until they eventually reach the temperature of their environment. They begin to feel "cold to the touch" (this is often reported by those who find them). In addition, chemical reactions begin to take place in the muscles after death occurs, resulting in stiffening and rigidity known as "rigor mortis." Dead people become rigid, retaining the shape they were in when they died. Finally, when the heart stops beating, blood begins to pool in the body, responding to the force of gravity. As a result, purple discoloration begins to become apparent in those areas of the body that are closest to the ground. In essence, dead bodies look, feel, and respond differently from living, breathing humans. Dead people, unlike those who are slipping in and out of consciousness, never respond to their injuries. They don't flinch or moan when touched. Is it reasonable to believe that those who removed Jesus from the cross, took possession of His body, carried Him to the grave, and spent time treating and wrapping His body for burial would not have noticed any of these conditions common to dead bodies?

In addition to this, the Gospel of John records the fact that the guard stabbed Jesus and observed both blood and water to pour from His body. That's an important observation, given that John was not a coroner or medical doctor. While I am certainly not a doctor, I've been to my share of coroners' autopsies, and I've spoken at length with coroner investigators at crime scenes. When people are injured to the point of death (such as the result of an assault or traffic accident), they often enter into some form of "circulatory shock" prior to dying (because their organs and body tissues are not receiving adequate blood flow). This can sometimes result in either "pericardial effusion" (increased fluid in the membrane surrounding the heart) or "pleural effusion" (increased fluid in the membrane surrounding the lungs). When Jesus was pinned to the cross in an upright position following the terrible flogging He received, it's reasonable to expect that this kind of effusion might have taken place in response to the circulatory shock He suffered prior to dying. These fluids would certainly pour out of His body if He were pierced with a spear. While the gospel writers might expect to see blood, their observation of the water is somewhat surprising. It is certainly consistent with the fact that Jesus was already dead when stabbed by the guard.

In addition to these concerns from the perspective of a homicide detective, there are other problems with the proposal that Jesus didn't actually die on the cross:

1. Many first-century and early second-century *unfriendly* Roman sources (i.e., Thallus, Tacitus, Mara Bar-Serapion, and Phlegon) and Jewish sources (i.e., Josephus and the Babylonian Talmud) affirmed and acknowledged that Jesus was crucified and died.

2. The Roman guards faced death if they allowed a prisoner to survive crucifixion. Would they really be careless enough to remove a living person from a cross?

3. Jesus would have to control His blood loss from the beatings, crucifixion, and stabbing in order to survive, yet was pinned to the cross and unable to do anything that might achieve this.

4. Jesus displayed wounds following the resurrection but was never observed to behave as though He was wounded, in spite of the fact that He appeared only days after His beating, crucifixion, and stabbing.

5. Jesus disappeared from the historical record following His reported resurrection and ascension and was never sighted again (as one might expect if He recovered from His wounds and lived much beyond the young age of thirty-three).

THE DISCIPLES LIED ABOUT THE RESURRECTION

Some non-Christians claim that the disciples stole the body from the grave and later fabricated the stories of Jesus's resurrection appearances.

THE PROBLEMS:

While this explanation accounts for the empty tomb and the resurrection observations, it fails to account for the transformed lives of the apostles. In my years working robberies, I had the opportunity to investigate (and break) a number of conspiracy efforts, and I learned about the nature of successful conspiracies. We'll examine the problem with conspiracy theories in chapter 7, but until then, let me simply say that I am hesitant to embrace any theory that requires the conspiratorial effort of a large number of people, over a significant period of time, when there is personally little or nothing to gain by their effort. This theory requires us to believe that the apostles were transformed and emboldened not by the miraculous appearance of the resurrected Jesus but by elaborate lies created without any benefit to those who were perpetuating the hoax.

In addition to this concern from the perspective of a detective, there are other concerns that have to be considered when evaluating the claim that the disciples lied about the resurrection:

> 1. The Jewish authorities took many precautions to make sure the tomb was guarded and sealed, knowing that the removal of the body would allow the disciples to claim that Jesus had risen (Matt. 27:62–66).
> 2. The people local to the event would have known it was a lie (remember that Paul told the Corinthians in 1 Corinthians 15:3–8 that there were still five hundred people who could testify to having seen Jesus alive after His resurrection).
> 3. The disciples lacked the motive to create such a lie (more on this in chapter 14).
> 4. The disciples' transformation following the alleged resurrection is inconsistent with the claim that the appearances were only a lie. How could their own lies transform them into courageous evangelists?

THE DISCIPLES WERE DELUSIONAL

Some skeptics believe that the disciples, as a result of their intense grief and sorrow, only imagined seeing Jesus alive after His death on the cross. These critics claim that the appearances were simply hallucinations that resulted from wishful thinking.

THE PROBLEMS:

This proposal fails to explain the empty tomb and only accounts for the resurrection experiences at first glance. As a detective, I frequently encounter witnesses who are related in some way to the victim in my case. These witnesses are often profoundly impacted by their grief following the murder. As a result, some allow their sorrow to impact what they remember about the victim. They may, for example, suppress all the negative characteristics of the victim's personality and amplify all the victim's virtues. Let's face it, we all have a tendency to think the best of people once they have died. But these imaginings are typically limited to the nature of the victim's character and not the elaborate and detailed events that involved the victim in the past. Those closest to the victim may be mistaken about his or her character, but I've never encountered loved ones who have collectively imagined an identical set of fictional events involving the victim. It's one thing to remember someone with fondness, another thing to imagine an elaborate and detailed history that didn't even occur.

Based on these experiences as a detective, there are other reasonable concerns when considering the explanation that the disciples hallucinated or imagined the resurrection:

1. While individuals have hallucinations, there are no examples of large groups of people having the exact same hallucination.

2. While a short, momentary group hallucination may seem reasonable, long, sustained, and detailed hallucinations are unsupported historically and intuitively unreasonable.

3. The risen Christ was reportedly seen on more than one occasion and by a number of different groups (and subsets of groups). All of these diverse sightings would have to be additional group hallucinations of one nature or another.

4. Not all the disciples were inclined favorably toward such a hallucination. The disciples included people like Thomas, who was skeptical and did not expect Jesus to come back to life.

5. If the resurrection was simply a hallucination, what became of Jesus's corpse? The absence of the body is unexplainable under this scenario.

THE DISCIPLES WERE FOOLED BY AN IMPOSTER

Some nonbelievers have argued that an imposter tricked the disciples and convinced them that Jesus was still alive; the disciples then unknowingly advanced the lie.

THE PROBLEMS:

While this explanation accounts for the resurrection observations and transformed apostles, it requires an additional set of conspirators (other than the apostles who were later fooled) to accomplish the task of stealing the body. Many of my partners spent several years investigating fraud and forgery crimes prior to joining us on the homicide team. They've learned something about successful con artists. The less the victim understands about the specific topic and area in which he or she is being "conned," the more likely the con artist will be successful. Victims are often fooled and swindled out of their money because they have little or no expertise in the area in which the con artist is operating. The perpetrator is able to use sophisticated language and make claims that are outside of the victim's expertise. The crook sounds legitimate, primarily because the victim doesn't really know what truly *is* legitimate. When the targeted victim knows more about the subject than the person attempting the con, the odds are good that the perpetrator will fail at his or her attempt to fool the victim.

For this reason, the proposal that a sophisticated first-century con artist fooled the disciples seems unreasonable. There are many concerns with such a theory:

> 1. The impersonator would have to be familiar enough with Jesus's mannerisms and statements to convince the disciples. The disciples knew the topic of the con better than anyone who might con them.
>
> 2. Many of the disciples were skeptical and displayed none of the necessary naïveté that would be required for the con artist to succeed. Thomas, for example, was openly skeptical from the beginning.
>
> 3. The impersonator would need to possess miraculous powers; the disciples reported that the resurrected Jesus performed many miracles and "convincing proofs" (Acts 1:2–3).
>
> 4. Who would seek to start a world religious movement if not one of the hopeful disciples? This theory requires someone to be motivated to impersonate Jesus other than the disciples themselves.
>
> 5. This explanation also fails to account for the empty tomb or missing body of Jesus.

THE DISCIPLES WERE INFLUENCED BY LIMITED SPIRITUAL SIGHTINGS

More recently, some skeptics have offered the theory that one or two of the disciples had a *vision* of the risen Christ and then convinced the others that these spiritual sightings were legitimate. They argue that additional sightings simply came as a response to the intense influence of the first *visions*.

THE PROBLEMS:

This proposal may begin to explain the transformation of the apostles, but it fails to explain the empty tomb and offers an explanation of the resurrection observations that is inconsistent with the biblical record. It's not unusual to have a persuasive witness influence the beliefs of other eyewitnesses (we'll discuss this in greater detail in chapter 4). I've investigated a number of murders in which one emphatic witness has persuaded others that something occurred, even though the other witnesses weren't even present to see the event for themselves. But these persuaded witnesses were easily distinguished from the one who persuaded them once I began to ask for their account of what happened. Only the persuader possessed the details in their most robust form. For this reason, his or her account was typically the most comprehensive, while the others tended to generalize since they didn't actually see the event for themselves. In addition, when pressed to repeat the story of the one persuasive witness, the other witnesses eventually pointed to that witness as their source, especially when pressured. While it's possible for a persuasive witness to convince some of the other witnesses that his or her version of events is the true story, I've never encountered a *persuader* who could convince everyone. The more witnesses who are involved in a crime, the less likely that all of them will be influenced by any one eyewitness, regardless of that witness's charisma or position within the group.

This theory also suffers from all the liabilities of the earlier claim that the disciples imagined the resurrected Christ. Even if the *persuader* could convince everyone of his or her first observation, the subsequent group *visions* are still unreasonable for all the reasons we've already discussed. There are many concerns related to the claim that a select number of *persuaders* convinced the disciples of resurrection:

1. The theory fails to account for the numerous, divergent, and separate group sightings of Jesus that are recorded in the Gospels. These sightings are described specifically with great detail. It's not reasonable to believe that all these disciples could provide such specified detail if they were simply repeating something they didn't see for themselves.

2. As many as five hundred people were said to be available to testify to their observations of the risen Christ (1 Cor. 15:3–8). Could all of these people have been influenced to imagine their own observations of Jesus? It's not reasonable to believe that a *persuader* equally persuaded all these disciples even though they didn't actually see anything that was recorded.

3. This explanation also fails to account for the empty tomb or the missing corpse.

THE DISCIPLES' OBSERVATIONS WERE DISTORTED LATER

Some unbelievers claim the original observations of the disciples were amplified and distorted as the legend of Jesus grew over time. These skeptics believe that Jesus may have been a wise teacher, but argue that the resurrection is a legendary and historically late exaggeration.

THE PROBLEMS:

This explanation may account for the empty tomb (if we assume the body was removed), but it fails to explain the early claims of the apostles related to the resurrection (more about this in chapters 11 and 13). Cold-case detectives have to deal with the issue of *legend* more than other types of detectives. So much time has passed from the point of the original crime that it seems possible that witnesses may now amplify their original observations in one way or another. Luckily, I have the record of the first investigators to assist me as I try to separate what the eyewitnesses truly saw (and reported at the time of the crime) from what they might recall today. If the original record of the first investigators is thorough and well documented, I will have a much easier time discerning the truth about what each witness saw. I've discovered that the first recollections of the eyewitnesses are usually more detailed and reliable than what they might offer thirty years later. Like other cold-case detectives, I rely on the original reports as I compare what witnesses once said to what these witnesses are saying today.

The reliability of the eyewitness accounts related to the resurrection, like the reliability of the cold-case eyewitnesses, must be confirmed by the early documentation of the *first investigators*. For this reason, the claim that the original story of Jesus was a late exaggeration is undermined by several concerns:

> 1. In the earliest accounts of the disciples' activity after the crucifixion, they are seen citing the resurrection of Jesus as their primary piece of evidence that Jesus was God. From the earliest days of the Christian movement, eyewitnesses were making this claim.
>
> 2. The students of the disciples also recorded that the resurrection was a key component of the disciples' eyewitness testimony (more on this in chapter 13).
>
> 3. The earliest known Christian *creed* or oral record (as described by Paul in 1 Cor. 15) includes the resurrection as a key component.
>
> 4. This explanation also fails to account for the fact that the tomb and body of Jesus have not been exposed to demonstrate that this late legend was false.

THE DISCIPLES WERE ACCURATELY REPORTING THE RESURRECTION OF JESUS

Christians, of course, claim that Jesus truly rose from the dead and that the Gospels are accurate eyewitness accounts of this event.

THE PROBLEMS:

This explanation accounts for the empty tomb, the resurrection observations, and the transformation of the apostles. It would be naive, however, to accept this explanation without recognizing the fact that it also has a liability that has been examined and voiced by skeptics and nonbelievers. The claim that Jesus truly rose from the dead presents the following concern and objection:

1. This explanation requires a belief in the supernatural, a belief that Jesus had the supernatural power to rise from the dead in the first place.

ABDUCTIVE REASONING AND THE RESURRECTION

I limited the evidence to four modest claims about the resurrection and kept my explanatory options open to all the possibilities (both *natural* and *supernatural*). The last explanation (although it is a miraculous, supernatural explanation) suffers from the least number of liabilities and deficiencies. If we simply enter into the investigation without a preexisting bias against anything supernatural, the final explanation accounts for all of the evidence without any difficulty. The final explanation accounts for the evidence most simply and most exhaustively, and it is logically consistent (if we simply allow for the existence of God in the first place). The final explanation is also superior to the other accounts (given that it does not suffer from all the problems we see with the other explanations).

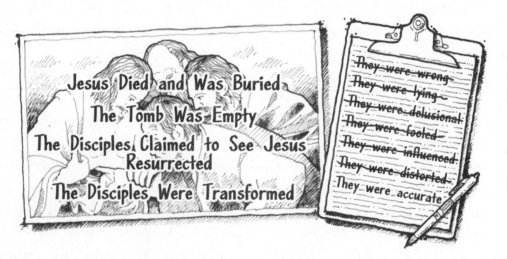

If we approach the issue of the resurrection in an unbiased manner (without the presuppositions described in the previous chapter) and assess it as we evaluated the dead-body scene, we can judge the possible explanations and eliminate those that are unreasonable. The conclusion that Jesus was resurrected (as reported in the Gospels) can be sensibly inferred from the available evidence. The resurrection is reasonable.

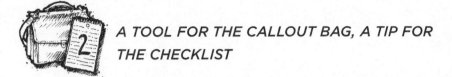

A TOOL FOR THE CALLOUT BAG, A TIP FOR THE CHECKLIST

Okay, let's add another tool to our callout bag: an attitude about *reason* that will help us as we examine and discuss the claims of Christianity. Like other nonbelievers in our world today, I used to think of *faith* as the opposite of *reason*. In this characterization of the dichotomy, I believed that atheists were reasonable "freethinkers" while believers were simple, mindless drones who blindly followed the unreasonable teaching of their leadership. But if you think about it, *faith* is actually the opposite of *unbelief*, not *reason*. As I began to read through the Bible as a skeptic, I came to understand that the biblical definition of faith is a well-placed and reasonable inference based on evidence. I wasn't raised in the Christian culture, and I think I have an unusually high amount of respect for evidence. Perhaps this is why this definition of faith comes easily to me. I now understand that it's possible for reasonable people to examine the evidence and conclude that Christianity is true. While my skeptical friends may not agree on how the evidence related to the resurrection should be interpreted, I want them to understand that I've arrived at my conclusions reasonably.

As I speak around the country, I often encounter devoted, committed Christians who are hesitant to embrace an *evidential* faith. In many Christian circles, faith that requires evidential support is seen as weak and inferior. For many, *blind faith* (a faith that simply trusts without question) is the truest, most sincere, and most valuable form of faith that we can offer God. Yet Jesus seemed to have a high regard for evidence. In John 14:11, He told those watching Him to examine "the evidence of the miracles" (NIV) if they did not believe what He said about His identity. Even after the resurrection, Jesus stayed with His disciples for an additional forty days and provided them with "many convincing proofs" that He was resurrected and was who He claimed to be (Acts 1:2–3 NIV). Jesus understood the role and value of evidence and the importance of developing an evidential faith. It's time for all of us, as Christians, to develop a similarly reasonable faith.

Chapter 3

Principle #3:

THINK "CIRCUMSTANTIALLY"

"I think we're done with this one," I said as I closed the cover of the red three-ring binder. I slipped it back onto the long shelf next to dozens of other *red books* in the homicide vault and looked at my partner. "Now I just have to tell Paula's family."

Our agency stores its cold cases next to our solved murders in a single storage room adjacent to the detective division. Solved homicides are stored in black binders, unsolved in red. The goal is to eventually fill the room with nothing but black binders. After a year with Paula's case, I was frustrated that it was still in a red book.

Paula Robinson was murdered in the spring of 1988. She was a junior in high school, and her murder was a true *whodunit*. The crime scene told us a lot about what happened prior to her death but little about who was responsible. We knew she voluntarily allowed the suspect to enter her parent's house. We knew that she had a sandwich with the killer, and he smoked a cigarette in the backyard. We also knew that the killer was with her in her bedroom where he tried to sexually assault her and eventually ended up killing her in a horrific rage. This crime scene was one of the worst in the history of our department.

While we knew a few things about the events leading up to the murder, we knew far less about the appearance and identity of the killer. Neighbors saw a young man leaving the residence following the crime, so we had a rough idea of how tall he was and about how much he weighed. But he was wearing a cap that covered his hair, and he fled so quickly that details related to his appearance were hard to come by. We did, however, recover a few of his hairs at the crime scene, and these hairs became our best lead.

The hair provided us with a partial DNA marker—not enough to enter into the statewide database, but enough to compare to anyone we might identify as a potential suspect. All we had to do was make a list of everyone and anyone who might be responsible for this and then go out and get his DNA. Sounds easy, right? Well, we spent a year identifying, locating, and then traveling around the country to collect DNA swabs from everyone we thought might have committed this crime. We swabbed thirty-four different men. All of them voluntarily agreed to be swabbed; we didn't have to write a single search warrant. Why? Because none of them murdered Paula Robinson; none of them had anything to fear. In the end, we ran out of potential suspects. Nearly twenty-five years after the murder, we simply exhausted our leads in the case and found ourselves without any viable options. It was time to suspend the case once again.

I traveled out to see Paula's mother one last time. Her hopes had been elevated when we reopened the case (and she learned that we might have a partial DNA marker). We tried to keep her expectations low, given the difficult nature of these kinds of cases, but she couldn't help but get excited about the possibilities.

"Sometimes we have a suspect that fits the evidence and we're able to put together a case, but this is not one of those situations," I tried to explain. "I don't need to have a DNA 'hit' in order to make a case, but in this situation, the DNA that we do have has actually eliminated everyone under consideration. I'm sorry." Paula's mother simply sat and wept.

In all my years working cold-case homicides, I've yet to encounter a case that was assisted by DNA. Most cold-case teams make a living with *DNA hits*, capitalizing on the latest technology and applying new science to old cases. I haven't been that lucky. My experiences with the latest scientific advances have produced results like Paula's case: a lot of work with no progress. Instead, I've been successful assessing cases that have little or no forensic evidence but are replete with what we call *circumstantial* evidence. I wish that Paula's case was only one such example.

DIRECT AND CIRCUMSTANTIAL EVIDENCE

Evidence typically falls into two broad categories. Direct evidence is evidence that can prove something all by itself. In California, jurors are given the example of a witness who saw that it was raining outside the courthouse. Jurors are instructed, "If a witness testifies he saw it raining outside before he came into the courthouse, that testimony is direct evidence that it was raining."[9]

This testimony (if it is trustworthy) is enough, in and of itself, to prove that it is raining. On the other hand, circumstantial evidence (also known as *indirect evidence*) does not prove something on its own, but points us in the right direction by proving something related to the question at hand. This related piece of evidence can then be considered (along with additional pieces of circumstantial evidence) to figure out what happened. Jurors in California are instructed, "For example, if a witness testifies that he saw someone come inside wearing a raincoat covered with drops of water, that testimony is circumstantial evidence because it may support a conclusion that it was raining outside."[10] The more pieces of consistent circumstantial evidence, the more reasonable the conclusion. If we observed a number of people step out of the courthouse for a second, then duck back inside, soaked with little spots of water on their clothing, or saw more people coming into the courthouse, carrying umbrellas, and dripping with water, we would have several additional pieces of evidence that could be used to make the case that it was raining. The more cumulative the circumstantial evidence, the better the conclusion.

Most people tend to think that direct evidence is required in order to be certain about what happened in a given situation. But what about cases that have no direct evidence connecting the suspect to the crime scene? Can the truth be proved beyond a reasonable doubt when all the evidence we have is circumstantial? Absolutely.

Jurors are instructed to make no qualitative distinction between direct and circumstantial evidence in a case. Judges tell jurors, "Both direct and circumstantial evidence are acceptable types of evidence to prove or disprove the elements of a charge, including intent and mental state and acts necessary to a conviction, and neither is necessarily more reliable than the other. Neither is entitled to any greater weight than the other."[11] Juries make decisions about the guilt of suspects in cases that are completely circumstantial every day, and I'm very glad that they do; all my cold-case homicides have been successfully prosecuted with nothing but circumstantial evidence. Let me give you an example of the power and role of circumstantial evidence in determining the truth of a matter.

MURDER, CIRCUMSTANTIAL EVIDENCE, AND CERTAINTY

Let's examine a hypothetical murder to demonstrate the power of direct and circumstantial evidence. I want you to put yourself on the jury as the following case is being presented in court. First, let's lay out the elements of the crime. On a sunny afternoon in a quiet residential neighborhood, the calm was broken by the sound of screaming coming from a house on the corner. The scream was very short and was heard by a neighbor who was watering her lawn next door. This witness peered through the large picture window of the corner house and observed a man assaulting her neighbor in the living room. The man was viciously bludgeoning the victim with a baseball bat. The witness next saw the suspect open the front door of the house and run from the residence with the bloody bat in hand; she got a long look at his face as he ran to a car parked directly in front of the victim's residence.

An Eyewitness Is 100% Certain She Can Identify the Suspect

If this witness was now sitting on the witness stand, testifying that the defendant in our case was, in fact, the man she saw murdering the victim, she would be providing us with a piece of direct evidence. If we came to trust what this witness had to say, this one piece of direct evidence would be enough to prove that the defendant committed the murder. But what if things had been a little bit different? What if the suspect in our case had been wearing a mask when he committed the murder? If this were the case, our witness would be unable to identify the killer directly (facially) and would be able to provide us with only scant information. She could tell us about the killer's general build and what kind of clothing he was wearing, but little more. With this information alone, it would be impossible to prove that any particular defendant was the true killer.

Now, let's say that detectives developed a potential suspect (named Ron Jacobsen) and began to collect information about his activity at the time of the murder. When detectives questioned Ron, he hesitated to provide them with an alibi. When he finally did offer a story, detectives investigated it and determined that it was a lie. On the basis of this lie, do you think Ron is guilty of this murder? He fits the general physical description offered by the witness, and he has lied about his alibi. We now have two pieces of circumstantial evidence that point to Ron as the killer, but without something more, few of us would be willing to convict him. Let's see what else the detectives were able to discover.

During the interview with Ron, they learned that he had recently broken up with the victim after a tumultuous romantic relationship. He admitted to arguing with her recently about this relationship, and was extremely nervous whenever detectives focused on her. He repeatedly tried to minimize his relationship with her. Are you any closer to returning a verdict on Ron? He fits the general description, has lied about an alibi, and has been suspiciously nervous and evasive in the interview. It's not looking good for Ron, but there may be other reasonable explanations for what we've seen so far. Even though we have three pieces of circumstantial evidence that point to Ron's involvement in this crime, there still isn't enough to be certain of his guilt.

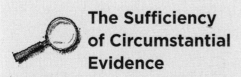

The Sufficiency of Circumstantial Evidence

"Before you may rely on circumstantial evidence to conclude that a fact necessary to find the defendant guilty has been proved, you must be convinced that the People have proved each fact essential to that conclusion beyond a reasonable doubt. Also, before you may rely on circumstantial evidence to find the defendant guilty, you must be convinced that the only reasonable conclusion supported by the circumstantial evidence is that the defendant is guilty. If you can draw two or more reasonable conclusions from the circumstantial evidence, and one of those reasonable conclusions points to innocence and another to guilt, you must accept the one that points to innocence. However, when considering circumstantial evidence, you must accept only reasonable conclusions and reject any that are unreasonable" (Section 224, *Judicial Council of California Criminal Jury Instructions*, 2006).

What if I told you that responding officers found that the suspect in this case entered the victim's residence and appeared to be waiting for her when she returned home? There were no signs of forced entry into the home, however, and detectives later learned that Ron was one of only two people who had a key to the victim's house, allowing him access whenever he wanted. Ron certainly seems to be a "person of interest" now, doesn't he? Ron matches the general description, has lied to investigators, is nervous and evasive, and had a way to enter the victim's house. The circumstantial case is growing stronger with every revelation.

What if you learned that the investigators were approached by a friend of Ron's who found a suicide note at Ron's house? This note was dated on the day of the murder and described

Ron's desperate state of mind and his desire to kill himself on the afternoon that followed the homicide. Ron apparently overcame his desire to die, however, and never took his own life. The fact that Ron was suicidal immediately following the murder adds to the cumulative case against him, but is it enough to tip the scales and convince you that he is the killer? It was certainly enough to motivate the detectives to dig a little deeper. Given all this suspicious evidence, a judge agreed to sign a search warrant, and detectives served this warrant at Ron's house. There they discovered a number of important pieces of circumstantial evidence.

First, they discovered a baseball bat hidden under Ron's bed. This bat was dented and damaged in a way that was inconsistent with its use as a piece of sporting equipment, and when the crime lab did chemical tests, detectives learned that while the bat tested negative for the presence of blood, it displayed residue that indicated it had been recently washed with bleach. In addition to this, investigators also discovered a pair of blue jeans that had been chemically spot cleaned in two areas on the front of the legs. Like the bat, the jeans tested negative for blood but demonstrated that some form of household cleaner had been used in two specific areas to remove something. Finally, detectives recovered a pair of boots from Ron's house. The witness described the boots she saw on the suspect and told responding officers that these boots had a unique stripe on the side. The boots at Ron's house also had a stripe, and after some investigation with local vendors, detectives learned that this unusual brand of boot

The Cumulative Nature of Circumstantial Evidence

The nature of circumstantial evidence is such that any one piece may be interpreted in more than one way. For this reason, jurors have to be careful not to infer something from a single piece of evidence. Circumstantial evidence usually accumulates into a powerful collection, however, and each additional piece corroborates those that came before until, together, they strongly support one inference over another.

An explanation derived from circumstantial evidence becomes more reasonable as the collection of corroborating evidence grows and the alternative explanations have been deemed unreasonable.

was relatively rare in this area. Only two stores carried the boot, and only ten pairs had been sold in the entire county in the past five years. Ron happened to own one of these ten pairs.

There are many pieces of circumstantial evidence that now point to Ron as the killer. He had access to the victim's house, lied about his activity on the day of the murder, behaved suspiciously in the interview, appeared suicidal after the murder, and was in possession of a suspicious bat matching the murder weapon, a pair of questionably spot-cleaned pants, and a set of rare boots matching the suspect's description. At this point in our assessment, I think many of you as jurors are becoming comfortable with the reasonable conclusion that Ron is our killer. But there is more.

Our eyewitness at the crime scene observed the suspect as he ran to his getaway car, and she described this car to the detectives. The witness believed that the suspect was driving a mustard-colored, early '70s Volkswagen Karmann Ghia. When executing the search warrant at Ron's house, detectives discovered (you guessed it) a yellow 1972 Karmann Ghia parked in his garage. After examining the motor vehicle records, they discovered that there was only one operational Karmann Ghia registered in the entire state.

Is Ron the killer? Given all that we know about the crime, the only reasonable conclusion is that Ron is the man who committed the murder. Is it *possible* that Ron is just unlucky enough to suffer from an unfortunate alignment of coincidences that make him appear to be guilty when he is not? Yes, anything is *possible*. But is it *reasonable*? No. Everything points to Ron, and when the evidence is considered cumulatively, Ron's guilt is the only reasonable conclusion. While there may be other explanations for these individual pieces of evidence, they are not reasonable when considered as a whole. Remember that as a juror, you are being asked to return a verdict that is based on what's reasonable, not what's possible.

Our case against Ron is entirely circumstantial; we don't have a single piece of forensic or eyewitness evidence that links him directly. These are the kinds of cases I assemble every year as I bring cold-case murderers to trial. The case against Ron is compelling and overwhelmingly sufficient. If you, as a juror, understand the nature and power of circumstantial evidence, you should be able to render a *guilty* verdict in this case.

THE COSMIC CIRCUMSTANTIAL CASE

The question of God's existence might be compared to our murder investigation. We assembled the circumstantial evidence and asked the question "How reasonable is it that this evidence can be interpreted in any way other than to indicate that Ron did this?" As the evidence accumulated, the likelihood of Ron's innocence shrank. Similarly, we can look at the evidence in our world (and in the universe) and ask, "How reasonable is it that this evidence can be interpreted in any way other than to confirm the existence of God?" We live in a universe filled with characteristics (evidences) that demand an explanation. Let's consider just a few of them:

A UNIVERSE WITH A BEGINNING

The vast majority of scientists continue to acknowledge that the universe came into being from nothing at some point in the distant past. Many have articulated this as the "big bang theory" (commonly referred to as the standard model of cosmology). But if the universe "began to exist," what "began" it? What caused the first domino to fall in the long sequence of cause-and-effect dominoes? If this first domino fell over as the result of being toppled by some other domino, how far back does this sequence go? Scientists understand the absurdity of an endless sequence of dominoes spanning back into infinite eternity; everyone is looking for an "uncaused first cause" that is capable of starting the domino run all by itself. This "uncaused first cause" must exist outside of space, time, and matter (as nothing has ever been observed to cause itself to exist). What could be uncaused and powerful enough to cause the universe? If the *caused universe* once was *not*, why is it here at all? As Gottfried Leibniz famously wrote, "Why is there something rather than nothing?"[12]

We typically think of God as an eternal, all-powerful Being who exists outside of space, time, and matter. The evidence of the finite universe (a universe that has a beginning) points

"Causal" Evidence

The Cosmological Argument:

1. Anything that begins to exist has a cause.

2. The universe began to exist.

3. Therefore, the universe must have a cause.

4. This cause must be eternal and uncaused.

5. God is the most reasonable explanation for such an uncaused first cause.

circumstantially to the existence of such a God. An incredibly powerful, uncaused first cause outside of space, time, and matter appears to be necessary to bring our universe into existence. If an eternal, all-powerful Being exists, Leibniz's famous question has an answer. A Being of this nature might freely choose to create a universe that demonstrated His power and served as a place where His cherished creatures could begin to understand His nature. The causal evidence of the universe is a significant piece of circumstantial evidence for God's existence.

A UNIVERSE WITH THE APPEARANCE OF DESIGN

Science has also helped us understand that the universe appears to be remarkably "fine-tuned" to support the existence of life. There are a number of forces in the cosmos that are precisely calibrated to work together to make life possible. The laws of electron mass, atomic mass, proton mass, strong nuclear force, weak nuclear force, speed of light, cosmological constant, gravity, mass of the universe, and many more are finely tuned to govern the universe and our world. Even within the atom itself, the precise relationship between protons, neutrons, and electrons appears to be fine-tuned and calibrated. According to Stephen Hawking, "If the proton-neutron mass difference were not about twice the mass of the electron, one would not obtain the couple of hundred or so stable nucleides that make up the elements and are the basis of chemistry and biology."[13] The forces in our universe, both small and large, appear to be fine-tuned to make life possible.

In addition to these cosmic and atomic forces, there are also specific conditions that are necessary for a planet to support life. If, for example, the size of the earth were altered slightly, life would not be possible on the planet. When a planet is too small, it loses internal heat and cannot keep its interior core active; if a planet is too large, it will have too much water and too thick of an atmosphere. As it turns out, the characteristics of a planet must be *just so* for life to be possible. The presence of liquid water, the proper distance from a star, the existence of a terrestrial crust, a properly proportioned magnetic field, the correct ratio of oxygen to nitrogen in the atmosphere, the existence of a large moon, and a mother star of a specific and particular size and type are all required. The path that leads to life on earth seems to be very narrow and difficult, yet the forces that govern the universe (and our world) appear to have a goal in mind: the production of a universe in which carbon-based life can emerge.

"Fine-Tuning" Evidence

The Anthropic Principle:

(1) The physical constants and laws of the universe appear to be uniquely and specifically related to one another (fine-tuned), making life possible on earth.

(2) The fine-tuned relationships of these laws and constants appear to be designed (as their existence by natural, unguided means seems improbable and unlikely).

(3) A design requires an intelligent designer; an incredibly vast and complex design requires an incredibly intelligent and powerful designer.

(4) God is the most reasonable explanation for such a vast, universal designer (and fine-tuner).

How can random forces be so conspicuously aligned and organized to support life? Is it merely a coincidence? That's certainly possible, but is it reasonable? If God exists, He is capable of fine-tuning the universe, and He just might have a reason to do so. The Bible, for example, describes God as the "Maker of heaven and earth" (Ps. 115:15), and describes Him as the Being who designed and created the universe with the earth in mind. The fine-tuning of the universe is another important piece of circumstantial evidence that points to the existence of an intentional, supernatural, powerful, and creative Being.

A UNIVERSE WITH COMPLEX LIFE

Scientists observe what they call the "appearance of design" in biological systems. Even Richard Dawkins (the renowned and vocal atheist and emeritus fellow of New College, Oxford) concedes that biological systems often appear designed[14] (although he proposes that a blind, natural process can somehow account for this appearance). There are many examples of cellular biological *machines* that demonstrate characteristics of "specified complexity" and bear a striking resemblance to systems and structures that have been designed

"Design" Evidence

The Teleological Argument:

(1) Structures and systems that (a) cannot be explained by some natural law requiring their appearance, (b) exist in spite of the high improbability they could result from chance, and (c) conform to an independently existing and recognizable pattern are most reasonably explained as coming from the design efforts of an intelligent agent.

(2) Biological systems possess characteristics (e.g., the information contained in the DNA code) that (a) cannot be explained by some natural law requiring their appearance, (b) exist in spite of the high improbability they could result from chance, and (c) conform to an independently existing and recognizable pattern of specified complexity.

(3) Biological systems are, therefore, most reasonably explained as coming from the design efforts of an intelligent agent.

(4) God is the most reasonable explanation for such an incredibly wise, all-powerful, intelligent agent.

by humans (intelligent agents). These characteristics lead many to the reasonable belief that unguided forces are simply insufficient to create such structures. William Dembski (the well-known mathematician, statistician, theologian, and intelligent-design advocate) has argued that specified complexity (and, therefore, the intervention of an intelligent agent) can be identified by using an "explanatory filter." If an object or event (1) cannot be explained by some natural law that necessitates its appearance, (2) exists in spite of the high improbability that it could occur as the result of chance, and (3) conforms to an independently existing and recognizable pattern, the most reasonable inference is that it is the product of an intelligent designer.[15]

Perhaps the most important evidence suggesting the involvement of an intelligent designer is the presence of DNA and the guiding role that this DNA plays in the formation of biological systems. Science has demonstrated that DNA is actually a digital code; DNA is specified *information*. DNA exhibits characteristics that, when examined through Dembski's explanatory filter, are best explained by the creative activity of an intelligent designer. As Stephen C. Meyer argues in his book *Signature in the Cell*, "Intelligence is the *only known cause* of complex functionally integrated information-processing systems" (italics original).[16] In other words, in the history of scientific and intellectual research, we can find no example in which information came from anything other than an intelligent source. If DNA is a form of specified information that guides the complex process of cellular formation and biological structures, "intelligent design stands as the best—most causally adequate—explanation for this feature of the cell, just as it stands as the best explanation for the origin of the information present in DNA itself."[17]

If biological systems display characteristics of design (in the form of specified complexity), it is reasonable to conclude that a designer has been involved in the process. What kind of designer could be responsible for the information, complexity, and specificity we see in biological systems? If God exists, He would certainly possess the characteristics and power to accomplish such a thing. The presence of specified information in biological systems is yet another piece of circumstantial evidence that points to the existence of God.

A UNIVERSE WITH OBJECTIVE MORALITY

Each and every one of us feels a certain obligation to *moral duty*. We have an intuitive sense of moral *oughtness*; we recognize that some things are right and some things are wrong, regardless of culture, time, or location. We understand that it's never morally *right* to lie, steal, or kill for the mere *fun* of it. These moral laws are transcendent and objective: their truth is not a matter of subjective opinion. Regardless of how you or I might *feel* about these laws, the truth of their moral status lies in the actions themselves, not in our subjective opinions about the actions. We may discover moral truth, but we do not invent it. Because of this, we are able to look across history and culture and make meaningful judgments about the moral *rightness* or *wrongness* of any given set of actions. We recognize that culture itself cannot be the source of moral law, and that there is instead a "law above laws" that transcends all of us. So, where does transcendent, objective moral truth come from?

"Moral" Evidence

The Axiological Argument:

(1) There is an objective, transcendent moral law.

(2) Every moral law has a moral lawgiver.

(3) Therefore, there is an objective, transcendent moral lawgiver.

(4) God is the most reasonable explanation for such a transcendent moral lawgiver.

All moral laws come from moral lawmakers. If there exists even one transcendent moral law (e.g., it's never morally *right* to kill someone for the mere *fun* of it), there must exist a transcendent moral *source*.

Darwinian evolution has great difficulty accounting for the existence of objective moral obligations for two reasons. First, if we live in a purely natural, physical world governed by the "cause and effect" relationships between chemical processes in our brains, "free will" is an illusion, and the idea of true moral choice is nonsensical. How can I, as a detective, hold a murderer accountable for a series of chemical reactions that occurred in his brain when he didn't have the freedom to escape the causal chain of biological events?

In addition to this, Darwinian evolution cannot produce truly objective morality. If moral truths are merely behavioral concepts that humans have created to aid their survival, morality is once again rooted in the subject (humans) rather than in the objective moral truth claim under consideration (e.g., whether it's ever morally *right* to kill someone for the mere *fun* of it). If morality is simply a convention of our species, we'd better hope that science-fiction writers are wrong about the possibility of sentient life in other parts of the universe. Unless there is a "law above the laws," an entity such as *Star Trek*'s United Federation of Planets would be powerless to stop immoral behavior. Objective morality must be rooted in something bigger than the evolutionary development of any one species.

If God exists, He would certainly transcend all species, cultures, locations, and moments in time. For this reason, the existence of transcendent moral truth is best explained by the existence of God as the transcendent source of such truth. Once again, we have an important piece of circumstantial evidence.

The cumulative circumstantial case for God's existence is much like the circumstantial case we made in our murder investigation. The more evidence we gathered, the clearer it was that Ron's involvement as the killer could account for all of it. Ron was either incredibly unlucky or incredibly guilty. At some point we recognized that the evidence made Ron's guilt in the matter the only reasonable inference, and we got there without a single piece of direct evidence. In a similar way, the circumstantial evidence in our universe is consistent with God's existence and involvement as the uncaused first cause, the fine-tuner, the designer, and the moral lawgiver required to account for all the evidence we observe. As in the homicide investigation, the more evidence we gather, the more reasonable our conclusion becomes. We've only briefly described four lines of circumstantial evidence for God's existence. Much more can (and has) been said about these areas of evidence by the *expert witnesses* listed at the end of this book. In addition to these evidences, investigators and philosophers have offered many additional arguments (including the Ontological Argument, the Transcendental Argument, the Argument from Religious or Aesthetic Experience, and many more). The cumulative circumstantial evidence pointing to God's existence is either incredibly coincidental or a compelling indication of the truth of the matter. At some point, God's existence is the only reasonable inference in light of the evidence, and like our homicide, we can get there without a single piece of direct (or forensic) evidence.

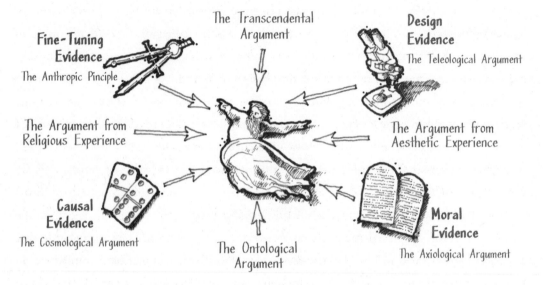

As the circumstantial case against Ron grew, the likelihood of his guilt also grew. As the circumstantial case for God grows, the likelihood of His existence also grows. If the evidence for Ron's guilt is compelling enough to reasonably conclude that he is guilty, the evidence for God's existence is compelling enough to reasonably conclude that He exists.

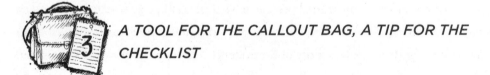

A TOOL FOR THE CALLOUT BAG, A TIP FOR THE CHECKLIST

It's time to add another principle to our investigative checklist as we assemble the tools we'll need to investigate and communicate the claims of Christianity. Circumstantial evidence has been unfairly maligned over the years; it's important to recognize that this form of evidence is not inferior in the eyes of the law. In fact, there are times when you can trust circumstantial evidence far more than you can trust direct evidence. Witnesses, for example, can lie or be mistaken about their observations; they must be evaluated before they can be trusted (we'll talk about that in the next chapter). Circumstantial evidence, on the other hand, cannot lie; it is what it is. You and I have the ability to assess and make an inference from the circumstantial evidence using our own reasoning power to come to a conclusion. It's not a coincidence that I was a nonbeliever before I learned anything about the nature of evidence. In those days, as I was evaluating the claims of Christianity, I demanded a form of evidence (direct evidence) that simply isn't available to anyone who is studying historical events. I failed to see that rejecting (or devaluing) circumstantial evidence would prevent me from understanding anything about history (when eyewitnesses of a particular event are unavailable for an interview). If I continued to reject (or devalue) circumstantial evidence, I would never have been able to successfully prosecute a single cold-case killer. All of us need to respect the power and nature of circumstantial evidence in determining truth so that we can be open to the role that circumstantial evidence plays in making the case for Christianity.

I'm alarmed sometimes when I hear Christians make inaccurate statements related to the nature of evidence. When discussing evidence with skeptics, we don't need to concede that a particular fact related to the Christian worldview is not a piece of evidence simply because it is not a piece of *direct* evidence. Even though a particular fact may not have the individual power to prove our case in its entirety, it is no less valid as we assemble the evidence. When we treat circumstantial evidence as though it is not evidence at all, we do ourselves a disservice as ambassadors for the Christian worldview. Circumstantial evidence is powerful if it is properly understood. When defending our belief in the existence of God, the resurrection of Jesus, or the validity of the Christian worldview, we may need to take some time to explain the nature, role, and power of circumstantial evidence. It's time well spent, because most of our friends, family members, and coworkers have not given this much thought. We need to help people understand the depth and quantity of the evidence that supports our view. Remember, circumstantial cases are powerful when they are cumulative. The more evidence that points to a specific explanation, the more reasonable that explanation becomes (and the more unlikely that the evidence can be explained away as coincidental). Take the time to discover and master the evidence for yourself so you can articulate the deep, rich, and robust evidential support for the claims of Christianity.

Chapter 4

Principle #4:

TEST YOUR WITNESSES

"Mr. Strickland, how can you be so sure that this man is the same man who robbed you?" The defendant's attorney stood up as he examined the witness and pointed to the man sitting next to him at the defense table. His questions were becoming more accusatory. "Isn't it true that the robbery occurred well after sunset?"

"Well, yes, it was about ten thirty at night." Jerry Strickland seemed to be preparing himself for an attack. He correctly interpreted the tone of the attorney's question and straightened himself in the witness box. He scratched his arm nervously. I knew that Strickland was a smart guy, and I was curious to see how he would hold up under this pressure. I had been working the robbery-homicide desk when I was assigned this case, and I knew it would all come down to Strickland's identification of the suspect.

"I notice you are wearing glasses today, but isn't it true that you weren't wearing those glasses on the night of the robbery?" The defense attorney began to walk slowly toward Mr. Strickland, his arms crossed, his chin slightly elevated as he glanced briefly at the jury.

"I had my glasses on to start with, but I got punched and they flew off my head," replied Strickland as he pushed his glasses up on his nose. "After that I'm not sure what happened to them." Jerry's testimony started off calmly enough under the direct questioning of the deputy district attorney, but now he seemed to be losing his confidence under the pressure of the cross-examination.

"How long did this episode with your attacker last?" the defense attorney asked.

"Just a few seconds," replied Strickland.

"So let me get this right. You're willing to send my client to jail for years, yet you only saw the suspect for a few seconds, late at night, in the dark, without the benefit of your glasses?" The defendant's attorney was now facing the jury. His question was rhetorical; he made his point and was now watching the jury to see if it had the impact he intended.

"Well, I-I'm not sure what to say," Strickland stammered hesitantly as he sank in his chair.

The prosecutor was an energetic, competent attorney who understood the value of this victim's eyewitness testimony. She waited for the defense attorney to return to his seat and then prepared for her redirect. "Mr. Strickland, you said earlier that you were robbed by this man. I want to ask you a question. Given your observations of the robber prior to the moment when he punched you; your observations of the suspect's height, the shape and features of his face, his body type, and the structure of his physique, I want you to rate your certainty about the identity of the suspect. On a scale of one to one hundred, how certain are you that this man sitting here at the defendant's table is the man who robbed you?"

Jerry Strickland sat up in his chair and leaned forward. He paused just slightly before answering. "I am 100 percent certain that this is the man who robbed me. There is no doubt in my mind."

The jury returned a verdict in less than thirty minutes and convicted the defendant, largely on the strength of Strickland's eyewitness testimony. While the defense attorney did his best to illustrate the potential limits of the victim's ability to accurately describe the suspect, the jury was convinced that Jerry Strickland was a competent eyewitness. They believed his testimony, and the rest was easy. Once you come to trust an eyewitness, you eventually must come to terms with the testimony that eyewitness has offered.

LEARNING TO TRUST AN EYEWITNESS

So, how do we come to trust what an eyewitness has to say? How can we evaluate a witness to make sure he or she is someone we can trust in the first place? Jurors are asked to evaluate witnesses in court cases every day. If you were sitting on a jury in the state of California today, the judge would give you some advice about assessing the witnesses who are about to testify before you. In fact, the judge would tell you that you ought to consider a number of factors and ask yourself the following questions:

1. How well could the witness see, hear, or otherwise perceive the things about which the witness testified?

2. How well was the witness able to remember and describe what happened?

3. What was the witness's behavior while testifying?

4. Did the witness understand the questions and answer them directly?

5. Was the witness's testimony influenced by a factor such as bias or prejudice, a personal relationship with someone involved in the case, or a personal interest in how the case is decided?

6. What was the witness's attitude about the case or about testifying?

7. Did the witness make a statement in the past that is consistent or inconsistent with his or her testimony?

8. How reasonable is the testimony when you consider all the other evidence in the case?

9. [Did other evidence prove or disprove any fact about which the witness testified?]

10. [Did the witness admit to being untruthful?]

11. [What is the witness's character for truthfulness?]

12. [Has the witness been convicted of a felony?]

13. [Has the witness engaged in (other) conduct that reflects on his or her believability?]

14. [Was the witness promised immunity or leniency in exchange for his or her testimony?][18]

These are the questions that jurors are encouraged to ask as they evaluate witnesses who testify in court. Sometimes these witnesses are testifying in trials that are a matter of life and death—trials that involve defendants who may ultimately face the death penalty. In the end, there are four critical areas of concern when it comes to evaluating an eyewitness:

WERE THEY EVEN THERE?

First, we've got to find out if the witness was even present to observe anything in the first place. This concern is captured by questions like "How well could the witness see, hear, or otherwise perceive the things about which the witness testified?" You might think that this is a silly issue to have to examine, but I can tell you from personal experience that there are times when people will claim to be a witness or participant in a case when they, in fact, were nowhere near the event. I once reopened a case from the early 1970s that my father helped investigate when he was working homicides. I remembered the case as a boy and the stress that it caused my dad when it went unsolved. The case was well known in the region and received an incredible amount of publicity. As I examined the cold case thirty years later, I discovered that the original investigators had been deceived by a man who came forward and confessed to being the killer. He sat with detectives over the course of many days and offered just enough detail to convince them that he had murdered the victim. In truth, he had nothing to do with the crime, but was seeking the attention and twisted fame it brought him. He was eventually exposed as a fraud, but his involvement in the case distracted the investigators long enough to take them off the trail of the real killer. This kind of thing happens in high-profile cases that offer fifteen minutes of fame. This is why we need to make sure that an eyewitness was truly present to see what he or she claims to have seen.

HAVE THEY BEEN HONEST AND ACCURATE?

The primary concern that most of us have when evaluating witnesses is the issue of credibility. A witness who was present at the time of the crime but who is lying about what happened is of no value. The jury instructions address this issue with questions like "Did the witness make a statement in the past that is consistent or inconsistent with his or her testimony?" In recent years, with the large number of court cases that have been publicized and broadcast nationally, we've all seen examples of witnesses who have been discredited as liars. When Michael Jackson was accused of child molestation in 2003, for example, the victim's mother took the stand as a witness. The defense exposed the fact that she had lied about a prior shoplifting incident in 1998. When the jurors discovered this, many (if not all) discredited her testimony in the 2003 case. When a witness is caught about a lie in the past, his or her testimony about the case can be called into question. It's important, however, to remember that jurors are also given this instruction by the judge:

> If you decide that a witness deliberately lied about something significant in
> this case, you should consider not believing anything that witness says. Or, if

you think the witness lied about some things, but told the truth about others, you may simply accept the part that you think is true and ignore the rest.[19]

Assume the Witness Is Trustworthy

Jurors have a duty to take an unbiased look at witnesses and assume the best in them until they have a reason to do otherwise. Jurors are told to set aside "any bias or prejudice [they] may have," including any based on the witness's gender, race, religion, or national origin. In addition jurors are instructed: "If the evidence establishes that a witness's character for truthfulness has not been discussed among the people who know him or her, you may conclude from the lack of discussion that the witness's character for truthfulness is good" (Section 105, *Judicial Council of California Criminal Jury Instructions*, 2006).

There may be a good reason for a witness to lie about something unrelated to the case (perhaps to avoid embarrassment or to protect the privacy of a loved one), yet still tell the truth about what he or she saw in the crime under consideration. Let's face it, all of us have lied about one thing or another. Jurors have to decide if a witness has simply lied on occasion (for some understandable reason) or is an untrustworthy, habitual liar. In the Michael Jackson case, the jurors seemed to have decided that the witness was the latter.

CAN THEY BE VERIFIED?

It's fair to ask if a witness's observations can be verified by some other piece of evidence or testimony. This concern is captured in questions like "How reasonable is the testimony when you consider all the other evidence in the case?" or "Did other evidence prove or disprove any fact about which the witness testified?" If a witness tells you that the defendant committed a robbery at a bank teller's window, and you come to find the defendant's fingerprints at that particular counter, you've got a piece of corroborating evidence that begins to verify what the eyewitness has to say. The direct evidence of additional eyewitnesses can also verify a statement, and circumstantial evidence (forensic or otherwise) can help validate what a witness has offered.

DO THEY HAVE AN ULTERIOR MOTIVE?

Finally, jurors have to figure out if a witness has a motive to lie. That's why the jury instructions include questions like "Was the witness's testimony influenced by a factor such as bias or prejudice, a personal relationship with someone involved in the case, or a personal interest in how the case is decided?" I've investigated a number of spousal-abuse cases involving husbands and wives who have assaulted each other. Trying to get to the truth of the matter was extremely difficult. Both sides were so angry with one another that they were willing to do or say anything to get the ex-spouse in trouble. Each appeared to have a motive to lie or exaggerate about the violent behavior of the other spouse, and jurors had difficulty discerning the truth amid all the anger and embellishment.

These four critical areas should be examined before we trust an eyewitness. If we can establish that a witness was present, has been accurate and honest in the past, is verified by additional evidence, and has no motive to lie, we can trust what the witness has to say.

SO, WHY CAN'T THEY AGREE?

If there's one thing my experience as a detective has revealed, however, it's that witnesses often make conflicting and inconsistent statements when describing what they saw at a crime scene. They frequently disagree with one another and either fail to see something obvious or describe the same event in a number of conflicting ways. The more witnesses involved in a case, the more likely there will be points of disagreement.

A Disagreement Is Not a Disqualifier

Jurors are instructed to be cautious not to automatically disqualify a witness just because some part of his or her statement may disagree with an additional piece of evidence or testimony: "Do not automatically reject testimony just because of inconsistencies or conflicts. Consider whether the differences are important or not. People sometimes honestly forget things or make mistakes about what they remember. Also, two people may witness the same event yet see or hear it differently" (Section 105, *Judicial Council of California Criminal Jury Instructions*, 2006).

I can remember a particular homicide that occurred in a restaurant parking lot in our town, late one rainy night, well after our homicide team went home for the day. Patrol officers responded to the scene and discovered that the suspect was already long gone. The officers located three witnesses and interviewed them very briefly. They quickly recognized that the murder investigation would require the involvement of our team. Radio dispatch called our sergeant, and he began waking us up by telephone, summoning four of us to handle the investigation. It took me nearly an hour to get into a suit and drive to the location of the crime. When I got there, I discovered that the officers gathered the witnesses and put them in the backseat of their police unit so they wouldn't get drenched in the rain. This simple act of kindness nearly ruined the case.

I learned many years ago the importance of separating witnesses. If eyewitnesses are quickly separated from one another, they are far more likely to provide an uninfluenced, pure account of what they saw. Yes, their accounts will inevitably differ from the accounts of others who witnessed the same event, but that is the natural result of a witness's past experience, perspective, and worldview. I can deal with the inconsistencies; I expect them. But when witnesses are allowed to sit together (prior to being interviewed) and compare notes and observations, I'm likely to get one harmonized version of the event. Everyone will offer the same story. While this may be tidier, it will come at the sacrifice of some important detail that a witness is willing to forfeit in order to align his or her story with the other witnesses. I'm not willing to pay that price. I would far rather have three messy, apparently contradictory versions of the event than one harmonized version that has eliminated some important detail. I know in the end I'll be able to determine the truth of the matter by examining all three stories. The apparent contradictions are usually easy to explain once I learn something about the witnesses and their perspectives (both visually and personally) at the time of the crime.

Let me give you an example. Many years ago I investigated a robbery in which a male suspect entered a small grocery store, walked up to the counter, and calmly contacted the cashier. The suspect removed a handgun from his waistband and placed it on the counter. He pointed it at the cashier, using his right hand to hold the gun on the counter, his finger on the trigger. The suspect quietly told the cashier to empty the register of its money and place it in a plastic bag. The cashier complied and gave the robber all the money in the drawer. The robber then calmly walked from the store. This robbery was observed by two witnesses, who were properly separated and interviewed apart from one another. When the crime report was assigned to me as the investigator, I read the officer's summary and wondered if the witnesses were describing the same robber:

Sylvia Ramos
38-yr.-old Female
Married with Kids
Interior Designer
Picking Up Milk on the Way Home from Work

Paul Meher
23-yr.-old Male
Single, No Kids
Apprentice Plumber
Visiting the Cashier on His Day Off

How They Described the Suspect

Younger Boy in His Teens	Man about 24–25 Years Old
Very Polite with Sweet Voice	Threatening Scowl
Did Not Have a Gun	Had a Ruger P95 9mm Handgun
Bought Something at the Store	Bought Nothing at the Store
Wore an Izod Polo Shirt	Might Have Worn a T-Shirt
Had No Vehicle	Ran to a '90s Tan Nissan

At first, these statements seemed to describe two different men committing two different crimes. But, the more I spoke with the witnesses, the more I realized that both were reliable in spite of the fact they seemed to be saying different things about the suspect. Sylvia Ramos was hurrying home from work and stopped at the store to purchase some milk and a few small items. She stood in line behind the suspect as he calmly committed the robbery. While she heard the tone of his voice, she never heard his words distinctly, and she never saw a gun. She described him as a polite young man in his teens. Based on the way the cashier handed the robber the bag, Sylvia believed that the robber made a purchase prior to committing the crime. Sylvia immediately recognized the suspect's blue shirt as a classic IZOD polo because many of the men in her office wore this style of shirt when she first started her career as a designer. In fact, she had recently purchased one for her husband. Sylvia watched the robber walk slowly out of the business and across the parking lot as he left the area. She was sure that he didn't have a "getaway" car.

Paul Meher was visiting the cashier when the robbery occurred. The cashier was an old friend from high school, and Paul was standing behind the counter with his friend at the time of the crime. Paul couldn't remember many details related to the suspect's clothing, but believed that he was wearing a T-shirt. He was certain, however, that the robber pointed a gun at his friend, and he recognized this pistol as a Ruger P95 because his father owned one that was identical. Paul focused on the gun during most of the robbery, but he also observed that the suspect scowled and had a menacing expression on his face. The robber spoke his words slowly and deliberately in a way that Paul interpreted as threatening. Paul described the man as just slightly older than him, at approximately twenty-four to twenty-five years of age. He was certain that the suspect made no effort to purchase anything prior to the crime, and afterward, Paul had a visual angle through the glass storefront that allowed him to see that the robber walked to the end of the parking lot, then ran to a tan-colored, 1990s Nissan four-door.

Once I interviewed these two witnesses, I understood why they seemed to disagree on several key points. In the end, many things impact the way witnesses observe an event. A lot depends on where a witness is located in relationship to the action. We've also got to consider the personal experiences and interests that cause some witnesses to focus on one aspect of the event and some to focus on another. Sylvia was older and had difficulty estimating the age of the suspect, but her design interests and experience with her husband helped her to correctly identify the kind of shirt the robber wore. Paul had personal experience with pistols and was sitting in a position that gave him an entirely different perspective as he watched the robbery unfold. As the detective handling the case, it was my job to understand each witness well enough to take the best they had to offer and come to a conclusion about what really happened. Every case I handle is like this; witnesses seldom agree on every detail. In fact, when two people agree completely on every detail of their account, I am inclined to believe that they have either contaminated each other's observations or are working together to pull the wool over my eyes. I expect truthful, reliable eyewitnesses to disagree along the way.

THE LAST WITNESS TO BE INTERVIEWED

Before I move away from this issue, it's important to add one final observation. I've worked a number of murder cases where there were many eyewitnesses who had to be interviewed. While at the scene, I took each witness off to the side to get his or her account without the input of other eyewitnesses. On one occasion, I discovered that an additional, previously unidentified witness was quietly standing within earshot of my interviews, waiting for an opportunity to talk to me. Up to this point, none of the officers or detectives was even aware of the fact that this person had seen anything, so while I was happy to hear what she had to say, it was clear that she had not been isolated. She was already aware of what others had described. When interviewed, she actually provided important information that the other witnesses had missed completely. I was grateful that she had been patient and waited to identify herself to us.

I observed something interesting about her statement, however. Because she had been eavesdropping on the interviews we were conducting and was already aware of what others said, she was inclined to skip over the details that had been offered by the first witnesses. She did an excellent job of *filling in the blanks*, but a poor job of covering the essential details of the crime that others had already described. If I had not repeatedly asked her to start at the beginning and tell me everything she saw, she would undoubtedly have given me an incomplete account that, if compared to the first statements of eyewitnesses, would have looked like a contradiction. In my years of collecting eyewitness statements, I've come to recognize that witnesses who are already aware of what has been offered are far more likely to simply supply the *missing details*. While this witness may offer something that's critical to the case and was previously unknown, he or she may also offer a version that is less detailed in many ways.

The Early Recognition of the Eyewitnesses

The early church fathers and leaders recognized that the Gospels were the eyewitness testimony of the apostles, and they set the Gospels apart for this reason. The ancient Christian author Tertullian wrote in AD 212: "The same authority of the apostolic churches will afford evidence to the other Gospels also, which we possess equally through their means, and according to their usage—I mean the Gospels of John and Matthew—whilst that which Mark published may be affirmed to be Peter's whose interpreter Mark was" (*Against Marcion*).

THE GOSPEL WRITERS AS EYEWITNESSES

Growing up as a skeptic, I never thought of the biblical narrative as an eyewitness account. Instead, I saw it as something more akin to religious mythology—a series of stories designed to make a point. But when I read through the Gospels (and then the letters that followed them), it appeared clear that the writers of Scripture identified themselves as eyewitnesses and viewed their writings as testimony. Peter identified himself as a "witness of the sufferings of Christ" (1 Pet. 5:1) and as one of many "eyewitnesses of His majesty" (2 Pet. 1:16–17). The apostle John claimed that he was writing as an eyewitness when he described the life and death of

Jesus. He identified himself as "the disciple who is testifying to these things and wrote these things" (John 21:24), and said that he was reporting "what we have heard, what we have seen with our eyes, what we have looked at and touched with our hands" (1 John 1:1). The apostles saw themselves first and foremost as a group of eyewitnesses, and they understood that their shared observations were a powerful testimony to what they claimed to be true. When Judas left the group, they quickly replaced him and demonstrated the high value they placed on their status as eyewitnesses. They set out to choose one "of the men who have accompanied us all the time that the Lord Jesus went in and out among us—beginning with the baptism of John until the day that He was taken up from us" (Acts 1:21–22). They replaced Judas with another eyewitness.

As I read through the book of Acts, I realized that the apostles repeatedly identified themselves as eyewitnesses and called upon their testimony as the foundation for all their preaching and teaching. In Peter's very first sermon at Pentecost, he told the crowd that the disciples "are all witnesses" of the fact of the resurrection (Acts 2:32), and he repeated this claim later at Solomon's Colonnade (Acts 3:15). When Peter and John were eventually arrested for testifying about the resurrection, they told the members of the Sanhedrin, "We cannot stop speaking about what we have seen and heard" (Acts 4:20), and they promptly returned to the streets where they "were giving testimony to the resurrection of the Lord Jesus" (Acts 4:33). Over and over again, the apostles clearly identified themselves as "witnesses of all the things He [Jesus] did both in the land of the Jews and in Jerusalem" (Acts 10:39), and used this status as the foundation for everything they taught. Even Paul relied on his status as an eyewitness. When Christian communities began to blossom across Asia Minor, Paul wrote to many of them and identified himself both as an apostle and as someone who could testify as an eyewitness. Paul said that

The Committed Biblical Witnesses

The New Testament accounts repeatedly use words that are translated as "witness," "testimony," "bear witness," or "testify." They are translated from versions of the Greek words *marturia* or *martureo*. The modern word *martyr* finds its root in these same Greek words; the terms eventually evolved into describing people who (like the apostolic eyewitnesses) remained so committed to their testimony concerning Jesus that they would rather die than recant.

Jesus "appeared to James, then to all the apostles; and last of all, as to one untimely born, He appeared to me also" (1 Cor. 15:7–8).

As the apostles began to write out their eyewitness observations, early Christians gave these accounts great authority and respect. In fact, as the "canon" of emerging New Testament Scripture was examined by the church fathers (the early leaders of the growing Christian community), the issue of *apostolic authority* was the first and foremost criterion for whether or not a particular writing made it into the collection. Was the text written by an apostolic eyewitness (Matthew, John, Peter, Paul, James, Jude, et al.) or by someone who at least had meaningful access to one or more of these eyewitnesses (e.g., Mark and Luke)? Only the accounts of the original eyewitnesses were given serious consideration, and the Gospels have always been understood as a set of eyewitness accounts.

The question, of course, is whether or not they can be trusted, and that's the focus of the second section of this book. We'll investigate the Gospels as eyewitness accounts, asking the same kinds of questions that judges encourage jurors to ask of witnesses in criminal proceedings. We'll ask if the apostolic eyewitnesses were present at the events that have been recorded. We'll ask if they were accurate and honest. We'll ask if their testimony can be verified in some way. Finally, we'll investigate whether or not they had an ulterior motive. When jury members conclude that a witness can be trusted, they must come to grips with what the witness has to say and use this testimony as the foundation for future decisions they may make about the truth of the case. If the gospel writers are found to be reliable, we can accept their statements as the foundation for future decisions we make about the truth of Jesus's life and God's existence.

THE EXPECTATIONS FROM EXPERIENCE

Before I ever examined the reliability of the gospel accounts, I had a reasonable expectation about what a dependable set of eyewitness statements might look like, given my experience as a detective. When more than one witness observes a crime, I expect to see the following characteristics in their statements:

THEIR STATEMENTS WILL BE PERSPECTIVAL

Each eyewitness will describe the event from his or her spatial and emotional perspective. Not everyone will be in the same position to see the same series of events or the same details. I will have to puzzle together statements that might at first appear contradictory; each statement will be colored by the personal experiences and worldviews of the witnesses.

THEIR STATEMENTS WILL BE PERSONAL

Each eyewitness will describe the event in his or her own language, using his or her own expressions and terms. As a result, the same event may be described with varying degrees of passion or with divergent details that are simply the result of individual tastes and interests.

THEIR STATEMENTS MAY CONTAIN AREAS OF COMPLETE AGREEMENT

Some aspects of each eyewitness statement may be completely identical. This is particularly true when witnesses describe aspects of the crime that were dramatic or important to the sequence of events. It's also true when later witnesses are aware of what others have offered and simply affirm the prior description by telling me, "The rest occurred just the way he said."

Perspectives and Biblical *Inerrancy*

The traditional definition of biblical *inerrancy* maintains that the Bible is accurate and completely free of error. Inerrancy does not require, however, that the biblical texts be free of any personal perspectives or idiosyncrasies. In fact, the existence of these distinctive features only helps us recognize the accounts as true eyewitness statements written by real people who revealed their human gifts (and limitations) along the way. These characteristics can help us have confidence in both the accuracy and the reliability of the accounts.

LATER STATEMENTS MAY FILL IN THE GAPS

Finally, as described earlier, I expect late witnesses who are aware of prior statements to simply *fill in* what has not been said previously.

It turns out that my expectations of true, reliable eyewitness accounts are met (at least preliminarily and superficially) by the Gospels. All four accounts are written from a different perspective and contain unique details that are specific to the eyewitnesses. There are, as a result, divergent (apparently *contradictory*) recollections that can be pieced together to get a complete *picture* of what occurred. All four accounts are highly personal, utilizing the distinctive language of each witness. Mark is far more passionate and active in his choice of adjectives, for example. Several of the accounts (Mark, Matthew, and Luke) contain blocks of identical (or nearly identical) descriptions. This may be the result of common agreement at particularly important points in the narrative, or (more likely) the result of later eyewitnesses saying, "The rest occurred just the way he said." Finally, the last account (John's gospel) clearly attempts to *fill in* the details that were not offered by the prior eyewitnesses. John, aware of what the earlier eyewitnesses had already written, appears to make little effort to cover the same ground. Even before examining the Gospels with the rigor we are going to apply in section 2, I recognized that they were consistent with what I would expect to see, given my experience as a detective.

THE *RELIABLE* BIBLE

In the end, it all comes down to the reliability of these accounts. When I was a nonbeliever, I heard Christians talk about the *inerrancy* or *infallibility* of the Bible, at least as these terms are typically applied to the original manuscripts that were composed by the authors. I examined these concepts in depth in seminary many years later, but as I first read the accounts in the Gospels, I was far more interested in evaluating their *reliability* as eyewitness accounts than their *inerrancy* as divine communiqués. I knew from my experience as a detective that the best eyewitness accounts contained points of disagreement and that this did not automatically invalidate their reliability.

If it was God's desire to provide us with an accurate and reliable account of the life of Jesus, an account we could trust and recognize as consistent with other forms of eyewitness testimony, God surely accomplished it with the four gospel accounts. Yes, the accounts are *messy*. They are filled with idiosyncrasies and personal perspectives along with common retellings of familiar stories. There are places where critics can argue that there appear to be contradictions, and there are places where each account focuses on something important to the author, while ignoring details of importance to other writers. But would we expect anything less from true, reliable eyewitness accounts? I certainly would not, based on what I've seen over the years.

Surely these apparent "contradictions" and curious peculiarities were present in the early texts and obvious to the earliest of Christians. The oldest gospel manuscripts we have display this sort of *eyewitness variability*, and there is no reason to think the originals were any less unique or idiosyncratic. The early believers could have destroyed all but one of the accounts, changed the *conflicting* details, or simply *harmonized* the Gospels. But these diverse accounts were preserved (as they are) because they are true; they display all the earmarks we would expect in true eyewitness testimony. If the early church had eliminated the four eyewitness perspectives and limited us to one tidy version, we would inevitably have missed some significant detail. If I had tried to *clean up* the apparent contradictions between Sylvia's and Paul's testimonies, I may have ignored the clear descriptions of the gun and the shirt. Instead, I took Sylvia and Paul at their word, learned about their personal perspectives, and wrote a search warrant for these two items. I recovered both the shirt and the pistol and eventually used these pieces of evidence to convict the robber in this case.

NOT ALL MEMORIES ARE CREATED EQUALLY

Sylvia and Paul were reliable eyewitnesses, even though their individual perspectives framed their observations of the robbery in unique ways. But what if many years passed before their testimony was required in court? Couldn't the passage of time impact their memories of the event? We've all forgotten details from past events; we understand what it is like to struggle with a particular memory. Isn't it possible, reasonable in fact, that Sylvia and Paul might forget or confuse some important detail of this robbery?

Much has been written in recent years about the "unreliability" of eyewitness testimony over time, especially as cases that previously hinged on eyewitness identification have been overturned by new DNA evidence. In fact, the New Jersey Supreme Court recently pointed to cases such as these and cited a "troubling lack of reliability in eyewitness identifications." As a result, the court issued new rules to make it easier for defendants to challenge eyewitness evidence in criminal cases.[20] Given that some eyewitness identifications have been overturned by DNA evidence, why should we trust eyewitness testimony about an event in the past?

In my experience as a cold-case detective, I've learned that not all memories are created equally. Let me give you an example. If you asked me what I did five years ago on Valentine's Day (February 14 here in the United States), I may or may not be able to remember many of the details. I probably took my wife out for dinner or maybe a short vacation. I could probably tax my memory and recall the day with some accuracy, but I may confuse it with other Valentine's Day memories; after all, I've got thirty-three memories of Valentine's Day with my wife to sift through (we started dating in 1979). This day was important to me, so it may *stick out* in my memory a bit more than other days in February, but if you ask me for specific chronological details, I may struggle to recall the particulars from Valentine's Day five years ago.

But if you ask me to recall the specifics of Valentine's Day in 1988, I can provide you with a much more accurate recollection. This was the day that Susie and I were married. It definitely *sticks out* in my mind. I can remember the details with much more precision because this event was unequaled in my life and experience. It's the only time I've ever been married, and the excitement and importance of the event were unparalleled for me. Valentine's Day stands out when compared to other days in February, but this Valentine's Day was even more special. Not all memories are equally important or memorable.

When eyewitnesses encounter an event that is similarly unique, unrepeated, and powerful, they are far more likely to remember it and recall specific details accurately. Sylvia and Paul had never observed a robbery prior to the one they observed in the liquor store. It was a unique, unrepeated event. As such, it stuck out in their minds and memories. This doesn't mean that their testimonies ought to be accepted without testing; the four criteria we've already described in this chapter must still be applied to Sylvia and Paul. We still have to determine if they were present to see the robbery and have a history of honesty and accuracy. We still need to determine if their testimonies can be corroborated by additional evidence and examine their motives to make sure they are not lying. If these criteria can be met, we have good reason to trust their testimonies as reliable.

THE UNEQUALED EVENTS OF THE NEW TESTAMENT

I remember the day I was married because it was unique, unrepeated, and personally important. Now put yourself in the shoes of the apostles as they witnessed the miracles and resurrection of Jesus. None of these eyewitnesses had ever seen anyone like Jesus before. He did more than teach them important lessons; He astonished the eyewitnesses with miracles that were unique and personally powerful. The apostles experienced only one Jesus in their lifetime; they observed only one man rise from the dead. The resurrection was unique, unrepeated, and powerful.

The gospel eyewitnesses observed a singularly powerful and memorable event and provided us with accounts that are distinctive, idiosyncratic, personal, and reliable. We simply have to take the time to understand the perspective and character of each eyewitness and then determine if the accounts are trustworthy given the four criteria we have described (more on that in section 2).

 ## A TOOL FOR THE CALLOUT BAG, A TIP FOR THE CHECKLIST

This may be one of the most important principles we can tuck away in our callout bag. Unless you've worked a lot with eyewitnesses and have become familiar with the nature of apparent contradictions in eyewitness accounts, it's easy to assume that people are lying (or are mistaken) simply because they don't agree on every detail or have ignored some facts in favor of others. If nothing else, we have to remember that an eyewitness account can be reliable in spite of *apparent* contradictions. While we might complain about two accounts that appear to differ in some way, we would be even more suspicious if there were absolutely no peculiarities or differences. If this were the case with the Gospels, I bet we would argue that they were the result of some elaborate collusion. As we examine the gospel accounts, we need to give the writers the same benefit of the doubt we would give other eyewitnesses. Human eyewitnesses produce human eyewitness accounts; they are often idiosyncratic and personal, but reliable nonetheless.

As a Christian, I recognize that the Bible is *God's Word*, but I also recognize that it was delivered to us through the observations and recollections of human eyewitnesses. Before I share that the Bible has something important to offer, I typically take the time to make a case for *why* the Bible has something important to offer. It's important for people to see that the writers identified themselves as *eyewitnesses*. They weren't writing *moral fiction*. They were recording what they saw with their own eyes, heard with their own ears, and touched with their own hands. Let's recognize the importance of biblical *reliability* and help our skeptical friends recognize the nature of personal, reliable eyewitness testimony. Many of us have seen or heard something during the course of our lives that forever changed the way we thought about the world around us. That's precisely what happened to the gospel writers. Their observations changed them forever, and their testimony can change the world we live in.

Chapter 5
Principle #5:

HANG ON EVERY WORD

After an exhausting day of interviews, we were really no closer to having a suspect in view. We were still looking for a *trailhead*, a direction that would lead us to the suspect who killed a beautiful young woman in our city in 1981. We managed to locate all the men and women who had been suspected of this crime many years ago and arranged interviews with them. Eight hours into these meetings, I was still undecided about who might be the most likely candidate for the murder. Then Scott Taylor said something that caught my attention.

Scott dated the victim about one year prior to the murder. He had been interviewed back in 1981, along with many other men who dated or knew her. The original investigators had been unable to single out any one of these men as a primary suspect. Today, Scott said something that seemed unusual. It wasn't anything big. In fact, my partner didn't catch it at all.

We asked each candidate how he or she "felt" about the victim's murder. We were careful to ask the question the same way each time we asked it; the responses were important to us as we tried to understand the relationships between the potential suspects and the victim. One responded, "I'm shocked that someone could have killed her." Another told us, "It's tragic; I hope you guys catch the killer." A third said, "Although we had problems, I was devastated when I learned about it." Scott said something very different.

"Let me ask you, Scott, how did you feel about her death? Did you have any feelings about it one way or the other?" I asked him casually, hoping to gauge his response.

Scott paused for a second, choosing his words. He shrugged his shoulders slightly and said, "Well, I was sorry to see her dead, you know. We didn't always get along, but it's never good to see anyone die."

Of all the possible responses that Scott could have offered, this one struck me as odd and a bit telling. It may have simply been a figure of speech that was common to Scott—I would have to interview him more thoroughly to see if I could provoke a similar response about something else—but it was interesting that Scott's first reply to our question was that he was "sorry to see her dead." We knew the killer stood over the victim's body and made sure she was dead by nudging her. It could reasonably be said that the killer "saw her dead" prior to leaving the scene. Was Scott inadvertently telling us something about his involvement in this crime?

It would be another year before we would complete our investigation. Ultimately, we learned a lot more about Scott's relationship with the victim, and we eventually determined that he killed her because he didn't want anyone else to date her following their breakup. We discovered a large amount of circumstantial evidence that came together to make our case. Scott's statement about "see[ing] her dead" pointed us in his direction and was eventually used in court (along with everything else we learned) to convict him. Was this statement enough, on its own, to make our case? Of course not. But it was consistent with Scott's involvement and truly reflected the way he felt in the moments following the murder.

Scott's case taught me the value of paying close attention to every word a suspect might offer. We all choose the words we use. Sometimes we choose as a matter of habit. Sometimes we choose words that reflect, either consciously or subconsciously, the truth about how we feel or the truth about what really happened. I've learned to hang on every word.

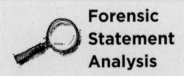

Forensic Statement Analysis

The careful study and analysis of the words (both written and spoken) provided by a suspect, witness, or victim. The purpose of Forensic Statement Analysis is to determine truthfulness or deception on the part of the person making the statement.

THE ART OF FORENSIC STATEMENT ANALYSIS

In my first years as an investigator, my department sent me to a number of classes, seminars, and training exercises to improve my skills. One of these classes was a course in Forensic

Statement Analysis (FSA). There I learned to refine my ability to hear and interpret every word offered by a suspect in a case. I began to employ FSA techniques almost immediately. I routinely asked suspects to write down what they did back on the day of the murder, accounting for their activity from the time they got up in the morning to the time they went to bed. I provided each suspect a blank piece of lined paper and a pen. Any alterations in their statement would have to be scratched out, and as a result, I was able to see what they initially wrote and where they were uncomfortable with their original choice of words. I would then examine this statement, asking several important questions. What kinds of words did the suspect use to describe the victim? Does the suspect ever inadvertently slip from the present to the past tense, giving away his or her presence or involvement at the scene of the crime? Does the suspect compress or expand the description of events in order to hide something or lie about how something occurred? Does the suspect over- or underidentify the victim in an effort to seem friendlier or disinterested in the victim? In essence, I examined every word to see if it provided any clue related to the suspect's involvement in the crime.

Let me give you an example. Imagine that we asked a suspect about his activity last night with his wife (who is now the victim of a murder). In describing what happened, the man responded:

"I took Amy, my beautiful wife of thirty-one years, out to dinner and a movie."

I've already learned something about their relationship in just this one sentence. Notice that the suspect told us his wife's name, and was apparently proud enough of her (or their relationship) to mention how long they had been together. Notice also that the suspect used the possessive expression "my beautiful wife" when he could easily have described her in some other way. Imagine, for example, if he had said this:

"I took my wife out to dinner and a movie."

While he still used a possessive expression ("my wife") in this response, he did not describe her as beautiful, and he reserved the information about her name and the length of their relationship. Maybe he's a private person who was uncomfortable with revealing personal details. Maybe he was not as proud of his wife or wanted to distance himself from her. We'd have to spend some time with him to learn more. Let's now imagine that he said this in response to our questioning:

"I took the wife out to dinner and a movie."

The suspect dropped the possessive language and described his wife as "the wife." Hmm. Why would he do that? Maybe this was just a figure of speech that he always used in describing anyone he had a relationship with, whether good or bad. Maybe he was distancing himself from his wife for some reason. Once again, we'd have to investigate this further. Finally, let's imagine that he said something like this:

"I took the old lady out to dinner and a movie."

Here, the suspect may simply have been using a figure of speech that was common to his region or his culture or even his family. He might, however, have been revealing something about his feelings toward his wife. He did not use possessive language, he gave us very little information about her, and he described her in a less-than-flattering manner. We would have to look at other areas of his statement to see if he used similar language when describing others or if he reserved these kinds of words for his wife alone. In any case, his use of words told us something important.

Clearly, this sort of word examination is more an *interpretive art* than a *hard science*, but the more we understand the importance of words, the better we become at discerning their meanings. Remember, all of us choose the words we use, and we've got lots of words to choose from. Our words eventually give us away.

THE FORENSIC GOSPELS

I had been interviewing and studying suspect and eyewitness statements for many years before I opened my first Bible. I approached the Gospels like I would any other forensic statement. Every little idiosyncrasy stood out for me. Every word was important. The small details interested me and forced me to dig deeper. As an example, the fact that John never mentioned the proper name of Jesus's mother (Mary) was curious to me. In his gospel, John repeatedly

What Is the Forensic Statement Analyst Trying to Achieve?

Forensic Statement Analysts carefully examine the words offered by witnesses and suspects in an effort to determine the following:

1. Is the writer (or speaker) more involved in the event than he or she might like us to believe?

2. Are there relational problems between the writer (or speaker) and the victim who is the subject of the case?

3. What are the hidden difficulties between the writer (or speaker) and the victim in the investigation?

4. Was the writer (or speaker) actually doing what he or she claimed to be doing at the time of the crime?

5. Should the writer (or speaker) be considered as a suspect in this crime under consideration?

referred to Mary as "Jesus's mother" or "the mother of Jesus" but never referred to her by name (as did the other gospel writers). Why would this be the case?

The answer might be found in the nineteenth chapter of John's gospel when Jesus entrusted Mary to John at the crucifixion. Jesus told John that Mary was now his mother, and He told Mary that John was now her son. John took Mary and cared for her (as he would his own mother) from this point on. Writing the gospel of John many years later, it just may be that John was uncomfortable calling his own mother by her formal name. I'm sure by this time in his life, John was referring to Mary as "my mother." It doesn't surprise me then that John would hesitate to call his adopted mother by her proper name in the gospel.

The more I read the Gospels, the more interested I was in taking a forensic approach in an effort to *read between* the lines of the gospel writers. My interest reached its peak in the gospel of Mark.

One of my Christian friends told me that Mark's gospel was really the eyewitness account of the apostle Peter. The early church seemed to agree. Papias (ca. AD 70–ca. 163), the ancient bishop of Hierapolis (located in western Turkey), claimed that Mark penned his gospel in Rome as Peter's scribe. He reported that "Mark, having become the interpreter of Peter, wrote down accurately, though not indeed in order, whatsoever he remembered of the things said or done by Christ."[21] Irenaeus (ca. AD 115–ca. 202), a student of Ignatius and Polycarp (two students of the apostle John) and the eventual bishop of Lugdunum (now Lyon, France), repeated this claim. He wrote, "Mark, the disciple and interpreter of Peter, did also hand down to us in writing what had been preached by Peter."[22] Justin Martyr (ca. AD 103–ca. 165), the famous early church apologist from Rome, also mentioned an early "memoir" of Peter and described it in a way that is unique to the gospel of Mark.[23] In addition, Clement of Alexandria (ca. AD 150–ca. 215), the historic leader of the church in North Africa, wrote that those who heard Peter's teaching "were not satisfied with merely a single hearing or with the unwritten teaching of the divine Gospel, but with all sorts of entreaties they besought Mark, who was a follower of Peter and whose Gospel is extant, to leave behind with them in writing a record of the teaching passed on to them orally."[24] These early church leaders and students of the apostles (from diverse geographic regions) were "closest to the action." They repeatedly and uniformly claimed that Mark's gospel was a record of Peter's eyewitness observations. But could a forensic statement analysis of the gospel of Mark verify these claims?

As I began to study Mark's gospel forensically, I observed a number of interesting anomalies related to Peter. These peculiarities seemed reasonable if Peter was, in fact, Mark's source for information. Let me share some of them with you.

MARK MENTIONED PETER WITH PROMINENCE

Peter is featured frequently in Mark's gospel. As an example, Mark referred to Peter twenty-six times in his short account, compared to Matthew, who mentioned Peter only three additional times in his much longer gospel.

MARK IDENTIFIED PETER WITH THE MOST FAMILIARITY

More importantly, Mark is the only writer who refused to use the term "Simon Peter" when describing Peter (he used either "Simon" or "Peter"). This may seem trivial, but it is important. Simon was the most popular male name in Palestine at the time of Mark's writing,[25] yet Mark made no attempt to distinguish the apostle Simon from the hundreds of other Simons known to his readers (John, by comparison, referred to Peter more formally as "Simon Peter" seventeen times). Mark consistently used the briefest, most familiar versions of Peter's name.

MARK USED PETER AS A SET OF "BOOKENDS"

Unlike in other gospel accounts, Peter is the first disciple identified in the text (Mark 1:16) and the last disciple mentioned in the text (Mark 16:7). Scholars describe this type of "bookending" as "inclusio"[26] and have noticed it in other ancient texts where a piece of history is attributed to a particular eyewitness. In any case, Peter is prominent in Mark's gospel as the first and last named disciple.

MARK PAID PETER THE UTMOST RESPECT

Mark also seemed to respect Peter more than any other gospel writer did; he repeatedly painted Peter in the kindest possible way, even when Peter made a fool of himself. Matthew's gospel, for example, describes Jesus walking on water and Peter's failed attempt to do the same (Matt. 14:22–33). In Matthew's account, Peter began to sink into the sea; Jesus described him as a doubter and a man "of little faith." Interestingly, Mark respectfully omitted Peter's involvement altogether (Mark 6:45–52). In a similar way, Luke's gospel includes a description of the "miraculous catch" of fish in which Peter was heard to doubt Jesus's wisdom in trying to catch fish when Peter had been unsuccessful all day. After catching more fish than his nets could hold, Peter said, "Go away from me Lord, for I am a sinful man!" (Luke 5:1–11). Mark's parallel account omits this episode completely (Mark 1:16–20). While other gospels mention Peter directly as the source of some embarrassing statement or question, Mark's gospel omits Peter's name specifically and attributes the question or statement to "the disciples" or some other similarly unnamed member of the group. When Peter made a rash statement (like saying that Jesus's death would never occur in Matthew 16:21–23), the most edited and least embarrassing version can be found in Mark's account (Mark 8:31–33). Over and over again, Mark offered a version of the story that is kinder to Peter.

MARK INCLUDED DETAILS THAT CAN BEST BE ATTRIBUTED TO PETER

Mark alone included a number of seemingly unimportant details that point to Peter's involvement in the shaping of the text. Mark alone told us that "Simon and his companions" were the ones who went looking for Jesus when He was praying in a solitary place (Mark 1:35–37). Mark is also the only gospel to tell us that it was Peter who first drew Jesus's attention to the withered fig tree (compare Matt. 21:18–19 with Mark 11:20–21). Mark alone seemed to be able to identify the specific disciples (including Peter) who asked Jesus about the timing of the destruction of the temple (compare Matt. 24:1–3 with Mark 13:1–4). While Matthew told us (in Matt. 4:13–16) that Jesus returned to Galilee and "came and settled in Capernaum," Mark said that Jesus entered Capernaum and that the people heard that He had "come home" (see Mark 2:1). Mark said this in spite of the fact that Jesus wasn't born or raised there. Why would Mark call it "home," given that Jesus appears to have stayed there for a very short time and traveled throughout the region far more than He ever stayed in Capernaum? Mark alone told us that Capernaum was actually Peter's hometown (Mark 1:21, 29–31) and that Peter's mother lived there. Peter could most reasonably refer to Capernaum as "home."

MARK USED PETER'S ROUGH OUTLINE

Many scholars have also noticed that Peter's preaching style (Acts 1:21–22 and Acts 10:37–41, for example) consistently seems to omit details of Jesus's private life. When Peter talked about Jesus, he limited his descriptions to Jesus's public life, death, resurrection, and ascension. Mark also followed this rough outline, omitting the birth narrative and other details of Jesus's private life that are found in Luke's and Matthew's gospels.

Mark used specific titles to describe Peter, gave him priority in the narrative, uniquely included information related to Peter, and copied Peter's preaching outline when structuring his own gospel. These circumstantial facts support the claims of the early church fathers who identified Peter as the source of Mark's information.

Peter is mentioned **frequently**

Peter is named **by the church fathers**

Peter's embarrassments **have been omitted**

Peter is **"bookended"**

Peter's knowledge **has been included**

SIMON PETER

Peter's outline **has been followed**

Peter is described **with familiarity**

By hanging on every word, we were able to construct a reasonable circumstantial case for the gospel of Mark as an eyewitness account. When combined with the testimony of the early church, this evidence becomes even more powerful.

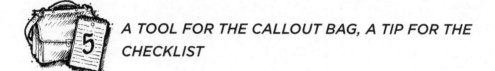

A TOOL FOR THE CALLOUT BAG, A TIP FOR THE CHECKLIST

Keep this principle in mind as you gather the tools in your *callout bag* and make your own investigative *checklist*. By paying close attention to the words witnesses use, we can learn a lot about the reliability and legitimacy of their statements. It's been fashionable recently to question the authenticity of the Gospels and the claims of the early church fathers related to their authorship. Were the Gospels intentionally misattributed to the apostles or their associates? Was there a conspiracy of some sort to make the Gospels seem authoritative? The *forensic* internal evidence of language can help us verify the claims of the early church related to these texts. The specific words used by the authors can teach us more than you might previously have thought possible. While it's been popular in the twenty-first century to try to cast doubt on what was so certain to those in the first and second centuries, thoughtful consideration of the words themselves will verify many of the claims of the early church leaders. We need to do our best not to trust others (including me) for this careful analysis. Instead, read the Gospels for yourself and examine every word. We each have the obligation to *do the heavy lifting* for ourselves.

I recognize that many of us, as Christians, are hesitant to treat *God's Word* as though it were a suspect or eyewitness statement that needs to be picked apart forensically. It almost seems to disrespect the holy nature of the text. I've even known brothers and sisters in the faith who were hesitant to write on the pages of their Bibles out of love and respect for the Word. I certainly understand this kind of reverence, and I also understand that it's easy for us to leave this kind of analysis to *experts* in the field. But you'll be amazed at how rich and deep your faith will become as a result of careful analysis and study. Some of us don't think we have enough training or experience to be able to examine the language of Scripture. But imagine for a minute that one of your sons wrote you a long letter describing something important to him.

As an interested reader, you would find yourself intuitively measuring his choice of words. You would inevitably "read between the lines" and find yourself gleaning far more from the letter than the simple content intended. We all have enough *expertise* to begin to question the use of specific words and develop a richer understanding of the biblical text if only we will become interested readers of Scripture. There are a number of reliable experts in the field who can help us sort out the language. We simply need to *raise the bar* on our approach to the biblical text. Yes, it's hard work, but it's our duty as ambassadors for Christ and as defenders of the faith.

Chapter 6

Principle #6:

SEPARATE ARTIFACTS FROM EVIDENCE

"Ladies and Gentlemen, the most important piece of forensic evidence the prosecution has in this case demonstrates the fact that the defendant had nothing to do with this murder." The defense attorney paused as his projector splashed an image of a cigarette butt on the courtroom screen. The jurors sat quietly with their eyes fixed on the photograph. Several jurors were taking notes.

I knew that this cigarette butt was going to be a problem for our case from the moment I first saw it in the collection of evidence. The victim in this crime had been murdered in his front yard in 1990. The murder occurred early in the morning, long before sunrise. When officers were called to the scene, they correctly taped off the area to preserve it for the criminal-ists. They were careful to *overestimate* the possible crime scene, capturing a large area within the tape, just to be sure that they didn't miss anything. While it is always wise to tape off the biggest possible area, it often results in an excessive collection of items. Some of these items are related to the crime and can be correctly identified as evidence; some of these items are simply uninvolved *artifacts* that get caught up incidentally. The jury will eventually have to decide which is which.

"The prosecution failed to perform a DNA test on this cigarette butt, even though they knew it was important to the case. They collected it, after all. Why would they do that unless they thought it was a piece of evidence?" The defendant's attorney paused with his hands on the podium, waiting for the jury members to turn their eyes back toward him. "As you know, our team conducted the appropriate tests and learned that there was, in fact, DNA on the cigarette, and this DNA, although it remains unidentified, does *not* belong to my client. The DNA belongs to the true killer. The police never even examined the DNA and missed the chance to find the real murderer."

It was true that we never tested the cigarette for DNA. It was also true that the partial DNA found by the defendant's team did not belong to the defendant and remained unidentified. But it was not true that the cigarette butt was a piece of evidence. Yes, we collected it because it was inside the tapeline at the crime scene. But that yellow tape captured both evidence and *artifacts*.

The cigarette butt was discovered in a neighbor's side yard, approximately fifty feet from the point of the murder. It was at the outmost edge of the taped area. If the officers had taped an area that was just six inches smaller in radius, this butt would not even be part of our case. The defense argued that the suspect was hiding in this location, fifty feet from the victim's front door, and must have smoked a cigarette while he was waiting for the victim to exit his house. They wanted the jury to view the cigarette butt as evidence of the killer's identity.

I knew better. The location of the cigarette was directly visible from the street and the front porch. If the suspect had been standing there, he would have been exposed and visible to anyone driving by (and to the victim as soon as he exited the front door). If the killer was relying on the darkness to hide his presence, the glowing ember of the cigarette and the smell of the smoke would be a sure giveaway. More importantly, I knew from the victim's family that this area was used by his daughter's friends to smoke cigarettes while they were visiting and working on their cars in the driveway. We never tested the cigarette as evidence in this case because we never viewed it as evidence in the first place. It was simply an artifact at the scene.

Like all our cases, this investigation was built on circumstantial evidence. I had no direct evidence, and the defense knew it. The defendant had been very careful and had gotten away without leaving a trace of his presence at the scene. While over thirty other pieces of circumstantial evidence pointed to the defendant as the killer, the only physical item collected at the scene happened to be an unrelated cigarette butt. The jury would now have to consider the circumstantial case surrounding the cigarette before it could consider the circumstantial case surrounding the defendant.

That's exactly what they did. The jury came back in less than three hours. They were able to distinguish between the evidence and the artifacts, and they properly kept the cigarette butt in its place as an artifact of the crime scene. They convicted the defendant of murder.

THE TEXTUAL ARTIFACTS OF THE BIBLE

Like crime scenes, historical scenes can be reconstructed with the evidence we have at our disposal. We have to be careful, however, to distinguish between evidence and artifacts. The testimony of an eyewitness can be properly viewed as evidence, but anything added to the account after the fact should be viewed with caution as a possible *artifact* (something that exists in the text when it shouldn't). The Gospels claim to be eyewitness accounts, but you may be surprised to find that there are a few added textual artifacts nestled in with the evidential statements. It appears that scribes, in copying the texts over the years, added lines to the narrative that were not there at the time of the original writing. Let me give you an example.

Most of us are familiar with the biblical story in the gospel of John in which Jesus was presented with a woman who had been accused of committing adultery (John 8:1–11). The Jewish men who brought the woman to Jesus wanted her to be stoned, but Jesus refused to condemn her and told the men, "He who is without sin among you, let him be the first to throw a stone at her." When the men leave, Jesus tells the woman, "I do not condemn you, either. Go. From now on sin

The Story of the Woman Caught in Adultery

The famous story of the woman caught in adultery (known as Pericope de Adultera) is found today in John 7:53–8:11. It was not present in the earliest known manuscripts of John's gospel, however, including Papyri 66 (ca. AD 200), Papyri 75 (early third century), Codex Sinaiticus (fourth century), and Codex Vaticanus (fourth century). It first appears in its entirety in the fifth century in Codex Bezae, but there are several other codices from that time in history that do not contain the story (e.g., Codices Alexandrinus, Ephraemi, Washingtonianus, and Borgianus). It appears in a different location (after John 21:25) in many ancient copies of the text, including a set of ancient gospels written in Greek known as "Family 1" that date from the twelfth to the fifteenth century. The story appears in the gospel of Luke (after Luke 24:53) in a group of Greek manuscripts known as "Family 13" that date from the eleventh to the fifteenth century.

no more." This story is one of my favorite passages in all of Scripture. Too bad that it appears to be an *artifact*.

While the story may, in fact, be absolutely true, the earliest copies of John's gospel recovered over the centuries fail to contain any part of it. The last verse of chapter 7 and the first eleven verses of chapter 8 are missing in the oldest manuscripts available to us. The story doesn't appear until it is discovered in later copies of John's gospel, centuries after the life of Jesus on earth. In fact, some ancient biblical manuscripts place it in a different location in John's gospel. Some ancient copies of the Bible even place it in the gospel of Luke. While there is much about the story that seems consistent with Jesus's character and teaching, most scholars do not believe it was part of John's original account. It is a biblical artifact, and it is identified as such in nearly every modern translation of the Bible (where it is typically noted in the margin or bracketed to separate it from the reliable account).

Should the existence of this textual artifact concern us? Do late additions to the biblical record disqualify the New Testament as a reliable manuscript? How can we call the Bible *inerrant* or *infallible* if it contains a late addition such as this? This passage is not the only textual artifact in the Bible. There are a number of additional verses that are considered to be artifacts by scholars and biblical experts. Let's take a look at a few of them to determine if their existence should cause us any alarm:

LUKE 22:43–44

"And there appeared an angel unto him from heaven, strengthening him. And being in an agony he prayed more earnestly: and his sweat was as it were great drops of blood falling down to the ground" (KJV).

These two verses do not appear in early manuscripts of Luke's gospel, and for this reason they have been omitted from some modern Bible translations (like the RSV). While the KJV does not isolate them as late additions, other translations (like the NIV, NASB, and NKJV) identify them as such in footnotes or special brackets.

JOHN 5:4

"For an angel went down at a certain season into the pool, and troubled the water: whosoever then first after the troubling of the water stepped in was made whole of whatsoever disease he had" (KJV).

Once again, this verse (along with the last few words of v. 3) does not appear in the best ancient manuscripts. Several modern translations have simply removed the verse (e.g., the NIV, RSV, and NRSV), while others have identified it in the footnotes (e.g., the NKJV and ESV).

1 JOHN 5:7

"For there are three that bear record in heaven, the Father, the Word, and the Holy Ghost: and these three are one" (KJV).

The second half of this verse ("the Father, the Word, and the Holy Ghost: and these three are one") does not appear in any manuscript of the Bible until the sixteenth century (and it appears in only two manuscripts at this point in history). It has been omitted from modern translations like the NASB and NIV and identified with a footnote in the NKJV.

ACTS 15:34

"Notwithstanding it pleased Silas to abide there still" (KJV).

The earliest and most reliable manuscripts do not contain this verse. Modern translations like the NIV, RSV, and NRSV have removed it, while the NASB, NKJV, and ESV have identified it with brackets or a footnote.

Skeptics have pointed to passages like these in an effort to demonstrate the unreliability of the biblical text as an eyewitness account. If these lines are fiction, how many more verses are also false? When I was an atheist, this was one of my prime complaints about the Bible, and I discovered that very few Christians were aware of the fact that these additions exist. I shook the faith of many of my Christian friends by simply demonstrating that these passages were not in the original biblical text.

SEPARATING THE ARTIFACTS FROM THE EVIDENCE

It wasn't until years later that I understood how to evaluate the existence of these late entries. I eventually learned that every crime scene presents its own set of unique questions and difficulties. Every scene contains important evidence that will guide us to the truth while also containing unrelated artifacts that will cause some uncertainty. I've never encountered a crime scene that was free of artifacts. In spite of these unrelated items, we, as detectives, were able to evaluate the case and determine what belonged to the crime and what did not. Yes, there were always a number of questions that needed to be answered. But our concerns were eventually resolved when we separated the artifacts from the evidence.

Doing this, of course, was sometimes quite difficult. Over the years, I've developed a number of strategies that have helped me to assess what is important in a crime scene and what is not.

Evidence and Artifacts

Judges try to help jurors understand the difference between evidence and unrelated artifacts by instructing them to disregard anything other than what was actually presented as part of the case:

"You must decide what the facts are in this case. You must use only the evidence that was presented in this courtroom [or during a jury view]. 'Evidence' is the sworn testimony of witnesses, the exhibits admitted into evidence, and anything else I tell you to consider as evidence....

"You must disregard anything you see or hear when the court is not in session, even if it is done or said by one of the parties or witnesses" (Section 104, *Judicial Council of California Criminal Jury Instructions*, 2006).

These principles can also be used to evaluate the textual artifacts that exist in the biblical accounts.

IDENTIFY THE LATE ADDITIONS

Responding officers typically tape off crime scenes immediately in preparation for the criminalists. The criminalists then photograph everything and document the scene thoroughly. Years later, if an item of evidence is discovered that was not present in the original photographs, we have good reason to identify it as a late addition to the case. Once we are certain that something is a late addition, we can simply ignore it as we assess the true evidence.

RECOGNIZE DIFFERENCES IN CHARACTER

But what if an item was at the scene from the very beginning? How can we determine if it is important to the case? There are some things that we recognize as unrelated from the very first moment we arrive. I've investigated many cases in which paramedics reached the scene even before the police. They made a valiant effort to save the dying victim prior to the arrival of the first responding officers. By the time the police got there, the crime scene was littered with the paraphernalia from the paramedic team. Bandage packaging, tubing, syringes, and a variety of other obvious medical items were now part of the scene and were photographed by the criminalists before my arrival at the location. These items became a part of the case but were quickly and easily recognized as artifacts. They stood out like a sore thumb; they were evidence of the rescue effort, not the crime.

LOOK FOR AN EXPLANATION

Many items at the scene may be explained by some unrelated cause that accounts for their presence and eliminates them as evidence. I once had a case in which a shoe print was photographed outside the victim's house. We initially thought it might belong to the killer until we matched it to the landlord, who first discovered the victim when he entered the residence to check on her. Once we had an explanation for the existence of the print, we recognized it as an artifact.

SEE WHAT HAPPENS IF YOU INCLUDE IT

There have been times when it was impossible for me to determine whether an item was a piece of evidence or simply an artifact of the scene. When this happens, I will sometimes create a hypothetical case that includes the item as evidence, just to see if its inclusion would change the outcome of the case. I once had a crime scene in which a pencil was recovered on the floor next to the victim. We weren't sure if it was part of the crime or if it belonged to the victim or the suspect. Forensic examinations provided nothing in the way of DNA or fingerprints. To be safe, I decided to think of it as evidence. I quickly realized that the pencil had no impact on the case; when I later assembled the evidence that pointed to a specific suspect, the presence of the pencil did nothing to either improve or weaken my case. There are times when we can be comfortable ignoring an item because it has no impact on the outcome, even if it were to be included.

RELY ON WHAT YOU KNOW

Some items in a crime scene present difficulties because they seem to contradict the larger group of confirmed items of evidence. Imagine that we are working a homicide and have recovered forty-two pieces of evidence that identify a man named Ben Rogers as the killer. Many of these pieces of evidence came from the crime scene, including his DNA on the victim, several of Ben's personal items left behind at the scene, and his fingerprints on the murder weapon. In addition to this, imagine that we have an eyewitness who saw him running from the victim's home, covered in blood. Now imagine that we also recovered a nametag belonging to Scotty

Nichols, a man who worked with the victim. This nametag was sitting on a nightstand about eight feet from the victim's body. When we question Scotty about the nametag, he tells us that he lost the item a day before the murder occurred, and he offers us a verifiable alibi for the day of the crime. He has no idea why his nametag is in the victim's home. What are we to do with this item? In cases like this we have to ask ourselves if the presence of the nametag impacts what we do know from the other evidence at the scene. When we have overwhelming evidence pointing in a particular direction, we may have to get comfortable with the fact that there is some ambiguity related to other items at the scene.

SO, CAN WE TRUST THE BIBLICAL EVIDENCE?

We can apply these principles as we examine the New Testament and evaluate questionable passages to determine if they are evidence or artifacts. Luckily, we have "photographs" of the early crime scene to help us. We have hundreds of early, ancient manuscripts that can give us a snapshot of what the text looked like before anyone added anything to the narrative. Once these late additions have been exposed in this way, we can simply choose to ignore the passages as artifacts and focus on the remainder as evidence.

Some biblical passages appear suspicious even before we find that they were missing in the earliest copies. These passages "stand out" because they seem to possess a different *character* (like the paramedic paraphernalia at our murder scene). Textual critics examined the story of the adulterous woman, for example, and recognized that the Greek words used in the narrative are far more similar to Luke's use of language than they are to John's. The passage seemed foreign to the gospel of John, even before the discovery that it was absent prior to the fifth century.

Next, we can look for reasonable explanations that might account for the addition of these passages (just as we did with the landlord's shoe print). Let's take a look at the four examples I've given from the New Testament and think through some of the reasonable explanations. Each addition to the text appears to be an effort on the part of a scribe to make something clear, to emphasize a point, or to add some detail known to the scribe but omitted by the apostle. In Luke 22:43–44, Jesus's agony is emphasized by the unusual description of blood in His sweat. This may simply have been an effort to make the agony more vivid, or perhaps the scribe was borrowing from a literary style of the time to make the account more robust. In John 5:4, the detail related to the pool at Bethesda may simply have been added to explain John 5:7, a legitimate verse that talks about the stirring of the water without additional explanation. In 1 John 5:7, the scribe may have succumbed to the strong temptation to take the one verse that most closely describes the Trinity and add a line that would make the doctrine irrefutable. While there are many verses that circumstantially point to the triune nature of God, this late insertion (if it were true) would remove all doubt. In Acts 15:34, the scribe added a detail about Silas staying in Antioch. This fact may have been known to the scribe (who may have been native to the area). As a result, he may have added it to the text to fill in a detail that would also be known to local readers of the account.

Some biblical passages, however, are more difficult to assess as artifacts. They may appear in some ancient texts, but not in others from the same period of time. When this is the case, we can choose to hypothetically include the passage as though it were reliable evidence (like the pencil in our murder scene) to see what effect it has on the larger case. If we chose, for example, to include the story of the adulterous woman as a reliable part of the biblical narrative, would it change what we know about any of the central claims of the Bible? No, it wouldn't. The story seems to be consistent with what we know about Jesus's character and teaching. We can imagine Jesus doing something like this, given what we know about Him from other passages. The story of the adulterous woman does not change our final understanding of the teaching of Scripture if it were to be included. In the vast majority of textual additions that have been made to the Bible over the centuries, the changes have been so insignificant as to have very little effect on the content of the narrative and virtually no impact on the important doctrinal claims of Christianity.

Reasons Why Scribes Sometimes Changed the Text

It's clear that scribes occasionally changed the biblical manuscripts when copying them. The vast majority of these changes were completely unintentional (simple misspellings or grammatical errors). Some, however, were intentional:

1. Some intentional alterations were performed in an effort to harmonize passages that describe the same event in two separate gospels (parallel passages).

2. Some intentional alterations were done to add detail known to the scribe but not clearly described by the apostolic author.

3. Some intentional alterations were made to clarify a passage of Scripture based on what a scribe thought the passage meant (the scribes were not always correct in their interpretations).

Finally, we have to learn to be comfortable with some ambiguity. No scene is free of artifacts, and the biblical *crime scene* is no different. There may be a few passages of Scripture that seem *out of place* or difficult to understand (like Scotty Nichols's nametag). At times like these, we have to ask ourselves if the reliable testimony of the biblical narrative is sufficient to accommodate an unexplained artifact. If we find that the biblical text (with the artifacts removed) makes a case that is strong and clear (we'll discuss this more is the second section of this book), we can allow ourselves the minor discomfort of a few unanswered questions.

PIECING TOGETHER THE PUZZLE

Let me give you an illustration to help you think about the relationship between evidence and artifacts. Imagine that tomorrow you open a drawer in your family room and empty its contents onto the table. You find that it contains all kinds of junk you haven't seen in quite some time, including keys and paper clips, batteries and coins. You also discover that it contains a number of puzzle pieces. In your curiosity about the puzzle pieces, you begin to sift through the contents of the drawer so you can assemble them. In order to bring together the puzzle, you're going to have to sort the related pieces from the items that are clearly not part of the puzzle. Some of these are obvious by their very nature. You immediately know that batteries and coins, like the paramedic paraphernalia, are not going to fit in the puzzle. As a result, you push these aside and start puzzling. But it turns out that there are two additional puzzle pieces in the drawer that simply don't fit the others. As you begin to assemble the image, you can see that these puzzle pieces don't fit this particular puzzle; they seem to belong somewhere else.

Now let me ask you a few questions. Does the mere presence of the non-puzzle pieces in the drawer invalidate the reliability of the puzzle pieces? No, the non-puzzle pieces can be quickly and easily identified and set aside. Does the presence of the non-puzzle pieces change the resulting image that has been pieced together? No, these additional "artifacts" are completely unrelated to the image on the puzzle. How about the two extra puzzle pieces that don't seem to match the rest? Does their presence in the drawer make the other puzzle pieces unreliable? No, the vast majority of pieces fit together nicely and demonstrate a coherent relationship to one another (in spite of the fact that there are two additional pieces that don't seem to fit). What if we accepted the two additional pieces as part of the puzzle and tried to force them in? Would they significantly change the final image? No, even if we were to accept these two pieces as part of the larger group and found a way to insert them into the puzzle, the image would still be obvious to us.

Crime scenes are a lot like this drawer full of items. There are pieces at the scene that are evidence of the crime in question, and there are extra artifacts that have nothing to do with the crime. When we successfully separate the artifacts from the evidence, we can determine what happened at the scene. The mere presence of the artifacts is not an insurmountable obstacle for us. The biblical text is also much like the drawer full of items. There are passages in the text that are evidence of the life of Jesus, and there are extratextual artifacts that must be separated. When we successfully separate the textual artifacts from the biblical evidence, we can determine what happened over two thousand years ago. The mere presence of the textual artifacts is not an insurmountable obstacle for us.

A TOOL FOR THE CALLOUT BAG, A TIP FOR THE CHECKLIST

As you form your own checklist of evidential principles, be sure to include this important approach to *artifacts*. When I was an atheist, I believed the existence of *scribal alterations* in the Bible invalidated the evidential value of the text altogether. I now understand that this is not the case. Every crime scene contains artifacts; if I refused to accept any explanation of the truth simply because an artifact was present along with the reliable evidence, I could never convict anyone of a crime. All ancient documents also contain textual artifacts. If we reject the entirety of Scripture simply because it contains artifacts of one kind or another, we had better be ready to reject the ancient writings of Plato, Herodotus, Euripides, Aristotle, and Homer as well. The manuscripts for these texts are far less numerous, and they are far less reliable. If we apply the same standard of perfection that some would demand of the Bible to other ancient histories, we're going to have to reject everything we thought we knew about the ancient past. More importantly, it's vital to see that we do actually have a methodology that allows us to uncover the artifacts and separate them from the original text. The art of *textual criticism* allows us to compare manuscripts to determine what belongs and what does not. The same process that revealed to me (as a skeptic) the passages that *couldn't* be trusted also revealed to me (as a believer) the passages that *can* be trusted. *Textual criticism* allows us to determine the nature of the original texts as we eliminate the textual artifacts. This should give us *more* confidence in what we have, not *less*.

I have many Christian friends who are reluctant to admit that the Bible contains *any* textual artifacts because they have always defended the Bible as either *inerrant* (containing no errors) or *infallible* (incapable of containing errors). But the presence of textual artifacts says nothing about the original text, and it's this original *autograph* that we have in view when we talk about inerrancy and infallibility in the first place. Christianity acknowledges that God used humans to deliver His truth to His people. In the Old Testament, God used prophets to speak to the nation of Israel. In the New Testament, God used the apostolic eyewitnesses to testify of His Son. Christianity recognizes the inerrancy of the original documents these eyewitnesses provided, even though they were filled with idiosyncrasies and personal perspectives (as we described previously). Humans were also involved in the transmission of these eyewitness accounts. Like the authors, the scribes had personal perspectives and human idiosyncrasies that may have impacted the way they copied the manuscripts. While they may have occasionally altered very minute portions of the text, we possess enough comparative copies of the ancient documents to identify these alterations and remove them from the reliable accounts. The textual artifacts testify to the gritty realism of the evidential account contained in the Bible. Like other real collections of evidence, there are artifacts embedded within the reliable evidence. Like other crime scenes, these artifacts need not hinder our ability to determine (and defend) the truth.

Chapter 7
Principle #7:

RESIST CONSPIRACY THEORIES

"Charlie, your roommate already told us where to find the green plaid shirt you were wearing last night." Charlie sat with his head down and his hands on his thighs. His body language communicated his continuing resistance to my questioning. This last statement, however, caused the first small reaction I had seen all afternoon. Charlie finally lifted his head and looked me in the eyes. "You and I both know I'm gonna find the victim's blood on that shirt," I said. Charlie sat there quietly. I could tell that he believed my lie about his roommate.

Eighteen hours earlier, Charlie and his roommate, Vic, attempted to rob Dennis Watkins as he was walking home from his girlfriend's house. A simple street robbery turned into a homicide when Dennis decided he was bigger than Charlie and struggled with him for his knife. Charlie stabbed Dennis only once, but the resulting chest wound was fatal. The robbery took place late at night in an alley to the rear of a fast-food restaurant in our town. There were no witnesses, and no one else was on the street at the time of the robbery, but Charlie was unknowingly recorded by a surveillance camera located on a bank across the alley. While the camera was too far away to identify the killer

Some Popular Conspiracy Theories

Lee Harvey Oswald didn't act alone when he killed President Kennedy.

The US government was involved in the 9/11 disaster.

The 1969 *Apollo* moon landing was fabricated.

A UFO crashed in Roswell, New Mexico.

facially, it did record the unusual green plaid shirt worn by one of the two attackers and captured an image of their general height and build. Several hours later (through a series of investigative efforts), we had Charlie and Vic in custody, but we had little evidence to corroborate their involvement. We needed a "cop-out" if we hoped to file the case with the district attorney.

We separated Charlie and Vic as soon as we arrested them; Vic was in a second interview room down the hall. I had not yet interviewed him; I lied to Charlie about the conversation. Vic didn't tell me where to find the plaid shirt. Charlie just happened to better match the physical build of the primary suspect I saw on the video, so I took a stab at him as the suspect who wore the shirt. I could tell I was right by Charlie's reaction. He was fidgeting in his chair and turned his gaze to the floor again. I stayed silent and let my statement hang in the air. Charlie finally looked up.

"Vic's lying about that. He's the one who gave me that shirt for my birthday, but he wears it more than I do." Charlie folded his arms again and leaned backward, trying to increase the distance between the two of us.

That was all I needed really—just another small piece of information. I left Charlie for a moment and entered the room with Vic. I pulled a chair up to the table that separated us, introduced myself, and got down to business.

"Vic, I just got done talking to Charlie. Murder is a serious crime, and he told me that you were the one who stabbed this guy. He told me about the green plaid shirt. He said that you gave that shirt to him for his birthday but you wear it more than he does. He told us where to find it. He said we'll find the victim's blood on the shirt and he's willing to testify against you, bud."

Within fifteen minutes, Vic told us all about the crime and confirmed what we had seen on the video. He provided many details about their prior plan to commit the robbery, and he confirmed his secondary involvement in the attack. He also told us that Charlie was the man who stabbed Dennis, and he provided us with the location of the knife. Vic believed everything I said about Charlie. I had just enough true information to make my lies sound believable; the combination was powerful enough to convince Vic that Charlie had "ratted him out." Vic was now willing to return the favor.

RULES FOR GOOD CONSPIRACIES

In my experience as a detective, I have investigated many conspiracies and *multiple-suspect* crimes. While successful conspiracies are the popular subject of many movies and novels, I've come to learn that they are (in reality) very difficult to pull off. Successful conspiracies share a number of common characteristics:

A SMALL NUMBER OF CONSPIRATORS

The smaller the number of conspirators, the more likely the conspiracy will be a success. This is easy to understand; lies are difficult to maintain, and the fewer the number of people who have to continue the lie, the better.

THOROUGH AND IMMEDIATE COMMUNICATION

This is key. When conspirators are unable to determine if their partners in crime have already given up the truth, they are far more likely to say something in an effort to save themselves from punishment. Without adequate and immediate communication, coconspirators simply cannot separate lies from the truth; they are easily deceived by investigators who can pit one conspirator against another.

Conspiracies

To prove that a defendant is part of a felonious conspiracy, prosecutors in the state of California must prove that

"1. The defendant intended to agree and did agree with [one or more of] (the other defendant[s]) ... to commit ... alleged crime[s];

2. At the time of the agreement, the defendant and [one or more of] the other alleged member[s] of the conspiracy intended that one or more of them would commit ... alleged crime[s];

3. (One of the) defendant[s] ... [or all of them] committed [at least one of] the alleged overt act(s) to accomplish the alleged crime" (Section 415, *Judicial Council of California Criminal Jury Instructions*, 2006).

A SHORT TIME SPAN

Lies are hard enough to tell once; they are even more difficult to repeat consistently over a long period of time. For this reason, the shorter the conspiracy, the better. The ideal conspiracy would involve only two conspirators, and one of the conspirators would kill the other right after the crime. That's a conspiracy that would be awfully hard to break!

SIGNIFICANT RELATIONAL CONNECTIONS

When all the coconspirators are connected relationally in deep and meaningful ways, it's much harder to convince one of them to "give up" the other. When all the conspirators are family members, for example, this task is nearly impossible. The greater the relational bond between all the conspirators, the greater the possibility of success.

LITTLE OR NO PRESSURE

Few suspects confess to the truth until they recognize the jeopardy of failing to do so. Unless pressured to confess, conspirators will continue lying. Pressure does not have to be physical in nature. When suspects fear incarceration or condemnation from their peers, they often respond in an effort to save face or save their own skin. This is multiplied as the number of coconspirators increases. The greater the pressure on coconspirators, the more likely the conspiracy is to fail.

Charlie and Vic's conspiracy was difficult to maintain for several reasons. While there were only two conspirators, they were unable to communicate with one another. Once they were separated, they were unable to monitor what the other was saying to the police. We were, therefore, able to deceive each of them without detection. In addition to this, Charlie and Vic were only roommates. The more we talked to them, the more obvious it was they were willing to give each other up to avoid punishment. Neither Charlie nor Vic had ever been to state prison, but both had served time in the county jail system. They'd heard stories from other inmates about the nature of California prisons, and the fear of serving time there was a significant motivation for them to cooperate. Conspiracies are most successful when all of the characteristics I've described are present. In this case, several key conditions were missing.

THE CHRISTIAN CONSPIRACY

When I was an atheist, I recognized that the most significant claim of the alleged apostolic *eyewitnesses* was their claim related to the resurrection. This was the big one; larger than any other alleged miracle ever performed by Jesus and the proof that the apostles seemed to trot out every time they talked about Jesus. I always assumed it was a lie. Maybe it was just my skeptical nature or my prior experience with people on the job. I understand the capacity people have to lie when it serves their purpose. In my view, the apostles were no different. In an effort to promote their cause and strengthen their own position within their religious community, I believed these twelve men concocted, executed, and maintained the most elaborate and influential conspiracy of all time. But as I learned more about the nature of conspiracies and had the opportunity to investigate and break several conspiracy cases, I started to doubt the reasonable nature of the alleged "Christian conspiracy."

The apostles faced far greater challenges than did Charlie and Vic, two thousand years later. The number of conspirators required to successfully accomplish the Christian conspiracy would have been staggering. The book of Acts tells us that there were as many as 120 eye-witnesses in the upper room following Jesus's ascension (Acts 1:15). Let's assume for a minute that this number is a gross exaggeration; let's work with a much smaller number to illustrate our point. Let's limit our discussion to the twelve apostles (adding Matthias as Judas's replace-ment). This number is already prohibitively large from a conspiratorial perspective, because none of the other characteristics of successful conspiracies existed for the twelve apostles.

The apostles had little or no effective way to communicate with one another in a quick or thorough manner. Following their dispersion from Jerusalem, the twelve disciples were scattered across the Roman Empire and, according to the most ancient accounts, were ulti-mately interrogated and martyred far from one another. Methods of communication in the first century were painfully slow, and unlike Charlie and Vic, the apostles were separated by far more than a hallway. From Peter in Rome, to James in Jerusalem, to Thomas in Mylapore, the apostles appear to have been ultimately interrogated in locations that prevented them from communicating with one another in a timely manner. They had no idea if any of their coconspirators had already "given up the lie" and saved themselves by simply *confessing* that Jesus was never resurrected. While skeptics sometimes claim that these recorded locations of martyrdom are unreliable because they are part of a biased Christian account, there isn't a

Peter
Crucified
upside down
in Rome

James
Killed by
the sword in
Jerusalem

Thomas
Killed by an
angry mob
in Mylapore

single non-Christian record that contradicts the claims of martyrdom offered by the local communities and historians.

In addition, the apostles would have been required to protect their conspiratorial lies for an incredibly long time. The apostle John appears to have lived the longest, surviving nearly sixty years after the resurrection. Charlie and Vic couldn't keep their conspiracy alive for thirty-six hours; the apostles allegedly kept theirs intact for many decades.

To make matters worse, many of them were complete strangers to one another prior to their time together as disciples of Jesus. Some were indeed brothers, but many were added over the course of Jesus's early ministry and came from diverse backgrounds, communities, and families. While there were certainly pairs of family members in the group of apostolic eyewitnesses, many had no relationship to each other at all. Philip, Bartholomew, Thomas, Simon the Canaanite, and Matthias had no family relationship to any of the other apostles. Whatever the relational connection between these men, the short years they spent together would quickly pale in comparison to the decades they would spend apart from one another prior to the time of their final interrogations. At some point, the bonds of friendship and community would be tested if their individual lives were placed in jeopardy.

Successful conspiracies are unpressured conspiracies. The apostles, on the other hand, were aggressively persecuted as they were scattered from Italy to India. According to the records and accounts of the local communities, each of them suffered unimaginable physical duress and died a martyr's death. Ancient writers recorded that Peter was crucified upside down in Rome, James was killed with the sword in Jerusalem, and Thomas was murdered by a mob in Mylapore. Each story of martyrdom is more gruesome than the prior as we examine the list of apostolic deaths. This pressure was far greater than the fear of state prison faced by Charlie and Vic, yet none of the Twelve recanted their claims related to the resurrection. Not one.

I can't imagine a less favorable set of circumstances for a successful conspiracy than those that the twelve apostles faced. Multiply the problem by ten to account for the 120 disciples in the upper room (Acts 1:15), or by forty to account for the five hundred eyewitnesses described by Paul (1 Cor. 15:6), and the odds seem even more prohibitive. None of these eyewitnesses ever recanted, none was ever trotted out by the enemies of Christianity in an effort to expose the Christian "lie."

Don't get me wrong, successful conspiracies occur every day. But they typically involve a small number of incredibly close-knit participants who are in constant contact with one another for a very short period of time without any outside pressure. That wasn't the case for the disciples. These men and women either were involved in the greatest conspiracy of all time or were simply eyewitnesses who were telling the truth. The more I learned about conspiracies, the more the latter seemed to be the most reasonable conclusion.

MARTYRDOM ISN'T ALWAYS A PROOF

Before I move on from this discussion of conspiracies, I want to address an issue that is sometimes raised related to the relationship between martyrdom and truth. History is filled with examples of men and women who were committed to their religious views and were willing to die a martyr's death for what they believed. The hijackers who flew the planes into the Twin Towers, for example, considered themselves to be religious martyrs. Does

The Martyrdom Traditions of the Apostles

Andrew was crucified in Patras, Greece.

Bartholomew (aka Nathanael) was flayed to death with a whip in Armenia.

James the Just was thrown from the temple and then beaten to death in Jerusalem.

James the Greater was beheaded in Jerusalem.

John died in exile on the island of Patmos.

Luke was hanged in Greece.

Mark was dragged by horse until he died in Alexandria, Egypt.

Matthew was killed by a sword in Ethiopia.

Matthias was stoned and then beheaded in Jerusalem.

Peter was crucified upside down in Rome.

Philip was crucified in Phrygia.

Thomas was stabbed to death with a spear in India.

this martyrdom testify to the truth of their beliefs in a manner similar to the martyrdom of the twelve apostles? No, there is an important distinction that needs to be made here. You and I might die for what we believe today, trusting in the testimony of those who were witnesses thousands of years ago. We were not there to see Jesus for ourselves, but we may believe that we have good reason to accept their testimony. Our martyrdom would therefore be a demonstration of this trust, rather than a confirmation of the truth.

The original eyewitnesses, however, were in a very different position. They knew firsthand if their claims were true or not. They didn't trust someone else for their testimony; they were making a firsthand assertion. The martyrdom of these original eyewitnesses is in a completely different category from the martyrdom of those who might follow them. If their claims were a lie, they would know it personally, unlike those who were martyred in the centuries that followed. While it's reasonable to believe that you and I might die for what we *mistakenly thought* was true, it's unreasonable to believe that these men died for what they *definitely knew* to be untrue.

A TOOL FOR THE CALLOUT BAG, A TIP FOR THE CHECKLIST

A healthy skepticism toward conspiracy theories is an important tool to include in our *callout* bag. We need to hesitate before we wholeheartedly embrace conspiratorial claims related to the apostles. Movies like *The God Who Wasn't There*[27] and *Zeitgeist, the Movie*[28] have popularized the notion that Christianity is simply a retelling of prior mythologies. In essence, these movies argue that a group of conspirators assembled the fictional story of Jesus from a number of preexisting mythologies (borrowing a little here and a little there) and perpetuated the elaborate lie until they died. While some of my skeptical friends may still reject the claims of Christianity, I hope I can at least help them recognize that successful, large-scale conspiracies are rare and that the notion of a "Christian conspiracy" is simply unreasonable.

As Christians, we need to recognize that our culture is fascinated by conspiracy theories. Many of our friends and family members are quick to jump to elaborate conspiratorial possibilities even when there are simpler explanations on the table. Given what I now know about the difficult nature of successful conspiracies, I can help the skeptics in my world as they assess the claims of the apostles. You can too. We all need to take the time to understand the elements of successful conspiracies so we can communicate them to others. But in order to be consistent in our beliefs and explanations, we're also going to need to resist the temptation to see a conspiracy around every corner of current events. If it is unreasonable for the resurrection to be the product of a conspiracy, it is just as unreasonable that other events requiring a large number of conspirators and the perfect set of conditions would be the result of a conspiracy. Let's be careful not to unreasonably embrace conspiracy theories related to secular issues, while simultaneously trying to make a case against the alleged conspiracy of the apostles. If we are consistent in our understanding and rejection of unreasonable conspiratorial explanations, we'll successfully communicate the truth of the resurrection to a skeptical world.

Chapter 8
Principle #8:

RESPECT THE "CHAIN OF CUSTODY"

"Detective Wallace, isn't it true that ..."

Something told me the question I was about to hear was intended to criticize my cold-case investigation. One of the state's most capable defense attorneys stood behind the podium, glaring at me with a dramatic expression of suspicion as he began his sixth day of questioning. By now I was familiar with the approach he was taking; his questions were more rhetorical than probative. He was trying to make a point, and he was doing his best to vilify the original detectives in the process. When a defense attorney begins a question in this way, odds are good that the next thing he says will be less than complimentary.

"Detective Wallace, isn't it true that there isn't a single crime-scene photograph of the alleged button you say was left at the murder scene in 1985?" He stood a little straighter and adjusted the waist of his pants, revealing the suspenders he wore underneath his suit jacket. He was sporting the finest suit I had seen in a courtroom in quite some time, and he occasionally strutted back and forth behind the podium to model it for the jury.

"Sir, I do believe there was one photograph taken by the original crime-scene investigators," I responded. While this was true, I knew my response would not satisfy him; I could see where this was headed.

The button was a key piece of evidence that pointed to the defendant. It was torn from his shirt during the murder and was discovered at the scene. Detectives later executed a search warrant and retrieved a shirt in the defendant's apartment that was missing a button. Forensic comparisons made it clear that the button at the crime scene matched the defendant's shirt. But we had a problem.

The CSI officers were using a 35mm camera in 1985, and they were limited by their technology. They would typically use rolls of film that had twelve, twenty-four, or thirty-six exposures each. As a result, I had fewer photographs than I would have liked (today our criminalists take hundreds of digital photographs with cameras that can store thousands of images). To make matters worse, photographers in 1985 had no way to preview the images they shot. They had to wait until the photographs were developed to know if they had images that were clear and focused. As it turned out, one of the most important photographs taken in this crime scene was the photograph taken of the button, and it was one of three photographs that were out of focus. The CSI officers shot only forty-eight photographs in total, and none of them displayed a clear image of the button.

Evidence Tampering

Defense attorneys sometimes insinuate that an officer has planted evidence in a case. In order to prove such an accusation, however, it must be demonstrated that

"(1) The [officer] willfully and intentionally … changed, planted, placed, made, hid, or moved … [a piece of evidence]. (2) The [officer] knew (he/she) was … changing, planting, placing, making, hiding, or moving … [a piece of evidence], and (3) When the [officer] … changed, planted, placed, made, hid, or moved … [the piece of evidence], (he/she) intended that (his/her) action would result in (someone being charged with a crime [or] [the piece of evidence] being wrongfully produced as genuine or true in a … court proceeding" (Section 2630, *Judicial Council of California Criminal Jury Instructions*, 2006).

"Come now, Detective Wallace, you know as well as I do that there isn't a single image of the button at the crime scene. You continue to point to these blurry images and expect the jury to believe that they contain your most important piece of evidence?" He had a good point. We didn't have a clear image of the button from the crime-scene photographs. In spite of this, we knew with certainty that the button was part of the murder scene. The first responding officers reported seeing it, and the detectives who arrived later also documented the button in their notes. CSI officers collected the button and booked it into evidence later in the day, along with other items from the scene and a number of items collected in the search warrant.

"Isn't it true that the first time this button was mentioned in a formal police report was in the property report completed by CSI officers *after* the search warrant was served?"

His implication was clear. If the button was not photographed at the scene, there was no way to be certain that officers didn't collect it at the search warrant, pull it from the defendant's shirt, and later claim that it first appeared at the murder scene. The attorney was carefully making the case that detectives had lied about the button in an effort to tamper with the evidence and frame his client.

I was concerned that the jury might accept this devious explanation of the button, but my fears were misplaced. After convicting the defendant, the jurors later told us that they believed the testimony of the responding patrol officers, CSI officers, and detectives who mentioned the button in their notes. The jury was unwilling to believe that a conspiracy of this size (involving seven different officers from three divisions) came together to frame the defendant. They convicted him, in spite of the fact that we didn't have a clear image of the button at the scene.

ESTABLISHING A "CHAIN OF CUSTODY"

Detectives quickly learn the importance of documenting and tracking key pieces of evidence. If the evidence isn't carefully handled, a number of questions will plague the case as it is presented to a jury. Was a particular piece of evidence truly discovered at the scene? How do we know it was actually there? How do we know that an officer didn't "plant" it there? These kinds of questions can be avoided if we respect and establish the "chain of custody." Every crime scene contains important pieces of evidence, and these items of evidence must eventually be delivered to a jury for consideration when the case is brought to trial. Our button, for example, had to find its way from the crime scene to the courtroom. Along the way, it spent years sitting in our police property room and was also handled by a number of specialists until I eventually checked it out from property and transported it to court.

Crime Scene   Courtroom

Each step in this process is a link in the chain that connects the crime scene to the court-room. If I can demonstrate that the links are all connected and well documented, the jurors will come to trust the fact that the button I am showing them in court is the same button we discovered at the crime scene. In an ideal investigation, the officer at the scene, after discover-ing the button, would document the discovery in his notes and ask a CSI officer to photograph the item. The CSI officer would then collect the button and book it into evidence, carefully packaging it and documenting his or her efforts in a report. The property room would then accept the button into evidence, citing the date and time it was booked in, along with the name of the officer who booked it. Each and every time the button was then removed from property to be examined by an expert, those handling it would document the movement of the button. Reports would be written and property logs would be maintained to track the button's movement from the point when it was first booked into property until it was finally checked out for trial. If this is done properly, the defense will not be able to claim that the button was planted.

Many of us still remember the infamous O. J. Simpson trial. Simpson was accused of killing Nicole Brown Simpson and Ron Goldman, and his defense team claimed that the police tampered with the evidence in order to implicate him. LAPD detective Mark Fuhrman testified that he found a bloodstained glove at the location where Nicole Brown Simpson and Ron Goldman were murdered. He also testified that later in the evening he traveled to O. J. Simpson's home and found the matching bloodstained glove on Simpson's estate, along with a number of blood drops that were ultimately connected to Nicole. The defense argued that Fuhrman transported the items from the scene of the murder and planted them at Simpson's residence. The chain of custody was at the center of the defense's argument.

A NEW TESTAMENT "CHAIN OF CUSTODY"

Those who are skeptical of the New Testament Gospels offer a similar objection based on the chain of custody. The Gospels claim to be eyewitness accounts of the life and ministry of Jesus Christ. These accounts were eventually entered into the "court record" when they were established as Scripture at the Council of Laodicea in AD 363. It was here that early Christian leaders first identified and codified the *canon* of the Christian Scripture, the official list of twenty-seven books and letters that became the New Testament. No council, prior to this meeting in the fourth century, formally acknowledged the list of accepted books and letters (including the Gospels); no "courtroom" recognized the evidence of the Gospels prior to this important church-council meeting. If the life of Jesus could be considered the Christian "crime scene," this council was undoubtedly the "courtroom" where the evidence of the eyewitness testimony was first formally acknowledged.

Crime Scene   Courtroom

Life of Jesus
(AD 1–33)

Council of Laodicea
(AD 363)

That's quite an expansive period of time between the "crime scene" and the "courtroom," don't you think? A lot could happen in 330 years. I thought it was tough to trace and track the evidence in my cases, and they were only decades old! Imagine tracking the evidence for ten times as many years. Skeptics have considered this period of time and argued that the eyewitness evidence of the Gospels was "planted." Like the defense attorney who argued that the button was added to the collection of evidence sometime *after* the crime occurred, skeptics often argue that the Gospels were written well after the life of Jesus. They are not true evidence; they were manufactured by conspirators who wanted to fool those who were not at the "crime scene."

The best way to counter this sort of a claim is to retrace the chain of custody to see if we can account for who handled the evidence from the point of the "crime scene" to its first appearance in the "courtroom."

EVIDENCE, HISTORY, AND REASONABLE EXPECTATIONS

While it may sound like an easy task to trace the chain of custody, it can be extremely difficult in cases that are very old. This is often my dilemma as a cold-case detective. When I open a case from the past, the first thing I try to do is collect all the original documents that were written during the first investigation. That should be easy, right? Well, not always. While these cases were important to our agency, there are times when unexpected issues, unrelated to the investigation, can make this task difficult. Sometimes things are lost when a records database is upgraded as the result of new storage technology. Sometimes notes or other reports have simply deteriorated to the point that they are no longer usable. Sometimes documents are accidentally destroyed or purged. The longer an event slips into the past, the more likely I may have a problem retrieving all the information I need to trace the chain of custody. In spite of this, I have been able to assemble enough of the chain of custody to demonstrate a level of responsibility to the jury. Given the age of the case, jurors understand that we simply cannot expect the same level of precise *record keeping* when outside forces cannot be controlled over long periods of time.

Something very similar happens when trying to trace the chain of custody for the gospel eyewitness accounts. Imagine trying to control outside forces for thousands of years instead of just a few decades. The "original reports" in the "Christian cold case" were written on papyrus, an excellent material if you are looking for something that was readily available in the first century, but a terrible material if you are looking for something that won't fall apart when handled frequently. As a result, we no longer have the original writings (sometimes called "autographs"). The first eyewitness accounts were copied repeatedly so that they could be distributed throughout the church and retained in spite of the nature of the papyrus that was available. It's now difficult to precisely retrace the movement of the Gospels over time and establish a chain of custody.

In order to have any success at all, we first need to identify the players who would be involved in such a chain. In cold-case homicide investigations, the *links* in the chain include the responding officers, the crime-scene investigators, the first detectives, the criminalists, and then the cold-case detectives, who ultimately bring the case to the prosecutor. But who would we expect to be involved in the gospel chain of custody?

The Apostolic Eyewitnesses

Disciple of the Disciple

Disciple of the Apostle

Disciples of the Disciple's Disciple

Life of Jesus (AD 1–33)

Council of Laodicea (AD 363)

To trace the New Testament Gospels, we are going to need to identify the original eyewitnesses and their immediate disciples, moving from one set of disciples to the next until we trace the Gospels from AD 33 to AD 363. The New Testament gospel chain of custody, if it exists, would provide us with confidence that the accounts we have today are an accurate reflection of what was observed at the "crime scene." This *link-by-link* approach to the history of the accounts would also help us respond to the objections of skeptics who claim that the Gospels were planted late in history. We will examine this issue in much more detail in section 2, and we will identify the historical links in this important chain.

A TOOL FOR THE CALLOUT BAG, A TIP FOR THE CHECKLIST

As a detective, I quickly learned the importance of the chain of custody, and I eventually pulled this principle from my callout bag as I investigated the reliability of the Gospels. Before I became a Christian, I seldom held the same level of skepticism for other ancient documents that I held for the biblical accounts. I can remember having an intense interest in ancient history from the time I was in high school. I had an "honors" class with a wonderful, sage-like teacher, Mr. Schultz, who had the ability to bring the past to life using the ancient written histories of Herodotus and Thucydides, among others. He taught from these accounts as if they were reliable and true, and I accepted them without much question. Mr. Schultz never talked about the fact that the earliest copies we have for these ancient writers appear in history approximately five hundred years after the events they claim to describe. There is no clear chain of custody for these historical accounts during this period of time. We don't know whom Herodotus, for example, entrusted with his writings. We don't know how Herodotus's record was preserved or what happened to it during these five hundred years. This is, of course, the nature of the vast majority of ancient historical accounts. Given that we accept these accounts as historically factual even though their history of transmission is missing for five centuries or more, wouldn't it be fair to reconsider our historical view of the gospel record if we discovered that the Gospels have a verifiable chain of custody? We need to keep this question in mind as we get ready to examine the issue more thoroughly in section 2.

Of all the documents written by Christians in the first and second centuries, the texts we most care about are those that made it into the *canon* of Scripture. Few of us are familiar with the *noncanonical* writings from the earliest period of Christian history. Many early Christian leaders wrote letters and documents that, while not considered *canonical*, are rich with theological content and historical detail. These *noncanonical* early church documents can tell us much about the teaching of the original eyewitnesses. They will eventually become part of the chain of custody as we examine the transmission of the Gospels in the first three centuries. We would be wise to have at least some understanding of the identity of the students and disciples of the apostles and some mastery of their writings. Many of these men (like Polycarp, Ignatius, and Clement) became known as the "early church fathers." They led the church following the deaths of the apostles, and their letters and writings are widely available online and in print form. The earliest works of these church fathers are often interesting and enriching. They are worth our time and effort, particularly as we make a case for the New Testament chain of custody and the reliability of the Gospels as eyewitness accounts.

Chapter 9

Principle #9:

KNOW WHEN "ENOUGH IS ENOUGH"

"I wasn't convinced," said Juror Number 8 as he looked across the table at the other jurors. Some of them laughed and shook their heads. Juror Number 8 stood his ground. "Hey, this is a big deal to me. I needed to be sure."

We sat together in the jury room, relaxing around a long table after the trial concluded and the verdict had been read. The jurors were assembled and eager to ask us questions. They looked exhausted but relieved. The trial took six weeks, and this jury conscientiously deliberated for another week before delivering a guilty verdict. I was nervous when the deliberation stretched beyond the first two days; I suspected that one (or more) of the jurors was delaying the verdict and that we might be headed toward a "hung jury." In California criminal trials, all twelve jurors must agree on the outcome. If there are any holdouts, no verdict will be reached and the case must be retried if the prosecutor hopes to convict the defendant. The longer the deliberation, the more likely the jury is divided. I was beginning to fear that the group was hung until the court clerk called us and told us that we had a verdict.

In all honesty, I thought the decision would come back much sooner. This case was overwhelming. We had nearly forty pieces of evidence that pointed to the defendant as the killer. In fact, he was actually caught trying to commit a very similar crime about ten days after he killed the victim in our town. He even had a knife that matched our victim's injuries when he was caught in this second crime. The case was robust and clear; I thought the jury would come back with a decision in less than a day. I typically join the prosecutor and interview the jurors following their work on one of our cases because I want to learn from their observations. What was evidentially powerful? What was relatively insignificant? What was it that finally "made the case" for them? Today I was eager to learn why it took them so long to come to a conclusion. They told me that after reviewing the evidence and taking their first vote, Juror Number 8 was the sole holdout. While everyone else was convinced the defendant was guilty, Juror Number 8 was not so sure.

"I take that 'reasonable doubt' stuff seriously," he said. "I mean, my gut was telling me that he was guilty, but I wasn't sure if we had enough evidence to make the 'standard' that the judge was talking about. I just needed to see the evidence one more time."

"What was it that finally convinced you?" I asked.

"The Band-Aid."

The Band-Aid? Really? I could hardly believe it. When the defendant committed the murder, he cut his finger. He went home and bandaged the injury and was wearing this Band-Aid when the detectives later interviewed him. He didn't want the detectives to notice the injury, so he slipped off the Band-Aid and left it in a corner of the interview room. The detectives noticed and collected the bandage only after the interview was completed. We later had the Band-Aid tested for DNA to demonstrate that it did, in fact, belong to the defendant. But I never considered this bandage to be an important part of the case. In fact, the prosecutor almost didn't include it in the presentation to the jury. Now I was very glad that he did.

WHERE'S THE TIPPING POINT?

You never know the impact that a particular piece of evidence will have on those who are considering your case. Sometimes the things that don't matter much to you personally are the very things that matter the most to someone else.

I've been producing a podcast and hosting a website (ColdCaseChristianity.com) for several years now, and people email me with their questions and doubts related to the evidence for the Christian worldview. Skeptics sometimes write to inform me that they simply don't believe there is enough evidence to prove that God exists. Christians sometimes write to tell me that they are struggling with doubt because they aren't sure if the evidence is sufficient. In many ways, all of these folks are struggling with the same question that jurors face in every case.

When is enough, enough? When is it reasonable to conclude that something is true? When is the evidence sufficient?

In legal terms, the *line* that must be crossed before someone can come to the conclusion that something is evidentially true is called the "standard of proof" (the "SOP"). The SOP varies depending on the kind of case under consideration. The most rigorous of these criteria is the "beyond a reasonable doubt" standard that is required at criminal trials. But how do we know when we have crossed the line and are "beyond a reasonable doubt"? The courts have considered this important issue and have provided us with a definition:

"Reasonable doubt is defined as follows: It is not a mere possible doubt; because everything relating to human affairs is open to some possible or imaginary doubt. It is that state of the case which, after the entire comparison and consideration of all the evidence, leaves the minds of the jurors in that condition that they cannot say they feel an abiding conviction of the truth of the charge."[29]

This definition is important because it recognizes the difference between *reasonable* and *possible* that we discussed earlier. There are, according to the ruling of the court, "reasonable doubts," "possible doubts," and "imaginary doubts." The definition acknowledges something important: every case has unanswered questions that will cause jurors to wonder. All the jurors will have doubts as they come to a decision. We will never remove

The Escalating Standard of Proof

"Some Credible Evidence"

The lowest possible standard (used in some child-protection hearings). This standard simply establishes that there is enough evidence to begin an inquiry, investigation, or trial.

"Preponderance of the Evidence"

This is the next standard of proof (used in most civil trials). This standard is established if a proposition is more likely to be true than untrue (i.e., 51 percent more likely to be true).

"Clear and Convincing Evidence"

This is an intermediate standard of proof (used in some civil and criminal proceedings). This standard is met when a proposition is significantly and substantially more likely to be true than untrue.

"Beyond a Reasonable Doubt"

This is the highest level of proof required by the law (usually reserved for criminal trials). This standard is met when there is no plausible reason to believe that a proposition is untrue.

every possible uncertainty; that's why the standard is not "beyond any doubt." Being "beyond a reasonable doubt" simply requires us to separate our *possible* and *imaginary* doubts from those that are *reasonable*.

"SHUNNING" THE TRUTH

There are many reasons why people may deny (or "shun") the truth. Not all reasons are based on evidence. Jurors can reject a truth claim for "ra'shun'al," "emo'shun'al," or "voli'shun'al" reasons. Sometimes jurors have *rational* doubts that are based on the evidence. Perhaps the defense has convinced them that an alternative explanation is better supported evidentially. Sometimes jurors have doubts that are purely *emotional*. I've been involved in cases where jurors had an emotional reaction to the prosecutor or defense attorney and struggled to over-come negative *feelings* so they could evaluate the case fairly. Sometimes jurors deny the truth for *volitional* reasons. They are willfully resistant and refuse to accept any position offered by the group. Attorneys on both sides do their best to identify *strong-willed* people such as these during the jury selection process to make sure that the jury is composed of people who will listen to the arguments of others. When making a decision that's based on evidence, it's important for us to understand the "shuns" we've described and limit our doubts to those that are rational and reasonable.

This makes the decision-making process much easier. When assessing the case, we simply need to examine our doubts and separate those that are based on evidence (rational doubts) from those that are not (emotional or volitional doubts). If the doubts we still possess fall into the second category, we can be comfortable with our decision. Once we identify the fact that our doubts are not reasonable, we can deliver a verdict, even though we may still have unanswered questions.

YOU'LL NEVER KNOW ALL THERE IS TO KNOW

It's important to remember that truth can be known even when some of the facts are missing. None of us has ever made a decision with *complete* knowledge of all the possible facts. There are always unanswered questions. I use a version of the puzzle illustration (from chapter 6) when trying to help jurors understand this truth. As we assemble a case that points to any particular defendant, we begin to collect pieces of evidence that slowly reveal the identity of the killer.

We begin to assemble the puzzle. While there might be a large amount of evidence in the prosecution's case, no criminal case possesses every possible piece of evidence. No prosecutor is able to answer every conceivable question.

Like this puzzle, every cold case I work has missing pieces. Some of these pieces are obvious and glaring. But notice that their absence doesn't keep us from having certainty about the image; we recognize the picture even though some things are missing. We have certainty because the pieces we *do* have reveal the killer's identity (in this case, Al Capone, the famous Chicago gangster and crime syndicate leader of the 1920s). We have certainty because additional pieces, even if they are different from what we might imagine, would not significantly change the identity we see in the puzzle. We have confidence in concluding that Al Capone is pictured here, even though there are unanswered questions about the puzzle.

For some, the idea of making a decision while there are still unanswered questions seems premature and even dangerous. What if there are outstanding facts that are yet unknown to us? What if new, additional information comes to light in a few years that contradicts the evidence that we have in front of us today? Wouldn't it be wiser for us to simply withhold judgment until every question can be answered (including those we haven't even thought of yet)? But juries understand the importance of acting on what they *do* know rather than fretting about what *could be* known. In courtrooms across America, jurors are asked to act (in the present) on the evidence available (from the past) to decide what ought to happen (in the future). They make these decisions because what they *do* know outweighs what might *possibly be known* if every question could be answered. Either the evidence is sufficient today or it is not; jurors must assess what they have in front of them at the moment rather than speculate about what they might find out later.

EVIDENTIAL SUFFICIENCY AND THE PROBLEM OF EVIL

A listener of the *Cold-Case Christianity Podcast* recently sent me an email expressing his doubts in the existence of an all-powerful and all-loving God, given the presence of evil in the world. This is a classic objection to theism. If God does exist, why would He allow people to do evil things? Either this "God" is unable to stop people from acting as they do (in which case He is not all-powerful), or He is unwilling to stop them (in which case He is not all-loving). The writer posed this question to me because he knew what I did for a living:

Epicurus and the Problem of Evil

The ancient Greek philosopher Epicurus is credited with first posing the "problem of evil" as it relates to the existence of God:

"Either God wants to abolish evil, and cannot; or he can, but does not want to. If he wants to, but cannot, he is impotent. If he can, but does not want to, he is wicked. If God can abolish evil, and God really wants to do it, why is there evil in the world?"

(According to Lactantius in *On the Wrath of God*, ca. AD 313)

"I bet you see many terrible things that people do to one another. How can you still believe in such a God?"

The problem of evil is perhaps the most difficult issue to address because it is emotionally loaded. It's at times like these that I try to help people walk through the distinctions between *reasonable doubts* (that are grounded rationally) and *possible doubts* (that are grounded emotionally). Let me explain.

We need to start by recognizing that there are many good reasons to believe that God exists (we talked about some of them in chapter 3). These pieces of the puzzle are already in place before we start talking about the issue of evil. Yes, there are some unanswered questions related to the existence of evil, but we have to begin our examination by recognizing that the puzzle is well on its way to completion even though this piece may seem to be missing. Next, we have to ask ourselves if the presence of evil truly represents a missing piece. Is it possible, instead, that the existence of evil may actually be an additional piece that helps make the puzzle more certain?

When people complain that there is evil in the world, they are not simply offering their opinion. They are instead saying that true, objective evil exists. They are complaining about evil behavior as though this behavior ought to be recognized by all of us, regardless of our personal likes, dislikes, or opinions about human conduct. If evil were a matter of opinion, we could eliminate it by simply changing our minds. People who complain about evil behavior must accept the premise that true, objective "right" and "wrong" exist in the first place. They must accept that some things are morally virtuous and some things are morally repulsive, no matter who you are, where you are located, or when you live in history. This kind of moral evil transcends all of us; if it doesn't, why complain in the first place? If evil is simply a matter of opinion, why doesn't the man who emailed me simply change his opinion?

You see, in order for true evil to exist (so that the writer has something legitimate to complain about), there must be a true barometer of right and wrong. In order for an act to be objectively "bad," there must be some standard of objective "good" by which to measure it. What might that standard be if not God? Can the standard come from some evolutionary process? Can it come from the slow development of cultural groups? If so, morals are simply a matter of opinion (albeit a largely held opinion), and there is nothing objectively evil to complain about. Remember that even the most heinous regimes of history identified their own behavior as morally virtuous. In order for true evil to exist, there must be a source of true good that transcends any and all groups that might make a claim about the existence of evil. In other words, the existence of true evil necessitates the presence of God as a standard of true virtue. It turns out that the existence of evil is actually another evidence for God's existence, another piece of the puzzle that reveals God's image.

But let's return to the very real issue of evil behavior. Why would God allow people to kill each other if He loves us and is powerful enough to stop it? While this question has emotional power, we have to ask ourselves if there might be a reasonable explanation. Are we thinking it through evidentially, or are we reacting emotionally? Are we rejecting the existence of God because there is no rational explanation for the existence of evil, or are we resisting volitionally because we stubbornly refuse to accept any explanation that might be offered?

I can think of a number of very good reasons why God would allow people to behave immorally, even though He loves His creation and is certainly powerful enough to stop evil.

Theodicy

"The theological discipline that seeks to explain how the existence of evil in the world can be reconciled with the justice and goodness of God" (*Webster's New World College Dictionary*, Wiley Publishing Inc., Cleveland, Ohio, 2010).

Ask yourself this question: Which is more loving, a God who creates a world in which love is possible or a God who creates a world in which love is impossible? It seems reasonable that a loving God would create a world where love is possible and can be experienced by creatures who are designed "in His image." But a world in which love is possible can be a dangerous place. Love requires freedom. True love requires that humans have the ability to freely choose; love cannot be forced if it is to be heartfelt and real. The problem, of course, is that people who have the freedom to love often choose to hate. That's why freedom of this nature is so costly. A world in which people have the freedom to love and perform great acts of kindness is also a world in which people have the freedom to hate and commit great acts of evil. You cannot have one without the other.

In addition to this, from a Christian perspective, we are all eternal creatures who will live beyond the grave. If this is true, then questions about why God might not stop evil are a bit premature. At best, we can say only that God hasn't stopped evil *yet*. But God has all eternity to act in this regard. Our eternal life provides the context for God to deal justly with those who choose hate and perform acts of evil. God *is* powerful enough to stop evil completely, and He *does* care about justice. But as an eternal Being, He may choose to take care of it on an eternal timeline. Compared to eternity, this mortal existence is but a vapor, created by God to be a wonderful place where love is possible for those who choose it.

If there are good reasons why God might permit evil in this life (such as the preservation of free will and the ability to love genuinely), concerns about His failure to act are simply unreasonable. Doubts about God's existence based on the problem of evil may have emotional appeal, but they lack rational foundation because reasonable explanations do, in fact, exist. While one can imagine *possible doubts* related to the problem of evil, careful consideration of the nature of objective evil reveals that these doubts are not *reasonable*. We ought to be able to move beyond our reservations here because the problem of evil does not present us with a *reasonable doubt*.

A TOOL FOR THE CALLOUT BAG, A TIP FOR THE CHECKLIST

In every investigation I've conducted, this principle related to *evidential sufficiency* has helped me evaluate my own conclusions and determine if they were reasonable; this important tool from our *callout* bag can also help us assess the claims of Christianity. All of us need to recognize that we make decisions every day with less-than-perfect knowledge and missing information. In our daily decisions, we act with certainty even though we don't know everything that could be known on any particular topic. We learn to trust our cars, even though we don't completely understand how they operate mechanically. We trust our mates and children, even though we don't know everything they are thinking or everything they are doing when we are away. We make a case for what we believe, and we accept the fact that we can't know everything. Criminal cases require the highest legal standard; they require juries to come to a decision that is "beyond a reasonable doubt." The decisions that juries make are often a matter of life and death for the defendants who have been accused. If this standard is appropriate for important cases involving *temporal* matters of life and death, it is reasonable to apply the standard to the case that will determine our *eternal* life or death. Juries are able to reach a verdict beyond a reasonable doubt, even though there are still some unanswered questions. They do this because the reasonable evidence they possess is greater than the possible questions that remain unanswered. Let's make sure that our objections and doubts are less emotional or volitional than they are rational. When I was an atheist, I never took the time to categorize my doubts into "rational" versus "emotional" classifications. I also never took the time to see if theism (or Christianity) offered a reasonable response to my doubts. Looking back at them, many of my doubts were merely *possible doubts* based on an emotional or volitional response.

I often get frustrated when sharing what I believe about God with my skeptical friends, coworkers, and family members. Those of us who are interested in making a rational, evidential case for our Christian worldview sometimes find our efforts to be completely unfruitful. Try as we might, even when we make a cogent, articulate, reasonable case for our view, our efforts seem to have no impact on our listeners. It's tempting to get frustrated and begin to doubt our own evidence. In times like these, it's important to remember the "shuns" of denial. Many of the people we are trying to reach are willing to deny the truth of God's existence on the basis of an emotional or volitional response, rather than on the basis of good evidence. This is not to say that all atheists are irrational, emotional, or willfully resistant. Many have taken the time to make a reasoned case of their own. It's our responsibility as Christians to make the effort to know our friends and family well enough to understand the nature of their denial. When they are resisting on the basis of evidence, let's examine the facts together and assess which explanations are the most reasonable. When they are resisting for other reasons, let's be sensitive enough to ask the kinds of questions that will help us understand where they are coming from before we overwhelm them with the evidence we are so eager to share. Don't expect someone to respond to your *reasoned* arguments when the *evidence* wasn't that important to him or her in the first place.

Chapter 10

Principle #10:

PREPARE FOR AN ATTACK

My partner sent me a joke involving a defense attorney and a murder trial; the joke's been circulating around our police agency for some time:

A defendant was on trial for a murder. There was overwhelming circumstantial evidence pointing to the defendant's guilt, in spite of the fact that the body of the victim was never recovered. After sitting through weeks of the trial, the defendant and his lawyer knew that he would probably be convicted. In an act of desperation, the defense attorney resorted to a trick.

"Ladies and Gentlemen of the jury, I have a surprise for you," the attorney proclaimed as he looked down at his watch. "Within sixty seconds, the person you thought had been murdered will walk into this courtroom."

He turned and looked toward the courtroom door. The jurors, surprised by the proclamation, turned and watched the door in anticipation. A minute passed. Nothing happened.

Finally the defense attorney said, "I need to admit to you that I lied about that last statement. But all of you turned with me and watched that door with eager anticipation. This demonstrates that you have a reasonable doubt in this case as to whether anyone was actually killed in the first place! I, therefore, insist that you return a verdict of not guilty."

The jury, openly rattled by the clever effort, retired to deliberate on the case. Moments later they returned and promptly delivered a verdict of guilty. The defense attorney was shocked.

"How could you return with a verdict so quickly?" he asked the jury. "You must have had some doubt; I saw all of you watch that door with expectation!"

The jury foreman replied, "Yes, we did look, but your client didn't."

I've been involved in a number of homicide trials over the years. Some of our cases have been evidentially overwhelming, and others have been more difficult to prove. In each and every case, the defendant has been represented by an articulate, intelligent, and committed defense attorney who carefully crafted a defense for his or her client. Many of these attorneys appeared to be incredibly confident, in spite of the overwhelming evidence that pointed to the guilt of their clients.

I'm never surprised by the enthusiasm and self-assurance of good defense attorneys. It's been my experience that there are many factors that can motivate an attorney to perform confidently and aggressively in behalf of a defendant. I suspect that some attorneys work diligently because they have a true belief in the innocence of their clients. Some attorneys probably work diligently because they have a true belief in the importance of fair and adequate representation in our criminal justice system, even if they don't personally believe that their clients are innocent. Some attorneys may work diligently because they have a true belief in advancing their careers. One thing is for sure, defense attorneys present the best case they can, even when they may not believe they are defending the truth.

THE GROWING ATTACK FROM SKEPTICS

I became a Christian in 1996. Until 2001, the Jim Wallace I knew prior to 1996 was the most sarcastic atheist I had ever known. I can remember some of my conversations with Christians prior to becoming a believer, and I am now embarrassed by the way I behaved; many of my coworkers continue to remind me of those days. But my own level of prior sarcasm was quickly eclipsed by the atheists who began to write and speak against religion following the attack on the World Trade Center in 2001. A new era in atheistic rhetoric began following that dreadful day, as prominent atheists responded to what they saw as evidence of the evil of "religious fundamentalism." A number of books flooded the shelves of local bookstores. Sam Harris wrote *The End of Faith: Religion, Terror and the Future of Reason* (2004) and *Letter to a Christian Nation* (2006). Richard Dawkins wrote *The God Delusion* (2006), and Christopher Hitchens wrote *God Is Not Great: How Religion Poisons Everything* (2007). The attack from atheists and skeptics grew and took on a new form of immediacy, aggression, and sarcasm.

Many Christians, especially those who had been believers for most of their lives, were caught off guard by the confidence and articulate opposition of these authors and those who shared their negative view of Christianity. The culture quickly seemed to embrace the winsome atheist criticisms; book sales for these three writers were phenomenal. The mere fact that anyone could offer a thoughtful and engaging defense of atheism seemed to shake the confidence of many believers who may have been taking their faith for granted. It wasn't as though these skeptics were offering anything new. Instead, they were presenting old arguments with new vigor, humor, cynicism, and urgency. They were much like the defense attorneys I had faced over the years.

I've discovered that good defense attorneys typically bring out the best in prosecutors and detectives, so I've learned to embrace the work of defense lawyers who have caused me to make sure my case is sound and reasonable. The fact that there is a defender on the opposite side of the issue who is arguing vociferously against us is no reason to believe that the defender possesses the truth. Defense attorneys operate that way even when they are defending what turns out to be a lie. The existence of a well-articulated defensive argument alone is no reason to surrender our position, but it ought to encourage us to know our case better than anyone else. Defense attorneys (just like those who oppose the claims of Christianity) ought to bring out the best in us.

THE DEFENSIVE STRATEGY

Defense attorneys approach each case differently, but I've noticed a number of general strategies that lawyers have taken when trying to defeat my cold-case investigations. By examining these defensive strategies and comparing them to the approach that is often taken by those who oppose Christianity, we can assess the validity of these tactics.

DEFENSE ATTORNEYS CHALLENGE THE NATURE OF TRUTH

If all truth is simply a matter of perspective and subjective opinion, it's virtually impossible to convict someone of a crime. We live in a culture that is more and more pluralistic with each passing generation. Many of our young adults have been taught (in universities and colleges and through movies, television, and books) that objective truth does not exist or simply cannot be known. As a result, relativism is a common feature of our cultural worldview. People are less and less comfortable accepting that one particular version of the truth is exclusively correct. In fact, many believe that such a view of truth is arrogant and narrow-minded. To make matters worse, a new cultural definition of "tolerance" has emerged. Tolerance used to be the attitude that we took toward one another when we disagreed about an important issue; we would agree to treat each other with respect, even though we refused to embrace each other's view on a particular topic. Tolerance is now the act of recognizing *and embracing* all views as equally valuable and true, even though they often make opposite truth claims. According to this redefinition of tolerance, anything other than acceptance and approval is narrow-minded and bigoted. Defense attorneys are capitalizing on these evolving redefinitions of truth and tolerance. If a lawyer can convince a jury that no version of what happened is better than another (because all truth is simply a matter of personal perspective and opinion), the jury is going to have trouble convicting the defendant with any level of confidence. For this reason, some defense attorneys begin by attacking the nature of truth before they ever attack the nature of the prosecution's case.

The erosion of the classic view of objective truth and tolerance is also taking its toll on those who hold a Christian worldview. The notion that there might be only one way to God (or only one truth about the identity and nature of God) is offensive and intolerant to many skeptics and nonbelievers. Like prosecutors who face similar misunderstandings about the nature of truth, Christians may also have to expose the logical problems inherent to the new cultural definitions. While some may argue that all religions are basically the same, this is simply untrue. The world's religions propose contrary claims related to the nature of God. Eastern religions propose the existence of an impersonal god, while the monotheistic religions of Judaism, Christianity, and Islam claim that God is personal. Judaism refuses to recognize Jesus as anything other than a "rabbi" or spiritual teacher, while Christianity claims that Jesus was God Himself. Islam

"Objective Truth"

While many truths are certainly a matter of opinion, some truths are completely independent of anyone's personal view. My statement "Police cars are the coolest cars on the road" may be true for me (given that I am often the one driving these cars), while completely untrue for you (especially when I pull you over for rolling through a stop sign). This statement is a matter of my "subjective" opinion; it is dependent on the "subject" who possesses it. The statement "Police cars are equipped to travel in excess of 100 mph" is not dependent on my opinion, however; this second statement is either true or false on the basis of the "object" itself. Police cars are equipped to travel this fast, and my "subjective" opinion has nothing to do with it.

denies that Jesus died on the cross, while Christianity claims that Jesus died at the crucifixion and then rose from the dead, verifying His deity. All of these claims about God and Jesus may be false, but they cannot all be true; they contradict one another by definition. The logical law of "noncontradiction" states that contradictory statements cannot both be true at the same time. Those who are evaluating the claims of the world's religions, like jurors evaluating a criminal case, must decide which of the views is supported by the evidence, rather than surrender the decision to an errant view of truth.

In addition to this, those who are investigating Christianity may want to rethink the latest cultural definitions of truth and tolerance. Those who claim that truth is a matter of perspective and opinion are proclaiming this as more than a matter of perspective and opinion. They would like us to believe that this definition is objectively true, even as they deny the existence of objective truth. When a statement fails to meet its own standard for being true, it is said to be "self-refuting." The claim that "objective truth does not exist" is self-refuting because it is, in fact, an objective claim about truth. The current redefinition of tolerance doesn't fare much better. Those who claim that tolerance requires all ideas and perspectives to be embraced as equally true and valuable simultaneously deny the classic view of tolerance. In other words, the new definition of tolerance is intolerant of the old definition. It cannot follow its own rules. It is just as self-refuting as the new redefinition of truth; we simply need to help people understand that this is the case.

DEFENSE ATTORNEYS FOCUS ON THE BEST THE PROSECUTION HAS TO OFFER

While circumstantial cases are built on many pieces of evidence that are evaluated as a group, some pieces are better (and more important to the case) than others. For this reason, defense attorneys focus their attention on the heart of the prosecution's case, the prominent and most condemning pieces of evidence that have been presented. If they can discredit or eliminate these key pieces of evidence, the foundation of the prosecution's case may begin to crumble. In fact, if I want to know what the defense thinks of my case (and what it considers to be the most devastating piece of evidence), I simply have to observe what it is attacking with the most vigor. If my case is thin or weak, the defense will be comfortable attacking the one piece it believes to be critical. If my case is substantial and strong, the defense will find itself trying to attack a much larger number of issues in an effort to limit the cumulative impact of the evidence. I know where my case is strong when I see what the defense has chosen to attack.

Skeptics do something similar when they attack the claims of Christianity. The Christian worldview is built on the eyewitness testimony of the gospel writers. For this reason, many skeptics attack the reliability of the Gospels as their primary tactic in trying to defeat the case for Christianity. This focused attack on the Gospels reveals the strength of our case. Like defense attorneys, skeptics recognize our most valuable piece of evidence. As a result, some critics attempt to undermine the reliability of the gospel writers as eyewitnesses (we'll talk more about that in section 2), while others seek to have this testimony "tossed out" as unreliable "hearsay" before it can even be evaluated. They argue that the gospel accounts fail to meet the judicial standard we require of eyewitnesses in criminal cases. Witnesses must be present in court in order for their testimony

What Makes It "Hearsay"?

A "hearsay" statement is anything said outside of the courtroom that is then offered inside the courtroom (during a court proceeding) as evidence of the truth of the matter asserted. Since jurors have to assess the credibility of a witness, courts generally require witnesses to be in the courtroom so (1) they can "swear" or promise that their testimony is true, (2) they can be personally present at the proceeding so the jury can assess them visually, and (3) they can be cross-examined by the opposition.

to be considered in a criminal trial. This often presents a problem for me as cold-case detective. I have a few cases that are now impossible to complete because key witnesses are dead and can no longer testify in court. It's not enough that I may have someone who heard what these witnesses once said about an event. If I called those "second level" witnesses into court, their testimony would be considered "hearsay." It would be inadmissible simply because the original witness was no longer available to be cross-examined for evaluation. This is a reasonable standard to hold for criminal trials; as a society, we hold that "it is better that ten guilty persons escape … than that one innocent suffer."[30] For this reason, we've created a rigorous (and sometimes difficult) legal standard for eyewitnesses.

But this standard is simply too much to require of historical eyewitness testimony. The vast majority of historical events must be evaluated in spite of the fact that the eyewitnesses are now dead and cannot come into court to testify. The eyewitnesses who observed the crafting and signing of the Constitution of the United States are lost to us. Those who witnessed the life of Abraham Lincoln are also lost to us. It's one thing to require eyewitness cross-examination on a case that may condemn a defendant to the gas chamber; it's another thing to hold history up to such an unreasonable necessity. If we require this standard for historical accounts, be prepared to jettison everything you think you know about the past. Nothing can be known about history if live eyewitnesses are the only reliable witnesses we can consult. If this were the case, we could know nothing with certainty beyond two or three living generations. Once the eyewitnesses die, history is lost. But we have great confidence about many historical events, in spite of the fact that the eyewitnesses have long been in their graves. As we evaluate the writers of any historical account, we must simply do our best to assess them under the four criteria we discussed in chapter 4 (we'll apply these criteria in section 2). Our goals are the same as we have for living courtroom eyewitnesses, but our expectations are appropriate to the examination of history. This is reasonable, given the nature of events that occurred in the distant past.

DEFENSE ATTORNEYS TARGET THE MICRO AND DISTRACT FROM THE MACRO

As we've already described, strong circumstantial cases are built on large collections of evidence; the more pieces of evidence that point to the suspect, the stronger the case. For this reason, defense attorneys attempt to distract juries from the larger collection by focusing them on individual pieces. The last thing the defense attorney wants the jury to see is how the pieces come together as a group to complete the puzzle. Instead, a defense lawyer wants jurors to examine each piece of the puzzle in isolation from all the rest, hoping that the item under consideration can be explained in some manner that won't implicate his or her client. If there is more than one reasonable way to interpret an individual piece of evidence, the law requires that juries decide in favor of the defendant's innocence. Defense attorneys, therefore, spend time trying to take the jury's eyes off the larger collection and focus the jury on the minutiae. A single puzzle piece, when examined in isolation, is difficult to understand without seeing the larger puzzle. One little puzzle piece might be part of any number of puzzles; there's just no way to know until we see how it fits with the rest. It's the job of defense attorneys to keep jurors from seeing how the pieces fit together.

Those who challenge the claims of Christianity take a similar approach. Let's take a look at the case for Peter's influence on the gospel of Mark as an example. Skeptics have noticed that Mark's account fails to include the fact that Peter got out of the boat and nearly drowned when Jesus was walking on water (as we described earlier, compare Mark 6:45–52 with Matt. 14:22–33). If this part of the puzzle is examined in isolation, it seems reasonable that Peter had no influence on the gospel of Mark at all (as many skeptics claim). How could Mark leave out this detail if he truly had access to Peter? Skeptics have used this passage of Scripture to argue against the eyewitness authorship and reliability of the Bible. But when this individual passage is examined alongside all the other verses involving Peter in the gospel of Mark, the more reasonable explanation emerges. It's only when examining all these passages as a group that we see Mark's consistent pattern of respect and stewardship toward Peter. It's in the larger context where we see that Mark consistently seeks to protect Peter's reputation and honor. When we combine this fact with the other pieces of the puzzle offered in chapter 5, the case for Peter's influence on Mark's gospel is substantial and reasonable. Like jurors in a criminal trial, we need to resist the effort of those who want us to focus on the individual puzzle pieces as though they were not part of a larger puzzle.

DEFENSE ATTORNEYS ATTACK THE MESSENGER

Nearly every piece of courtroom evidence is submitted through the involvement of a human agent. Eyewitness testimony is one obvious example of this, but even forensic evidence is depen-

"Ad Hominem" Attacks

Ad hominem (Latin for "to the man") is an abbreviated form of Argumentum ad hominem. It describes what is normally seen as a logical fallacy: the attempt to discredit the truth of a claim by pointing out some negative characteristic, behavior, or belief of the person who is making the claim. Dictionary.com describes ad hominem as "attacking an opponent's character rather than answering his argument."

dent on human participation: a detective who first observed it or a criminalist who later examined it. Defense attorneys sometimes attack the person presenting the evidence when they don't like what the evidence says about their client. This is why you often see a vigorous (and critical) cross-examination of key witnesses; defense attorneys typically vilify these witnesses, claiming some bias or highlighting potentially offensive behavior in the witness's professional or personal life. If the defense can get the jury to hate the witness, it may be able to get the jury to hate the evidence the witness has presented.

This has become a prominent tactic of skeptics who deny the claims of Christianity. There can be no doubt that history is replete with examples of people who claimed to be Christians, yet behaved poorly. In fact, many people have committed great violence in the name of Christianity, claiming that their Christian worldview authorized or justified their actions, even though the teaching of Jesus clearly opposed their behavior. But a fair examination of history will also reveal that Christians were not alone. Groups holding virtually every worldview, from theists to atheists, have been equally guilty of violent misbehavior. Atheists point to the Crusades and the Spanish Inquisition when making a case against Christians; theists point to the atheistic regimes of Joseph Stalin and Mao Tse-tung when making a case against atheists. Death statistics are debated in an effort to argue which groups were more violent, but all this seems to miss the point. The common denominator in this violent misbehavior was not worldview; it was the presence of humans.

If we are going to decide what's true on the basis of how people behave, we're in big trouble, because every worldview suffers from examples of adherents who have behaved inconsistently and poorly. I expect that news headlines will continue to feature the apparent hypocrisy of those who claim to be Christians. Jesus certainly predicted that there would be counterfeit Christians ("weeds") living alongside those who were true followers of Christ ("wheat") in the parable of the weeds (Matt. 13:24–30 NIV). I also expect that skeptics will continue to use incidents involving "counterfeit Christians" to their advantage, seeking to vilify these people in order to invalidate the evidence itself. Discourse and dialogue related to Christianity seem to become more vitriolic and demeaning with each passing year. Public debates are often less about substantive arguments than they are about ad hominem attacks. In the end, however, it's all going to come down to the evidence. That's why prosecutors warn juries about the difference between personal attacks and reasoned explanations. Tactics that rely on sarcasm and ridicule must not be allowed to replace arguments that rely on evidence and reason.

DEFENSE ATTORNEYS WANT PERFECTION

Every criminal investigation (and prosecution) is a serious matter, and juries understand this. Defense attorneys sometimes capitalize on the appropriately serious attitude of jurors by criticizing the fact that the prosecution's case was something less than perfect. Given the grave importance of these kinds of cases, shouldn't the authorities have done everything conceivable to conduct a perfect, flawless investigation? Shouldn't every imaginable piece of evidence have been recovered? Shouldn't every possible witness have been located? By identifying the imperfections and limitations of the investigation, attorneys hope to reveal a lack of concern and accuracy that might undermine the prosecution's case.

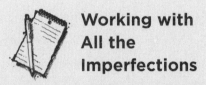

Working with All the Imperfections

Juries must understand that there is no such thing as a "perfect" case. Jurors are told in advance, for example, that they will not have access to everything that could be known about a case. Judges instruct juries that "neither side is required to call all witnesses who may have information about the case or to produce all physical evidence that might be relevant" (Section 300, *Judicial Council of California Criminal Jury Instructions*, 2006). Juries are not allowed to speculate about what is missing, but must focus instead on the reasonable inferences that can be drawn from what is not.

Something similar occurs when skeptics point to the allegedly "imperfect" or "incomplete" historical evidence supporting the claims of Christianity. Why, for example, don't we have a complete set of documents from all the apostles who wrote in the first century? Why don't we have some of the missing letters mentioned in the New Testament, like Paul's prior letter to the Corinthian church described in 1 Corinthians 5:9 or John's letter to Diotrephes's church cited in verse 9 of 3 John? Why isn't there more evidence from sources outside the biblical record corroborating the events described in the Bible (more on this in chapter 12)?

While expectations of perfection may assist defense attorneys as they attack the prosecution's case and skeptics as they attack the claims of Christianity, these kinds of expectations are unreasonable. I've never seen a "perfect" investigation, and I've certainly never conducted one. All inquiries and examinations of the truth (including historical investigations) have their unique deficiencies. Jurors understand that they must work with what they have in front of them. Either the evidence is sufficient or it is not. Jurors can't dwell on what "might have been" or what "could have been done," unless they have evidence and good reason to believe that the truth was lost along the way. Juries cannot assume there is a better explanation (other than the one offered by the prosecution) simply because there were imperfections in the case; reasonable doubts must be established with evidence. In a similar way, skeptics cannot reject the reasonable inferences from the evidence we *do* have, simply because there may possibly be some evidence we *don't* have; skeptics also need to defend their doubt evidentially.

DEFENSE ATTORNEYS PROVIDE ALTERNATIVE "POSSIBILITIES"

Defense attorneys do their best to prevent jurors from accepting the prosecution's version of events. Sometimes it's not enough to simply "poke holes" in the prosecution's case in an effort to distract the jury from the totality of the evidence. Defense attorneys will sometimes provide an alternative theory about what happened in a particular crime, building their own evidential case for a completely different explanation. More often than not, however, the defense will simply imply an alternative explanation by asking suggestive questions that open up a number of alternate "possibilities," even though these "possibilities" are not supported by any evidence. The goal here is to provide jurors with some way to assemble a narrative that does not involve the defendant's guilt. Prosecutors have to help jurors assess the difference between "possible" and "reasonable" in times like this and encourage jurors to limit their deliberations to reasonable inference from the evidence rather than speculating on unsupported possibilities.

Alternative Explanations

Judges instruct juries to be wary of explanations that are not reasonably supported by the evidence. Judges advise jurors that they "must be convinced that the only reasonable conclusion supported by the circumstantial evidence is that the defendant is guilty. If you can draw two or more reasonable conclusions from the circumstantial evidence, and one of those reasonable conclusions points to innocence and another to guilt, you must accept the one that points to innocence. However, when considering circumstantial evidence, you must accept only reasonable conclusions and reject any that are unreasonable" (Section 224, *Judicial Council of California Criminal Jury Instructions,* 2006).

Those who deny the historicity of Jesus sometimes take an approach that's similar to that of defense attorneys. Some skeptics have denied the existence of Jesus altogether by proposing an alternative possibility. Citing the similarities between Jesus and other "savior mythologies" of antiquity, they've argued that Jesus is simply another work of fiction, created by people who wanted to start a new religious tradition. Many of these critics point to the ancient deity Mithras as a prime example of the fictional borrowing they claim occurred in the formation of Christianity. They describe Mithras as a savior who appeared nearly four hundred years prior to the first Christians, and they point to the following similarities:

Mithras was born of a virgin.

Mithras was born in a cave, attended by shepherds.

Mithras had twelve companions or disciples.

Mithras was buried in a tomb and after three days rose again.

Mithras was called "the Good Shepherd."

Mithras was identified with both the Lamb and the Lion.

While these similarities are striking and seem to sustain an alternative theory related to the historicity of Jesus, a brief investigation quickly reveals that they are unsupported by the evidence. There is no existing "Mithraic scripture" available to us today; all our speculations about the Mithras legend are dependent on Mithraic paintings and sculptures and on what was written about Mithras worshippers by the Christians who observed them between the first and third centuries. Even with what little we do know, it is clear that Mithras was not born of a virgin in a cave. Mithras reportedly emerged from solid rock, leaving a cave in the side of a mountain. There is also no evidence that Mithras had twelve companions or disciples; this similarity may be based on a mural that places the twelve personages of the Zodiac in a circle around Mithras. There is no evidence that Mithras was ever called the "Good Shepherd," and although Mithras was a "sun-god" and associated with Leo (the House of the Sun in Babylonian astrology), there is no evidence that he was identified with the Lion. There is also no evidence that Mithras ever died, let alone rose again after three days. These claims of skeptics (like the "possibilities" offered by defense attorneys) are not supported by the evidence. It's important to remember that a "possible" response is not necessarily a "plausible" refutation.

DEFENSE ATTORNEYS EMPLOY A CULTURALLY WINSOME ATTITUDE

Most defense lawyers understand the importance of "first impressions." I've been involved in a number of high-profile cases with prominent defense attorneys. These attorneys were brutally aggressive, sarcastic, and rancorous in the preliminary hearings, while personable, endearing, and charismatic in the jury trials. What's the difference? The presence of a jury; jurors are not present at preliminary hearings. Defense lawyers understand that style is often as important as substance. How you deliver a claim is sometimes more important than the claim itself. For this reason, defense attorneys are often keen observers of the culture; they borrow mannerisms and language that will effectively endear their persona and message to the jury they are trying to convince. The facts are sometimes of secondary importance.

A Presentation Is Not a Piece of Evidence

Jurors are also advised that the words of the attorneys are not to be considered as evidence: "Nothing that the attorneys say is evidence. In their opening statements and closing arguments, the attorneys will discuss the case, but their remarks are not evidence. Their questions are not evidence. Only the witnesses' answers are evidence. The attorneys' questions are significant only if they help you understand the witnesses' answers. Do not assume that something is true just because one of the attorneys asks a question that suggests it is true" (Section 104, *Judicial Council of California Criminal Jury Instructions*, 2006).

The skeptics in our midst are equally savvy. Christians are not the only people who take an urgent, evangelical approach to their worldview. Many popular atheists are equally interested in proselytizing those around them. They are keenly aware of what is popular. As a part of the culture they are trying to reach, they understand what people are watching on television and on the Internet. They've seen the hit movies and purchased the best-selling music. They've mastered the language and are shaping the art, music, and literature of our society. They often portray Christians as antiquated, backward-thinking "dinosaurs" who are out of touch with progressive concepts and the current culture. They recognize and capitalize on the well-intentioned desire of many Christians to resist the things of the world in favor of the things of God (1 John 2:15). Skeptics often have an advantage in communicating their opposition and alternative theories simply because they are more aligned with the culture they are trying to influence.

This is often revealed most glaringly in televised debates between Christians and nonbelievers. The most effective skeptics are those who (like effective defense attorneys) make a winsome connection with the audience. They are endearing. They are entertaining. They understand and highlight the doubts and concerns that people have about Christianity. They use persuasive rhetoric to make their points. I've seen a number of debates in which the

Christian representative possessed the best arguments and mastery of the evidence, yet seemed less influential from the perspective of communication. In a culture where image is more important than information, style more important than substance, it is not enough to possess the truth. Case makers must also master the media.

When the prosecution presents a case in the courtroom, the defense is left with three possible responses: it can declare, destroy, or distract. On rare occasions, the defense declares a robust alternative theory to explain what happened in a particular case. This is difficult, however, because it requires the defense to substantiate its alternative scenario with evidence. In essence, they've got to build their case the same way the prosecution has already built a case against their client. More often than not, defense attorneys take a different approach; they focus on destroying the prosecution's case by discrediting the evidence. If they can find legitimate shortcomings in the individual pieces of evidence, they can undermine the prosecution's case, piece by piece. A third tactic is often just as effective in circumstantial cases, however. Using the tactics we've discussed in this chapter, defense lawyers can distract the jury from the cumulative impact of the circumstantial evidence.

By attacking the nature of truth, targeting the foundation of the prosecution's case, focusing on the micro rather than the macro, disparaging the prosecution's witnesses, raising the expectation of perfection, offering unsupported possibilities, and delivering all of this in a winsome way, defense attorneys attempt to distract juries from the larger picture. They don't want the jury to see the forest through the trees. They don't want the jury to see the connected and reasonable nature of the cumulative circumstantial case.

Those who oppose the claims of Christianity often take a very similar approach. Like defense attorneys, they sometimes ignore the larger connected nature of the case for Christianity and focus on possibilities and claims that either are untrue or have no impact on the evidence.

 ## A TOOL FOR THE CALLOUT BAG, A TIP FOR THE CHECKLIST

While the tactics of defense attorneys may not seem like tools appropriate for your investigative *callout* bag, think of them as *precautionary* principles for your *checklist*. If these tactics are inappropriate for defense attorneys, they're equally inappropriate for those of us who are presenting the claims of Christianity. Let's hold ourselves to a high standard, even as we require our opponents to recognize their own reasonable responsibilities. It's well known that the "burden of proof" in criminal trials rests upon the prosecution. Defendants are presumed innocent until found guilty; they are under no obligation to mount any defense at all. But if, for example, a defendant in a murder trial wants the jury to believe that he simply committed the homicide in self-defense, the burden to raise this doubt falls on the defense team. Skeptics have long claimed that the burden of proof for the truth of the Christian worldview (e.g., the existence of God or the deity of Jesus) belongs to Christians; naturalism is the default position that need not be proved. That's fine if they limit their resistance to *destruction* or *distraction* tactics, but once they declare an alternative possibility (e.g., that Jesus is a re-creation of Mithras), the burden of raising this alternative doubt clearly shifts. *Possible alternatives are not reasonable refutations*. If they're not offering a declaration that can be supported by evidence, they're probably attempting to *destroy* or *distract*. It's my hope that my skeptical friends will see the deficiencies of these two approaches. Destruction tactics that try to disqualify the Gospels would also disqualify other historical texts. If skeptics applied an equal standard to other documents of antiquity, they would be hard pressed to believe anything about the ancient past. In addition to this, any efforts to distract from the cumulative case for Christianity by redefining truth or vilifying Christians, while potentially effective, does nothing to demonstrate the truth of naturalism. I've known many defense attorneys who worked hard because they truly believed that their clients were innocent. I've known some who worked hard for other reasons. I have skeptical friends who are in a similar position. Some reject Christianity because they believe it is evidentially false, and they are prepared to declare (and argue) an alternative case. On the other hand, some reject Christianity for another reason (perhaps some past personal experience or a desire to live their life without religious restrictions). When this is the case, they often resort to *destroy* or *distract* tactics. Let's help our doubting friends examine the character of their objections. All of us ought to be willing to argue the merits of our case without resorting to tactics unbecoming of our worldviews.

While I grew up as an atheist, many of my Christian friends either grew up in the church or lived in areas of the country where they met little or no opposition to their Christian worldview. As a result, some were shaken when they had their first encounter with someone who not only opposed them but also did so tactically and winsomely. For some Christians, their first encounter with atheistic opposition occurs at the university level, as either a student or the parent of a student. The number of young Christians who reject Christianity in college is alarming, according to nearly every study that has been done on the topic. Part of this is a matter of preparation. While we are often willing to spend time reading the Bible, praying, or participating in church programs and services, few of us recognize the importance of becoming good Christian *case makers*. Prosecutors are successful when they master the facts of the case and then learn how to navigate and respond to the tactics of the defense team. Christians need to learn from that model as well. We need to master the facts and evidences that support the claims of Christianity and anticipate the tactics of those who oppose us. This kind of preparation is a form of worship. When we devote ourselves to this rational preparation and study, we are worshipping God with our mind, the very thing He has called us to do (Matt. 22:37).

EXAMINE THE EVIDENCE

*Applying the principles of investigation to
the claims of the New Testament*

I was lying in bed, staring at the ceiling.

"I think it may be true," I said to my wife.

"What may be true?" she asked.

"Christianity." I'm sure she was weary of my growing obsession. For several weeks now, it was all I could think about, and I had already talked her ears off on several occasions. She knew I was more serious about this than I had ever been in the past, so she patiently tolerated my obsession and constant conversation. "The more I look at the Gospels, the more I think they look like real eyewitness accounts," I continued. "And the writers seem to have believed what they were writing about."

I knew I was standing on the edge of something profound; I started reading the Gospels to learn what Jesus taught about living a good life and found that He taught much more about His identity as God and the nature of eternal life. I knew that it would be hard to accept one dimension of His teaching while rejecting the others. If I had good reasons to believe that the Gospels were reliable eyewitness accounts, I was going to have to deal with the stuff I had always resisted as a skeptic. What about all the miracles that are wedged in there between the remarkable words of Jesus? How was I going to separate the miraculous from the remarkable? And why was it that I continued to resist the miraculous elements in the first place?

The initial step in my journey toward Christianity was an evaluation of the Gospels. I spent weeks and weeks examining the gospel accounts as I would any eyewitness account in a criminal case. I used many of the tools that I've already described to make a decision that changed my life forever. I'd like to share some of that investigation with you.

Chapter 11

WERE THEY PRESENT?

Why was the tomb supposedly empty? I say supposedly because, frankly, I don't know that it was. Our very first reference to Jesus' tomb being empty is in the Gospel of Mark, written forty years later by someone living in a different country who had heard that it was empty. How would he know?[31]

—Bart Ehrman, New Testament scholar, professor of
religious studies, and author of *Jesus Interrupted*

The so-called Gospel of John is something special and reflects … the highly evolved theology of a Christian writer who lived three generations after Jesus.[32]

—Geza Vermes, scholar, historian, and author of *The Changing Faces of Jesus*

No work of art of any kind has ever been discovered, no painting, or engraving, no sculpture, or other relic of antiquity, which may be looked upon as furnishing additional evidence of the existence of these gospels, and which was executed earlier than the latter part of the second century.[33]

—Charles Burlingame Waite, historian and author of *History
of the Christian Religion to the Year Two Hundred*

IF THE GOSPELS ARE LATE, THEY'RE A LIE

When I was a nonbeliever, I eagerly accepted the skeptical claims of people like Ehrman, Vermes, and Waite. In fact, I often made similar statements (although mine were much less articulate) as I argued with Christian friends and coworkers at the police department. Like the skeptics quoted here, I was inclined to reject the Gospels as late works of fiction. I considered them to be mythological accounts written well after all the true eyewitnesses were dead. They were late, and they were a lie.

I worked in our Gang Detail in the early 1990s and investigated a variety of gang-related assaults. One of them involved a stabbing between members of two rival gangs; both parties were armed with knives. It was hard to determine which of the two gang members was actually the victim, as both were pretty seriously injured and no eyewitnesses were willing to come forward to testify about what really happened. About a year after the case was assigned to me, I got a telephone call from a young woman who told me that she witnessed the entire crime and was willing to tell me how it occurred. She said that she had been deployed as a member of the army for the past year, and, for this reason, she had been unaware that the case was still unresolved. After a little digging, I discovered that this "eyewitness" was actually a cousin of one of the gang members. After a lengthy interview with her, she finally admitted that she was training in another state at the time of the stabbing. She didn't even hear about it until about a week before she contacted me. She was lying to try to implicate the member of the rival gang and protect her cousin. Clearly, her story was a late piece of fiction, created long after the original event for the express purpose of achieving her goal. She wasn't even available or present at the crime to begin with, and for this reason, she was worthless to me as a *witness*.

As a skeptic, I believed that the Gospels were penned in the second century and were similarly worthless. If they were written that late, they were not eyewitness accounts. It's really as simple as that; true eyewitnesses to the life of Jesus would have lived (and written) in the first century. The first criterion of eyewitness reliability requires us to answer the question "Were the alleged eyewitnesses present in the first place?" Like the unbelieving scholars, I answered this question by arguing that the Gospels were written in the second or third century, much closer to the establishment of Christianity in the Roman Empire than to the alleged life of Jesus:

Life of Jesus (AD 1–33)

Gospel Writers

Council of Laodicea (AD 350–363)

Before I could ever take the Gospels seriously as eyewitness accounts, I needed to decide where they fell on this timeline. If the writers first appeared toward the right (closer to the church councils and the formal establishment of the Catholic Church), there was good reason to doubt that they were true witnesses to the sufferings of Christ (1 Pet. 5:1) or that they actually saw Jesus with their own eyes (1 John 1:1–3). If, on the other hand, they appeared to the left of the timeline, I could at least begin to consider them earnestly. The closer they appeared to the life and ministry of Jesus, the more seriously I could consider their claims.

INCHING BACK ON THE TIMELINE

There are many pieces of circumstantial evidence that form a compelling case for the early dating of the Gospels. There are several good reasons to believe that the gospel writers are standing on the left side of the timeline. The more I examined this evidence, the more I came to believe that the Gospels were written early enough in history to be taken seriously as eyewitness accounts. Let's take a look at this evidence before we locate each piece on the timeline.

THE NEW TESTAMENT FAILS TO DESCRIBE THE DESTRUCTION OF THE TEMPLE

We begin with perhaps the most significant Jewish historical event of the first century, the destruction of the Jerusalem temple in AD 70. Rome dispatched an army to Jerusalem in response to the Jewish rebellion of AD 66. The Roman army (under the leadership of Titus) ultimately destroyed the temple in AD 70,[34] just as Jesus had predicted in the

Gospels (in Matt. 24:1–3). You might think this important detail would be included in the New Testament record, especially since this fact would corroborate Jesus's prediction. But no gospel account records the destruction of the temple. In fact, no New Testament document mentions it at all, even though there are many occasions when a description of the temple's destruction might have assisted in establishing a theological or historical point.

THE NEW TESTAMENT FAILS TO DESCRIBE THE SIEGE OF JERUSALEM

Even before the temple was destroyed, the city of Jerusalem was under assault. Titus surrounded the city with four large groups of soldiers and eventually broke through the city's "Third Wall" with a battering ram. After lengthy battles and skirmishes, the Roman soldiers eventually set fire to the city's walls, and the temple was destroyed as a result.[35] No aspect of this three-year siege is described in any New Testament document, in spite of the fact that the gospel writers could certainly have pointed to the anguish that resulted from the siege as a powerful point of reference for the many passages of Scripture that extensively address the issue of *suffering*.

LUKE SAID NOTHING ABOUT THE DEATHS OF PAUL AND PETER

Years before the siege of Jerusalem and the destruction of the temple, another pair of events occurred that were significant to the Christian community. The apostle Paul was martyred in the city of Rome in AD 64, and Peter was martyred shortly afterward in AD 65.[36] While Luke wrote extensively about Paul and Peter in the book of Acts and featured them prominently, he said nothing about their deaths. In fact, Paul was still alive (under house arrest in Rome) at the end of the book of Acts.

LUKE SAID NOTHING ABOUT THE DEATH OF JAMES

Luke featured another important figure from Christian history in the book of Acts. James (the brother of Jesus) became the leader of the Jerusalem church and was described in a position of prominence in Acts 15. James was martyred in the city of Jerusalem in AD 62,[37] but like the deaths of Paul and Peter, the execution of

James is absent from the biblical account, even though Luke described the deaths of Stephen (Acts 7:54–60) and James the brother of John (Acts 12:1–2).

LUKE'S GOSPEL PREDATES THE BOOK OF ACTS

Luke wrote both the book of Acts and the gospel of Luke. These two texts contain introductions that tie them together in history. In the introduction to the book of Acts, Luke wrote:

The first account I composed, Theophilus, about all that Jesus began to do and teach, until the day when He was taken up to heaven, after He had by the Holy Spirit given orders to the apostles whom He had chosen. (Acts 1:1–2)

It's clear that Luke's gospel (his "first account") was written prior to the book of Acts.

PAUL QUOTED LUKE'S GOSPEL IN HIS LETTER TO TIMOTHY

Paul appeared to be aware of Luke's gospel and wrote as though it was common knowledge in about AD 63–64, when Paul penned his first letter to Timothy. Note the following passage:

The elders who rule well are to be considered worthy of double honor, especially those who work hard at preaching and teaching. For the Scripture says, "You shall not muzzle the ox while he is threshing," and "The laborer is worthy of his wages." (1 Tim. 5:17–18)

Paul quoted two passages as "scripture" here—one in the Old Testament and one in the New Testament. "You shall not muzzle the ox while he is threshing" refers to Deuteronomy 25:4, and "The laborer is worthy of his wages" refers to Luke 10:7. It's clear that Luke's gospel was already common knowledge and accepted as scripture by the time this letter was written. To be fair, a number of critics (like Bart Ehrman) have argued that Paul was not actually the author of 1 Timothy and maintain that this letter was written much later in history. The majority of scholars, however, recognize the fact that the earliest leaders of the church were familiar with 1 Timothy at a very early date.[38]

PAUL ECHOED THE CLAIMS OF THE GOSPEL WRITERS

While some modern critics challenge the authorship of Paul's pastoral letters, even the most skeptical scholars agree that Paul is the author of the letters written to the Romans, the Corinthians, and the Galatians. These letters are dated between AD 48 and AD 60. The letter to the Romans (typically dated at AD 50) reveals something important. Paul began the letter by proclaiming that Jesus is the resurrected "Son of God." Throughout the letter, Paul accepted the view of Jesus that the gospel eyewitnesses described in their own accounts. Just seventeen years after the resurrection, Jesus was described as divine. He is God incarnate, just as the gospel eyewitnesses described in their own accounts. In fact, Paul's outline of Jesus's life matches that of the Gospels. In 1 Corinthians 15 (written from AD 53 to 57), Paul summarized the gospel message and reinforced the fact that the apostles described the eyewitness accounts to him:

> For I delivered to you as of first importance what I also received, that Christ died for our sins according to the Scriptures, and that He was buried, and that He was raised on the third day according to the Scriptures, and that He appeared to Cephas, then to the twelve. After that He appeared to more than five hundred brethren at one time, most of whom remain until now, but some have fallen asleep; then He appeared to James, then to all the apostles; and last of all, as to one untimely born, He appeared to me also. (1 Cor. 15:3–8)

In his letter to the Galatians (also written in the mid-50s), Paul described his interaction with these apostles (Peter and James) and said that their meeting occurred at least fourteen years prior to the writing of his letter:

> But when God, who had set me apart even from my mother's womb and called me through His grace, was pleased to reveal His Son in me so that I might preach Him among the Gentiles, I did not immediately consult with flesh and

blood, nor did I go up to Jerusalem to those who were apostles before me; but I went away to Arabia, and returned once more to Damascus. Then three years later I went up to Jerusalem to become acquainted with Cephas, and stayed with him fifteen days. But I did not see any other of the apostles except James, the Lord's brother. (Gal. 1:15–19)

Then after an interval of fourteen years I went up again to Jerusalem with Barnabas, taking Titus along also. (Gal. 2:1)

This means that Paul saw the risen Christ and learned about the gospel accounts from the eyewitnesses (Peter and James) within five years of the crucifixion (most scholars place Paul's conversion from AD 33 to 36, and he visited Peter and James within three years of his conversion, according to Gal. 1:19). This is why Paul was able to tell the Corinthians that there were still "more than five hundred brethren" who could confirm the resurrection accounts (1 Cor. 15:6). That's a gutsy claim to make in AD 53–57, when his readers could easily have accepted his challenge and called him out as a liar if the claim was untrue.

PAUL QUOTED LUKE'S GOSPEL IN HIS LETTER TO THE CORINTHIANS

Paul also seems to have been familiar with the gospel of Luke when he wrote to the Corinthian church (nearly ten years earlier than his letter to Timothy). Notice the similarity between Paul's description of the Lord's Supper and Luke's gospel:

For I received from the Lord that which I also delivered to you, that the Lord Jesus in the night in which He was betrayed took bread; and when He had given thanks, He broke it and said, "This is My body, which is for you; do this in remembrance of Me." In the same way He took the cup also after supper, saying, "This cup is the new covenant in My blood." (1 Cor. 11:23–25)

And when He had taken some bread and given thanks, He broke it and gave it to them, saying, "This is My body which is given for you; do this in remembrance of

Me." And in the same way He took the cup after they had eaten, saying, "This cup which is poured out for you is the new covenant in My blood." (Luke 22:19–20)

Paul appears to be quoting Luke's gospel—the only gospel that has Jesus saying that the disciples are to "do this in remembrance of Me." If Paul is trying to use a description of the meal that was already well known at the time, this account must have been circulating for a period of time prior to Paul's letter.

LUKE QUOTED MARK (AND MATTHEW) REPEATEDLY

Luke, when writing his own gospel, readily admitted that he was not an eyewitness to the life and ministry of Jesus. Instead, Luke described himself as a historian, collecting the statements from the eyewitnesses who were present at the time:

Inasmuch as many have undertaken to compile an account of the things accomplished among us, just as they were handed down to us by those who from the beginning were eyewitnesses and servants of the word, it seemed fitting for me as well, having investigated everything carefully from the beginning, to write it out for you in consecutive order, most excellent Theophilus; so that you may know the exact truth about the things you have been taught. (Luke 1:1–4)

As a result, Luke often repeated or quoted entire passages that were offered previously by either Mark (350 verses from Mark appear in Luke's gospel) or Matthew (250 verses from Matthew appear in Luke's account).[39] These passages were inserted into Luke's gospel as though they were simply copied over from the other accounts. It's reasonable, therefore, to conclude that Mark's account was already recognized, accepted, and available to Luke prior to his authorship of the gospel.

MARK'S GOSPEL APPEARS TO BE AN EARLY "CRIME BROADCAST"

Mark's gospel bears a striking resemblance to a "crime broadcast." When first-responding officers arrive at the scene of a crime, they quickly gather the details related to the crime and the description of the suspect, then "clear the air" with the radio dispatchers so they can broadcast these details to other officers who may be in the area. This first *crime broadcast* is brief and focused on the essential elements. There will be time later to add additional details, sort out the order of events, and write lengthy reports. This first broadcast is driven by the immediacy of the moment; we've got to get the essentials out to our partners because the suspects in this case may still be trying to flee the area. There is a sense of urgency in the first broadcast because officers are trying to catch the bad guys before they get away.

Although Mark's gospel contains the important details of Jesus's life and ministry, it is brief, less ordered than the other gospels, and filled with "action" verbs and adjectives. There is a sense of urgency about it. This is what we might expect, if it was, in fact, an early account of Jesus's ministry, written with a sense of urgency. It is clear that the eyewitnesses felt this urgency and believed that Jesus would return very soon. Paul wrote that "salvation is nearer to us than when we believed" (Rom. 13:11), and James said, "The coming of the Lord is near" (James 5:8). Peter, Mark's mentor and companion, agreed that "the end of all things is near" (1 Pet. 4:7). Surely Mark wrote with this same sense of urgency as he penned Peter's experiences in his own gospel. Mark's account takes on the role of "crime broadcast," delivering the essential details without regard for composition or stylistic prose. Papias confirmed this in his statement about Mark's efforts:

> Mark, having become the interpreter of Peter, wrote down accurately, though not indeed in order, whatsoever he remembered of the things said or done by Christ. For he neither heard the Lord nor followed him, but afterward, as I said, he followed Peter, who adapted his teaching to the needs of his hearers, but with no intention of giving a connected account of the Lord's discourses, so that Mark committed no error while he thus wrote some things as he remembered them. For he was careful of one thing, not to omit any of the things which he had heard, and not to state any of them falsely.[40]

The accuracy of the account was more important to Mark than anything else; for all Mark knew, Jesus would return before there would be any need to write an ordered *biography* of sorts. Mark was in charge of the essential *crime broadcast*. As the years passed and the eyewitnesses aged, others made a more deliberate effort to place the narrative in its correct order. Papias seems to indicate that this was Matthew's intent:

Therefore Matthew put the *logia* in an ordered arrangement in the Hebrew language, but each person interpreted them as best he could.[41]

Luke also seems to be doing something similar according to the introduction of his own gospel:

> *It seemed fitting for me as well, having investigated everything carefully from the beginning, to write it out for you in consecutive order. (Luke 1:3)*

Both Matthew and Luke appear to be writing with a much different intent than Mark. Their accounts are more robust and ordered. While Mark seems to be providing us with the initial "crime broadcast," Matthew and Luke are more concerned about the "final report."

MARK APPEARS TO BE PROTECTING KEY PLAYERS

We've already talked about how important it is to "hang on every word." In my years as an investigator, there have been many times when a witness carefully chose his or her words to avoid dragging someone else into the case. This was particularly true when working gang cases. There were a number of times when a witness had the courage to come forward with information, but was less than forthcoming about the identity of others who might have seen something similar. Driven by the fear that these additional witnesses might be in a position of jeopardy, the witness would mention them in his or her account but refuse to specifically identify them. Most of the time the witnesses were simply trying to protect someone who they thought was defenseless and vulnerable.

I experienced just the opposite in some of my cold-case investigations. When reinterviewing witnesses who spoke to investigators years earlier, I found that they were now willing to provide me with the identities of people whom they previously refused to identify. Sometimes this was because they developed some animosity toward these people over the years; this was especially true when boyfriends and girlfriends broke up and were eventually willing to talk about each other. Sometimes it was a matter of diminishing fear; when the suspect in a case died, it wasn't unusual to have people come forward and identify themselves simply because they were no longer afraid to do so.

Many careful readers of Mark's gospel have observed that there are a number of unidentified people described in his account. These *anonymous* characters are often in key positions in the narrative, yet Mark chose to leave them unnamed. For example, Mark's description of the activity in the garden of Gethsemane includes the report that "one of those who stood by [the arrest of Jesus] drew his sword, and struck the slave of the high priest and cut off his ear" (Mark 14:47). Mark chose to leave both the attacker and the man attacked unnamed in his description, even though John identified both (Peter as the attacker and Malchus as the person being attacked) in his gospel account. Similarly, Mark failed to identify the woman who anointed Jesus at the home of Simon the leper (Mark 14:3–9), even though John told us that it was Mary (the sister of Martha), who poured the perfume on Jesus's head.[42] While skeptics have offered a number of explanations for these variations (arguing, for example, that they may simply be late embellishments in an effort to craft the growing mythology of the Gospels), something much simpler might be at work. If Mark, like some of the witnesses in my gang cases, was interested in protecting the identity of Peter (as Malchus's attacker) and Mary (whose anointing may have been interpreted as a proclamation of Jesus's kingly position as the Messiah), it makes sense that he might leave them unnamed so that the Jewish leadership would not be able to easily target them. In fact, Mark never even described Jesus's raising of Mary's brother, Lazarus. This also makes sense if Mark was trying to protect Lazarus's identity in the earliest years of the Christian movement, given that the resurrection of Lazarus was of critical concern to the Jewish leaders and prompted them to search for Jesus in their plot to kill him. If Mark wrote his gospel early, while Mary, Lazarus, Peter, and Malchus were still alive, it is reasonable that Mark might have wanted to leave them unnamed or simply omit the accounts that included them in the first place.

Scholars generally acknowledge John's gospel as the final addition to the New Testament collection of gospel accounts. It was most likely written at a time when Peter, Malchus, and Mary were already dead. John, like some of the witnesses in my cold cases, had the liberty to identify these important people; they were no longer in harm's way.

THEY WERE EARLY ON THE TIMELINE

Given these eleven pieces of circumstantial evidence, what reasonable inference can be drawn about the dating of the Gospels? First we've got to account for the suspicious absence of several key historical events in the New Testament record: the destruction of the temple, the siege of Jerusalem, and the deaths of Peter, Paul, and James. These omissions can be reasonably explained if the book of Acts (the biblical text that ought to describe these events) was written prior to AD 61–62. These events are missing from the accounts because they hadn't happened yet.

We know from the introductory lines of the book of Acts that Luke's gospel was written prior to Acts, but we must use the remaining circumstantial evidence to try to determine *how* much prior. The fact that Paul echoed the description of Jesus that was offered by the gospel writers is certainly consistent with the fact that he was aware of the claims of the Gospels, and his quotations from Luke's gospel in 1 Timothy and 1 Corinthians reasonably confirm the early existence of Luke's account, placing it well before AD 53–57. Paul was able to quote Luke's gospel and refer to it as scripture because it was already written, circulating at this time, and broadly accepted. Paul's readers recognized this to be true as they read Paul's letters.

Luke told us that he was gathering data from "those who from the beginning were eyewitnesses and servants of the word" (Luke 1:2). As a result he either referred to or quoted directly from over five hundred verses that are found in either the gospel of Mark or the gospel of Matthew. It is reasonable to infer that these accounts were in existence prior to Luke's investigation. If this is the case, Mark's gospel would date much earlier than Luke's, and can be sensibly placed in either the late 40s or very early 50s. This then explains some of the characteristics we see in Mark's gospel. There appears to be a sense of urgency in the gospel, similar to the *crime broadcasts* that are made by responding officers, and Mark appears to be protecting key players in the account as if they were still alive at the time of his writing.

Let's place the evidence on the timeline to see where the gospel accounts are located relative to the life of Jesus:

Life of Jesus | Mark writes his gospel AD 45–50 | Luke writes his gospel AD 50–53 | Paul quotes Luke AD 53–57 | Luke writes Acts AD 57–60 | Deaths of James, Peter, and Paul AD 61–65 | Siege of Jerusalem AD 67–70 | Temple destroyed AD 70
(AD 1–33)

The reasonable inference from the circumstantial evidence is that the Gospels were written very early in history, at a time when the original eyewitnesses and gospel writers were still alive and could testify to what they had seen. This is why Mark was careful not to identify key players and Paul could reasonably point to five hundred living eyewitnesses who could still testify to their observations of Jesus's resurrection. While skeptics would like to claim that the Gospels were written well after the alleged life of the apostles and much closer to the councils that affirmed them, the evidence indicates something quite different.

The circumstantial evidence supports an early dating for the Gospels. The gospel writers appear in history right where we would expect them to appear if they were, in fact, eyewitnesses. This early placement alone does not ensure that the Gospels are reliable accounts, but it keeps them "in the running" and becomes an important piece of circumstantial evidence, in and of itself, as we determine the reliability of the gospel writers.

SO, WHY DO SOME CONTINUE TO DENY IT?

Some are still skeptical of the early dating of the Gospels, in spite of the circumstantial evidence that supports such a conclusion. Many skeptics are quick to embrace alternative explanations that place the Gospels so late in history that they simply could not have been written by eyewitnesses. As with any process of *abductive reasoning*, we need to examine the alternative *possibilities* to see if any of them are *reasonable* (based on evidence). Let's examine some of the reasons why skeptics like Ehrman, Vermes, and Waite claim that the Gospels were written either "forty years later," "three generations after Jesus," or in "the latter part of the second century."

THE AUTHORS OF THE GOSPELS ARE ANONYMOUS

Some have argued that the Gospels are late because none of the authors specifically identifies himself in the accounts. This lack of identification is seen as evidence that the accounts were not actually written by anyone in the first century, but were falsely attributed to these authors much later in an effort to legitimize the forgeries.

BUT ...

The Gospels are not the only ancient documents that fail to identify the author within the text of the manuscripts. Tacitus (the Roman senator and historian who lived from AD 56 to AD 117) wrote a history of the Roman Empire from the reign of Augustus Caesar to Nero entitled *Annals*. Tacitus was, in fact, present during much of this period of time, but failed to include himself in any of his descriptions or identify himself as the author. Like the Gospels, the *Annals* are written *anonymously* yet are attributed to Tacitus without reservation by historical scholars. Why? Because, like the Gospels, Tacitus's authorship is supported by external evidence (such as the claims of other early writers who credited Tacitus with the work). The Gospels were also attributed to their traditional authors quite early in history (Papias, living in the late first century and early second century, is one such example).

In fact, no one in antiquity ever attributed the Gospels to anyone other than the four traditionally accepted authors. That's a powerful statement, in and of itself, especially considering the fact that early Christians consistently recognized, identified, and condemned the false writings of forgers who tried to credit false gospels to the apostolic eyewitnesses. *The Traditions of Matthias* (AD 110–160), for example, was identified as a forgery by early Christians and was eventually included in a list with other forgeries (including the gospels of Thomas and Peter) by Eusebius, the "Father of Church History."

One might also wonder why, if these gospel accounts were falsely attributed to the authors we accept today, the second- or third-century forgers would not have picked better *pseudonyms* (false attributions) than the people who were ultimately accredited with the writings. Why would they pick Mark or Luke when they could easily have chosen Peter, Andrew, or James? Mark and Luke appear nowhere in the gospel records as eyewitnesses, so why would early forgers choose these two men around which to build their lies when there were clearly better candidates available to legitimize their work?

It's not as if the Gospels of Mark, Matthew, Luke, and John have been discovered in some ancient collection under someone else's name. The only copies we possess of these Gospels, regardless of antiquity or geographic location, are attributed to one of the four traditional authors. No early church leader has ever attributed these Gospels to anyone other than Mark, Matthew, Luke, or John. There is no alternative ancient tradition that claims, for example, that the gospel of Mark is actually written by anyone other than Mark.

While it is *possible* that the Gospels were not written by the traditional first-century authors and were given these attributions only much later in history, it is not evidentially *reasonable*. If skeptics were willing to give the Gospels the same "benefit of the doubt" they are willing to give other ancient documents, the Gospels would easily pass the test of authorship.

THE TEMPLE DESTRUCTION IS PREDICTED

While the absence of any description of the temple's destruction can reasonably be interpreted as a piece of circumstantial evidence supporting the early dating of the New Testament accounts, skeptics sometimes use this fact to make just the opposite case. Many have proposed that Jesus's prediction related to the destruction was inserted to legitimize the text and make it appear that He had some prophetic power. If this was the case, the Gospels would clearly date to *after* the event (post AD 70), as the writers already knew the outcome before they cleverly inserted the prediction.

BUT ...

This sort of skepticism is clearly rooted in the presupposition we described in chapter 1. If we begin from a position of philosophical naturalism (the presumption that nothing supernatural is possible), we have no choice but to describe the supernatural elements we find in the Gospels as lies. From a naturalistic perspective, prophetic claims are impossible. The skeptic, therefore, must find another explanation for Jesus's prediction related to the temple; critics typically move the date of authorship beyond the date when the prophecy was fulfilled to avoid the appearance of supernatural confirmation. But as we described earlier, a fair examination of the evidence that supports supernaturalism must at least allow for the possibility of supernaturalism in the first place. The naturalistic bias of these critics prevents them from accepting any dating that precedes the destruction of the temple in AD 70 and forces them to ignore all the circumstantial evidence that supports the early dating.

When explaining why the destruction of the temple itself was not included in the gospel record, skeptics have argued that the gospel writers intentionally omitted the fulfillment to make the accounts look like they were written early. But if this was the case, why were the gospel writers unafraid to describe the fulfillment of prophecy in other passages in the Gospels? Over and over again we see the fulfillment of Old Testament messianic prophecies that are attributed to Jesus in one manner or another. In addition to this, on several occasions Jesus predicted His own resurrection. The gospel writers readily described the fulfillment of these predictions in the resurrection accounts. Why would they be willing to describe this aspect of fulfilled prophecy, but shy away from discussing the destruction of the temple?

In addition, Luke freely admitted that he was not an eyewitness to the events in his gospel. He told us from the onset that he was writing at some point well after the events actually occurred, working as a careful historian. Why not include the siege of Jerusalem and the destruction of the temple? There was no reason to be shy here. Other Old Testament authors wrote from a perspective that followed the events they described and were unafraid to say so. Moses, Joshua, and Samuel, for example, repeatedly reported on events that took place well before their written account; they often wrote that the conditions they were describing continued from the point of the event "to this day" (indicating the late point at which they were actually writing). Why wouldn't Luke take a similar approach to the destruction of the temple, especially given the fact that he made no pretense about writing as a historian?

While it is certainly *possible* that the Gospels were all written after the destruction of the temple, it is not evidentially *reasonable*. In fact, the primary motivation for denying the early authorship of the Gospels is simply the bias against supernaturalism that leads skeptics to redate the Scriptures to some point following the fulfillment of Jesus's prophecy.

THE ACCOUNTS ARE REPLETE WITH MIRACULOUS EVENTS

Many critics have also pointed to the presence of the miraculous to make a case for late dating. Surely the miracles are works of fiction. If the gospel accounts were written early, eyewitnesses to the life of Jesus would have exposed these miracles as fictitious, right? Much of this critical analysis comes from a literary discipline known as "form criticism." Form critics attempt to classify portions of Scripture on the basis of their literary "type," "pattern," or "form." Once these pieces are isolated within the larger narrative, form critics attempt to explain their origin. In the case of the Gospels, form critics have argued that the supernatural elements are different from those parts of the narrative that can be trusted as accurate history. They explain the "paradigms,"[43] "sayings,"[44] "miracle stories,"[45] and "legends"[46] as late additions inserted by local Christian communities to make a particular theological case or to present Jesus as something more than He was.

BUT ...

By now you probably recognize that the presupposition of naturalism (and the bias against supernaturalism) is once again the impetus behind this criticism. The *form critics* of history (a movement that was most popular in the mid-twentieth century) simply rejected the possibility that any description of a miracle could be factually true. It turns out that it was the miraculous "content" of these passages, rather than their common literary *style* or *form*, that caused critics to identify the verses they thought should be removed or handled with suspicion. In fact, they often selected passages that were very different from one another in terms of their stylistic forms. Sometimes they identified passages that did not fit neatly into one of their categories (or appeared to be a blend of more than one literary form), and they often disagreed with one another about the identity of particular types of literary *forms* and passages. They did agree on one thing, however: passages that contain miraculous events were not to be taken seriously as part of the original narrative.

These skeptics evaluate the gospel accounts with the assumption (based on the presence of the miraculous) that Christians must have written them in the second or third century, unafraid that their lies would be detected by those who lived in the first century. This proposal ignores, of course, all the evidence that supports an early dating for the New Testament documents. It also assumes that the gospel accounts are false until proved true. This is just the opposite approach we take with witness testimony when it is presented in court. We ought to presume that witnesses are telling us the truth until we discover otherwise, and the presence of the miraculous alone should not cause us to believe that the gospel eyewitnesses were lying.

There is no evidence, aside from the existence of supernatural elements within the gospel accounts, to support the assumption of late dating that form critics have proposed. While the insertion of miraculous elements late in history might be *possible*, it is not evidentially *reasonable*. Once again, the primary motivation for denying the early authorship of the Gospels is simply the bias against supernaturalism.

THERE WAS A SECOND-CENTURY BISHOP IN ANTIOCH NAMED "THEOPHILUS"

Some have tried to argue that the "Theophilus" described by Luke in the introduction to his gospel and the book of Acts was actually Theophilus, the bishop of Antioch (who served in that city from approximately AD 169 to 183). They support this claim by pointing out that some ancient authorities maintained that Luke originally came from this city, and the fact that Theophilus of Antioch wrote a defense of Christianity that discussed the canon of the New Testament (which, of course, would have included the gospel of Luke). Skeptics who argue for this identification of Theophilus also point to the opening sentence of Luke's gospel, where Luke wrote, "Many have undertaken to compile an account of the things accomplished among us." Isn't it possible that Luke was referring to the many late-second-century heretical, false gospels (like the gospel of the Egyptians) that caused Theophilus of Antioch to write his own defense in the first place? If this is true, Luke's gospel ought to be dated in the second century, after the appearance of these heretical gospels and during the tenure of Theophilus of Antioch.

BUT ...

Luke addressed Theophilus as "most excellent" in his gospel introduction. This is a title of authority, indicating that Theophilus held a position of leadership. If Theophilus were already in a position of lifetime Christian leadership (governing the church of Antioch as a bishop and deserving of Luke's title), would he really know so little about the life of Jesus that Luke would need to send him an account "in consecutive order" so he could "know the exact truth about the things [he had] been taught"? Luke's introduction makes it sound as if Luke was in a position of greater knowledge than Theophilus and seems completely inconsistent with the possibility that Theophilus was someone already knowledgeable enough to have ascended to such an important position of Christian leadership.

It does appear, however, that Theophilus was in some position of leadership, given the way that Luke addressed him. Are there any reasonable first-century explanations consistent with

the other pieces of circumstantial evidence placing the gospel in the first century? Yes, in fact, there are. Luke used the same "most excellent" title when addressing Felix (in Acts 24:3) and Festus (in Acts 26:25), both of whom were Roman officials. Theophilus may, therefore, have been a Roman official of some sort. It's interesting to note that Luke did not use this title when addressing Theophilus in the book of Acts. This may reflect the fact that Theophilus was serving a short-term position in the Roman government (rather than a lifetime position as a bishop in Antioch). Perhaps Theophilus began to serve his term of office during the time when Luke was writing the gospel. Such positions of leadership were certainly available in the first-century government of the Roman Empire.

Roman officials of the first century aren't the only reasonable candidates for Theophilus's identity. There were a number of Jewish leaders in the first century who possessed the name, including Theophilus ben Ananus (the Roman-appointed high priest of the Jerusalem temple between AD 37 and AD 41).[47] If this was, in fact, the Theophilus whom Luke was addressing, it might explain why Luke began his gospel with a description of another priest, Zechariah, and his activity in the temple. This might also explain why Luke alone spent so

Who Is "Theophilus"?

Many have tried to identify "Theophilus." While no one knows the answer for sure, there are many reasonable possibilities:

He's Every "Friend of God"

Some have observed that the word *Theophilus* is Greek for "Friend of God." For this reason, they propose that Luke wrote his works for all those who were friends of God and interested in the claims of Jesus.

He's a Roman Official

Since Luke uses the expression "most excellent" only when addressing Roman officials, many believe that Theophilus must have held some similar Roman position. Paul Maier, in his novel *The Flames of Rome*, makes a case for Titus Flavius Sabinus II as the person to whom Luke wrote.

He's a Jewish High Priest

Others have identified a pair of Jewish high priests who lived in the first century (Theophilus ben Ananus or Mattathias ben Theophilus), arguing that Luke's focus on the temple and Jewish customs related to the Sadducees could best be explained if one of these two priests was his intended audience.

much time writing about the way that Joseph and Mary took Jesus to the temple following His days of purification and then again when He was twelve years old. It might also explain why, interestingly, Luke failed to mention Caiaphas's role in the crucifixion of Jesus (Caiaphas was Theophilus ben Ananus's brother-in-law).

While it is *possible* that Luke was writing to Theophilus of Antioch late in the second century, it is not evidentially *reasonable*. Even if we don't have enough evidence to identify the *true* Theophilus with precision, there are some reasonable first-century explanations available, and the manner in which Luke described Theophilus in Luke 1 is inconsistent with Theophilus of Antioch.

LUKE AGREED WITH MUCH OF WHAT JOSEPHUS REPORTED

Some skeptics have examined the writings of Titus Flavius Josephus, the first-century Roman-Jewish historian who lived from AD 37 to approximately AD 100 and wrote about life in the area of Palestine, including the siege of Jerusalem and the destruction of the temple. Josephus wrote *Antiquities of the Jews* in the early 90s (AD 93–94). Critics cite a number of similarities between Luke and Josephus and argue that Luke actually used Josephus as a source for his own work. This, of course, would place the date of Luke's work sometime after the early 90s, perhaps even as late as the early second century.

BUT ...

The fact that Josephus mentioned historical details that are also described by Luke (e.g., the census taken under Quirinius, the death of Herod Agrippa, the identity of the tetrarch Lysanias, and the famine during the reign of Claudius) does not necessarily mean that Luke was using Josephus as his source. Josephus may, in fact, be referencing Luke's work; both may be referencing the work of someone who preceded them; or each may simply be citing the facts of history independently. In any case, the dual citations we see here ought to give us confidence that Luke's record is historically accurate.

If Luke was using Josephus as a source (in a manner similar to his use of Mark or Matthew), why didn't he quote Josephus? This would certainly be consistent with his introductory proclamation that he was referencing other sources to compile his history. Luke readily quoted Mark and inserted many parallel accounts that are also found in Matthew's record; why not quote or mirror Josephus in a similar way? Luke never did this, however, and his work demonstrates no similarity with Josephus's literary style.

While it is certainly *possible* that Luke was borrowing from Josephus, it is not evidentially *reasonable*. There are a number of unrelated pieces of circumstantial evidence that point to an early date for Luke's gospel, nearly forty years prior to the work of Josephus. All the alleged *evidence* that supports the claim that Luke referenced Josephus can also be used to defend the claim that Josephus referenced Luke. The cumulative circumstantial case for early dating can help us determine which of these possibilities is the most reasonable.

THE MOST REASONABLE CONCLUSION

We can now employ some *abductive reasoning* as we try to determine which explanation related to dating is the most sensible. Like our dead-body scene described in chapter 2, we begin by listing all the evidence that we've examined so far, including the evidence that has been identified by skeptics. Next, we list the two possible explanations that might account for this evidence:

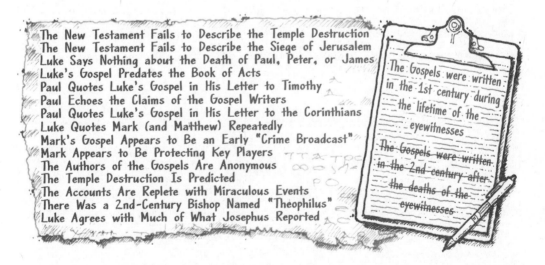

The New Testament Fails to Describe the Temple Destruction
The New Testament Fails to Describe the Siege of Jerusalem
Luke Says Nothing about the Death of Paul, Peter, or James
Luke's Gospel Predates the Book of Acts
Paul Quotes Luke's Gospel in His Letter to Timothy
Paul Echoes the Claims of the Gospel Writers
Paul Quotes Luke's Gospel in His Letter to the Corinthians
Luke Quotes Mark (and Matthew) Repeatedly
Mark's Gospel Appears to Be an Early "Crime Broadcast"
Mark Appears to Be Protecting Key Players
The Authors of the Gospels Are Anonymous
The Temple Destruction Is Predicted
The Accounts Are Replete with Miraculous Events
There Was a 2nd-Century Bishop Named "Theophilus"
Luke Agrees with Much of What Josephus Reported

The Gospels were written in the 1st century during the lifetime of the eyewitnesses

The Gospels were written in the 2nd century after the deaths of the eyewitnesses

Using the lifetime of the alleged eyewitnesses (the gospel writers) and the destruction of the temple as a point of differentiation, the evidence can allow for two possible inferences: either the Gospels were written prior to the destruction of the temple (and during the span of time in which the alleged eyewitnesses were alive), or the Gospels were written well after the destruction of the temple and after the alleged eyewitnesses would have been long in the grave. If we accept the first explanation, we can integrate and embrace all the evidence without any contradiction or friction between pieces. The second explanation may explain the last five pieces of evidence, but has great difficulty (at best) explaining the first eleven. The inference that the Gospels were written in the first century, prior to the destruction of the temple (and during the lifetime of those who claimed to see Jesus), is the best explanation. The explanation is *feasible*, *straightforward*, and *logical*. It *exhausts* all the evidence we have assembled, and it is *superior* to the alternative explanation. It meets the five criteria we established for abductive reasoning; we can have confidence that we've arrived at the most reasonable explanation.

THE GOSPELS PASS THE FIRST TEST

Juries are encouraged to evaluate eyewitnesses in the four categories we described in chapter 4. They begin by making sure that witnesses were truly present at the time of the crime. When evaluating the gospel writers, the most reasonable inference from the evidence is an early date of authorship. Does this mean that they are reliable? Not yet; there's much more to consider. But the Gospels have passed the first test; their testimony appears early enough in history to confirm that the gospel writers were actually present to see what they said they saw.

Chapter 12

WERE THEY CORROBORATED?

*The word god is for me nothing more than the expression and
product of human weaknesses, the Bible a collection of honourable,
but still primitive legends which are nevertheless pretty childish. No
interpretation no matter how subtle can (for me) change this.*[48]
—Albert Einstein, father of modern physics

*Is there an intelligent man or woman now in the world who believes
in the Garden of Eden story? If there is, strike here (tapping his
forehead) and you will hear an echo. Something is for rent.*[49]
—Robert Green Ingersoll, the nineteenth-century American
political leader known as "The Great Agnostic"

*I think that the people who think God wrote a
book called the Bible are just childish.*
—Bill Maher, comedian, television host, and political commentator

THERE OUGHT TO BE SOME SUPPORT

Christian Scripture is not merely a collection of proverbs or commandments related to moral
living, although the New Testament certainly contains these elements. The Bible is a claim

about history. Like other eyewitness accounts, the Bible tells us that something happened in the past in a particular way, at a particular time, with a particular result. If the accounts are true, they are not merely "legends" or "childish" stories, even though they may contain miraculous elements that are difficult for skeptics to accept. It's not surprising that those who reject the supernatural would doubt those who claimed to see something miraculous. It's also not surprising that these skeptics would want miraculous claims to be corroborated.

While there are times when an eyewitness is the only piece of evidence I have at my disposal, most of my cases are buttressed by other pieces of evidence that corroborate the eyewitness. I once had a case from 1982 in which a witness (Aimee Thompson) claimed to see a murder suspect (Danny Herrin) standing in the front yard of the victim's house just minutes before the murder took place. At the time of the original investigation, Aimee identified Danny from a "six-pack photo lineup," a series of six photographs of men (complete strangers to Aimee), arranged in two rows in a photo folder. Aimee did not know Danny personally, but she recognized his face in the photo. She remembered that he was wearing a popular concert T-shirt with a logo from the musical band Journey, announcing its tour in support of the *Escape* album. In addition to this, she told me that the man she observed stood in a peculiar way, hunched over just slightly as if he had some sort of physical injury. I knew that Danny also had this unusual posture and fit her description. Given this identification, I traveled out to the city where Danny lived for an interview. When I spoke with Danny, he denied that he was anywhere near the victim's house. In fact, he claimed that he wasn't even in the same city as the victim on that particular day. While it would have been nice to find some forensic evidence at the scene that corroborated Aimee's observations, this was unfortunately not the case. The original investigators did, however, find a gas receipt in Danny's car that had been issued from a gas station on the day of the murder, just a quarter mile from the victim's house. In addition to this, I later interviewed Danny's sister; she told me that Danny mentioned stopping by to see the victim on the day of the murder.

Now it's true that the gas receipt and his sister's statement alone would not prove that Danny murdered the victim, but these two additional facts did corroborate Aimee's claims; if nothing else, her assertions were made more reasonable by her observations of Danny's unusual stance and these additional supporting facts. There were two forms of corroboration working here. First, there was corroboration that was *internal* to Aimee's statement. She described something that was true about the suspect (his stance), and could not have been known by Aimee unless she was actually present as she claimed. In addition to this internal evidence, there was also *external* evidence that corroborated her claim. The gas receipt and Danny's sister's statement were independent of Aimee, but still supported her assertions. Together, the internal and external evidence *agreed* with Aimee's primary claims as an eyewitness.

CORROBORATION FROM THE "INSIDE OUT"

As it turns out, there is similar corroboration available to us when we examine the claims of the gospel accounts. Some of this corroboration is *internal* (evidences from within the gospel documents that are consistent with the claims of the text), and some is *external* (evidences that are independent of the gospel documents yet verify the claims of the text). Much has been written about the internal evidences that support the reliability of the New Testament authors; scholars have studied the use of language and Greek idioms to try to discover if the writing styles of each author corroborate the New Testament claims related to the authors. Is John's use of language consistent with that of a first-century fisherman? Is Luke's language consistent with that of a first-century doctor? While these exercises are interesting from a scholarly perspective, they did not pique my investigative curiosity as a detective. Two areas of internal evidence, however, did interest me as someone who has interviewed hundreds of witnesses.

THE GOSPEL WRITERS PROVIDED UNINTENTIONAL EYEWITNESS SUPPORT

As we discussed in chapter 4, one of the most important tasks for a detective is to listen carefully when multiple eyewitnesses provide a statement about what they observed at the scene of a crime. It's my job to assemble the complete *picture* of what happened at the scene. No single witness is likely to have seen every detail, so I must piece together the accounts, allowing the observations of one eyewitness to *fill in the gaps* that may exist in the observations of another eyewitness. That's why it's so important for eyewitnesses to be separated before they are interviewed. True, reliable eyewitness accounts are never completely parallel and identical. Instead, they are different pieces of the same puzzle, unintentionally supporting and complementing each other to provide all the details related to what really happened.

When I first read through the Gospels forensically, comparing those places where two or more gospel writers were describing the same event, I was immediately struck by the inadvertent

More "Unintentional Support"

There are many examples of "undesigned coincidences" in the gospel eyewitness accounts. Here are a few more:

Question: Matthew 8:16

Why did they wait until evening to bring those who needed healing?

Answer: Mark 1:21; Luke 4:31

Because it was the Sabbath.

Question: Matthew 14:1–2

Why did Herod tell his servants that he thought Jesus was John the Baptist, raised from the dead?

Answer: Luke 8:3; Acts 13:1

Many of Jesus's followers were from Herod's household.

Question: Luke 23:1–4

Why didn't Pilate find a charge against Jesus even though Jesus claimed to be a King?

Answer: John 18:33–38

Jesus told Pilate that his kingdom was not of this world.

support that each writer provided for the other. The accounts *puzzled together* just the way one would expect from independent eyewitnesses. When one gospel eyewitness described an event and left out a detail that raised a question, this question was unintentionally answered by another gospel writer (who, by the way, often left out a detail that was provided by the first gospel writer). This interdependence between the accounts could be explained in one of two ways. It may have been that the writers worked together, writing at precisely the same time and location, to craft a clever lie so subtle that very few people would even notice it at all. The second possibility is that the Gospels were written by different eyewitnesses who witnessed the event and included these unplanned supporting details; they were simply describing something that actually happened.

As someone who was new to the Bible, I began to investigate whether or not anyone else had observed this phenomenon and found that a professor of divinity named J. J. Blunt wrote a book in 1847 entitled *Undesigned Coincidences in the Writings of the Old and New Testament, an Argument of Their Veracity; with an Appendix, Containing Undesigned Coincidences between the Gospels and Acts, and Josephus.* This was one of the first books about the Bible I ever purchased. In his section related to the Gospels and the book of Acts, Blunt identified the very same inadvertent parallel passages I discovered when examining the Gospels forensically. Blunt described the phenomenon as a series of "undesigned coincidences" and identified over forty locations in the New Testament where this feature of unintentional eyewitness support could be seen on the pages of Scripture. Let me give you a few examples of what we are talking about here.

THE CALLING OF THE DISCIPLES

As someone unfamiliar with the Bible, the calling of Peter, Andrew, James, and John seemed odd to me when I first read it in the gospel of Matthew:

> *Now as Jesus was walking by the Sea of Galilee, He saw two brothers, Simon who was called Peter, and Andrew his brother, casting a net into the sea; for they were fishermen. And He said to them, "Follow Me, and I will make you fishers of men." Immediately they left their nets and followed Him. Going on from there He saw two other brothers, James the son of Zebedee, and John his brother, in the boat with Zebedee their father, mending their nets; and He called them. Immediately they left the boat and their father, and followed Him. (Matt. 4:18–22)*

That's it? Jesus walked up and said, "Follow Me," and they dropped everything "immediately"? Who would do that? How did they even know who Jesus was or if anything about Him was worthy of that kind of dedication? If Matthew's account was the only testimony available to us (and for many communities in the ancient world, it *was* the only testimony available, at least for a number of years), this would remain a mystery. I do believe there is a clue in Matthew's version of events (the mending of the nets), but the questions raised by Matthew aren't answered for us until we hear from Luke:

> *Now it happened that while the crowd was pressing around Him and listening to the word of God, He was standing by the lake of Gennesaret; and He saw two boats lying at the edge of the lake; but the fishermen had gotten out of them and were washing their nets. And He got into one of the boats, which was Simon's, and asked*

him to put out a little way from the land. And He sat down and began teaching the people from the boat. When He had finished speaking, He said to Simon, "Put out into the deep water and let down your nets for a catch." Simon answered and said, "Master, we worked hard all night and caught nothing, but I will do as You say and let down the nets." When they had done this, they enclosed a great quantity of fish, and their nets began to break; so they signaled to their partners in the other boat for them to come and help them. And they came and filled both of the boats, so that they began to sink. But when Simon Peter saw that, he fell down at Jesus' feet, saying, "Go away from me Lord, for I am a sinful man!" For amazement had seized him and all his companions because of the catch of fish which they had taken; and so also were James and John, sons of Zebedee, who were partners with Simon. And Jesus said to Simon, "Do not fear, from now on you will be catching men." When they had brought their boats to land, they left everything and followed Him. (Luke 5:1–11)

The disciples didn't just *jump in* with Jesus on a whim after all. Matthew was interested in describing how the disciples were called, but Luke was interested in providing a bit more detail. When the testimony of all the witnesses is considered in unison, we get the complete picture. The disciples heard Jesus preach and saw the miracle of the abundant catch of fish. This harvest of fish was so impressive and large that it broke their nets. Only after returning to the shore (and while James and John were mending their torn nets) did Jesus call them to follow Him. They left their lives as fishermen on the basis of the things Jesus taught and the miracle Jesus performed.

THE STRIKING OF JESUS

In the next example, let's examine the description of Jesus's beating that Matthew offered in chapter 26 of his gospel. In this scene, describing Jesus's examination before Caiaphas, Matthew told us that the chief priests and the members of the council struck Jesus and slapped Him when he "blasphemed" by identifying Himself as the "Son of Man":

Then they spat in His face and beat Him with their fists; and others slapped Him, and said, "Prophesy to us, You Christ; who is the one who hit You?" (Matt. 26:67–68)

This question posed by members of the council seems odd. Jesus's attackers were standing right in front of Him; why would they ask Him, "Who is the one who hit You?" It doesn't seem like much of a challenge, given that Jesus could look at His attackers and identify them easily. Luke told us more, however:

Now the men who were holding Jesus in custody were mocking Him and beating Him, and they blindfolded Him and were asking Him, saying, "Prophesy, who is the one who hit You?" And they were saying many other things against Him, blaspheming. (Luke 22:63–65)

Once again, one gospel eyewitness unintentionally supported the other in what J. J. Blunt called an "undesigned coincidence." Matthew's narrative makes sense once we read in Luke's account that Jesus was blindfolded. Imagine for a moment that you are one of the earliest converts to Christianity, at a time and place in history where the gospel of Matthew was the only available account

More "Unintentional Support"

There are many examples of "undesigned coincidences" in the gospel eyewitness accounts. Here are a few more:

Question: Matthew 26:71

Why did the maid notice Peter?

Answer: John 18:16

A disciple spoke with her when he brought Peter inside.

Question: Mark 15:43

Why did Mark say Joseph of Arimathea acted "boldly" (NIV)?

Answer: John 19:38

Joseph was previously a secret disciple who was in fear of the Jews.

(in chapter 13, for example, we'll hear a report of the gospel of Matthew used in the early days of Christianity to teach new believers east of Africa). This passage would be puzzling; it would raise a question that might never be answered unless you had access to the other eyewitness accounts. As a cold-case detective, I've experienced something similar to this a number of times. Often, questions an eyewitness raises at the time of the crime are left unanswered until we locate an additional witness years later. This is a common characteristic of true, reliable eyewitness accounts.

THE FEEDING OF THE FIVE THOUSAND

Perhaps the finest example of *unintentional support* is found in an episode described in all four gospels: the miracle of the "feeding of the five thousand." Mark's account of this miracle raises a question when considered without input from the other gospel writers. Mark wrote that just prior to this event, Jesus sent out the disciples to preach repentance in the local towns and villages. When they returned, they found themselves surrounded by a multitude of people:

> *The apostles gathered together with Jesus; and they reported to Him all that they had done and taught. And He said to them, "Come away by yourselves to a secluded place and rest a while." (For there were many people coming and going, and they did not even have time to eat.) They went away in the boat to a secluded place by themselves. The people saw them going, and many recognized them and ran there together on foot from all the cities, and got there ahead of them. When Jesus went ashore, He saw a large crowd, and He felt compassion for them because they were like sheep without a shepherd; and He began to teach them many things. When it was already quite late, His disciples came to Him and said, "This place is desolate and it is already quite late; send them away so that they may go into the surrounding countryside and villages and buy themselves something to eat." But He answered them, "You give them something to eat!" And they said to Him, "Shall we go and spend two hundred denarii on bread and give them something to eat?" And He said to them, "How many loaves do you have? Go look!" And when they found out, they said, "Five, and two fish." And He commanded them all to sit down by groups on the green grass. They sat down in groups of hundreds and of fifties. And He took the five loaves and the two fish, and looking up toward heaven, He blessed the food and broke the loaves and He kept giving them to the disciples to set before them; and He divided up the two fish among them all. They all ate and were satisfied, and they picked up twelve full baskets of the broken pieces, and also of the fish. There were five thousand men who ate the loaves. (Mark 6:30–44)*

According to Mark, many people were coming and going in the area, even before Jesus and His disciples became the focal point of this crowd. Why was this crowd in the area in the first place? Mark never said. The question Mark's account raised isn't answered until we hear John's testimony:

> *After these things Jesus went away to the other side of the Sea of Galilee (or Tiberias). A large crowd followed Him, because they saw the signs which He was performing on those who were sick. Then Jesus went up on the mountain, and there He sat down with His disciples. Now the Passover, the feast of the Jews, was near. Therefore Jesus, lifting up His eyes and seeing that a large crowd was coming to Him, said to Philip, "Where are we to buy bread, so that these may eat?" This He was saying to test him, for He Himself knew what He was intending to do. Philip answered Him, "Two hundred denarii worth of bread is not sufficient for them, for everyone to receive a little." One of His disciples, Andrew, Simon Peter's brother, said to Him, "There is a lad here who has five barley loaves and two fish, but what are these for so many people?" Jesus said, "Have the people sit down." Now there was much grass in the place. So the men sat down, in number about five thousand. Jesus then took the loaves, and having given thanks, He distributed to those who were seated; likewise also of the fish as much as they wanted. When they were filled, He said to His disciples, "Gather up the leftover fragments so that nothing will be lost." So they gathered them up, and filled twelve baskets with fragments from the five barley loaves which were left over by those who had eaten. (John 6:1–13)*

John answered the question raised by Mark. The large crowd was the result of two circumstances: First, John alone told us that the people searched for Jesus because they knew He had been performing miraculous healings. Second, John alone said that it was nearly Passover, the holy Jewish holiday that caused thousands to travel through this area to arrive at Jerusalem for the celebration. While Mark mentioned the crowd, only John told us why it was there in the first place. But in unintentionally answering the question raised by Mark,

John raised an unanswered question of his own. John's account mentioned Philip and Andrew specifically. This stood out to me, only because the use of pronouns and proper names is an important focus of Forensic Statement Analysis. Andrew and Philip are not major characters in the Gospels; the gospel writers seldom mention them, especially when compared with Peter, John, and James. For this reason, their appearance here raises a couple of questions. Why did Jesus ask Philip where they ought to go to buy bread? Why did Andrew get involved in the answer? In addition to this, John also mentioned a detail that was not found in Mark's briefer account. John said that the disciples fed the crowd "barley loaves." John also repeated Mark's testimony that there was "much grass" in the area. In order to make sense of the questions John raised and the role of the grass and the barley, let's finish with an examination of Luke's account:

"Harmonization" or "Interpolation"?

When an investigator considers two or more eyewitness accounts, it's the duty of the detective to "harmonize" the accounts. The details from each account must be assembled without modifying the statements or adding details that are foreign to the observations of the witnesses. In the end, the final "harmony" will provide us with a version of events in which the voices of all the eyewitnesses can be heard clearly and distinctly, even though they may be providing different details. Detectives must avoid "interpolation," the insertion of additional or extraneous material into the eyewitness record.

> *When the apostles returned, they gave an account to Him of all that they had done. Taking them with Him, He withdrew by Himself to a city called Bethsaida. But the crowds were aware of this and followed Him; and welcoming them, He began speaking to them about the kingdom of God and curing those who had need of healing. Now the day was ending, and the twelve came and said to Him, "Send the crowd away, that they may go into the surrounding villages and countryside and find lodging and get something to eat; for here we are in a desolate place." But He said to them, "You give them something to eat!" And they said, "We have no more than five loaves and two fish, unless perhaps we go and buy food for all these people." (For*

there were about five thousand men.) And He said to His disciples, "Have
them sit down to eat in groups of about fifty each." They did so, and had
them all sit down. Then He took the five loaves and the two fish, and look-
ing up to heaven, He blessed them, and broke them, and kept giving them to
the disciples to set before the people. And they all ate and were satisfied; and
the broken pieces which they had left over were picked up, twelve baskets
full. (Luke 9:10–17)

Luke is the only one who told us that this event occurred when Jesus withdrew to the
city of Bethsaida. This revelation unlocks the mystery of Philip and Andrew's prominence
in John's testimony; they were both from Bethsaida (according to John 1:44). We learned
this detail not from Luke (who told us that the miracle occurred in Bethsaida) but from
John (who mentioned it without any connection to the miracle). Jesus asked Philip about
sources for the bread because He knew that Philip was from this part of the country. Philip
and Andrew naturally tried their best to respond, given that they were uniquely qualified to
answer Jesus's question.

What about the grass and barley? Why were these details included in the narrative? Are
they consistent with what eyewitnesses might have actually seen or experienced? As it turns
out, the Passover occurred at a time (in April) that followed five of the rainiest months for the
area of Bethsaida. In addition to this, the Passover occurred at the end of the barley harvest.[50]
These meaningless details are just what I would expect to hear from eyewitnesses who were
simply describing what they saw, including the details that don't really matter in the larger
narrative.

THE GOSPEL WRITERS REFERENCED NAMES CORRECTLY

When I interview eyewitnesses, I listen carefully to their descriptions of the
suspect and the environment in which the crime took place. Their observations
of the scene, if they are genuine, should reflect the true nature of the time and
location of the crime. When Aimee told me about her observations of the suspect in 1982, she
described a Journey concert shirt that promoted an album (*Escape*) that was released in 1981.
The description of the shirt was consistent with the time frame of the murder. If Aimee had

described a shirt that was unavailable until 1990, for example, I would have been concerned that her statement was either inadvertently inaccurate or deliberately false.

Something similar can be observed in the gospel accounts. The gospel writers are believed to have written from a number of geographic locations. Mark probably wrote from Rome, Matthew may have written from Judea, Luke from either Antioch or Rome, and John from Ephesus.[51] Skeptics have argued that these accounts were not written by people who had firsthand knowledge of the life and ministry of Jesus but were simply inventions written generations later by people who weren't all that familiar with the locations they were describing. All of the gospel writers described a large number of people as they wrote out their testimonies, and often identified these individuals by name. As it turns out, these names provide us with important clues to help us determine if the writers of the Gospels were actually familiar with life in first-century Palestine.

Richard Bauckham[52] examined the work of Tal Ilan[53] and used Ilan's data when investigating the biblical use of names. Ilan assembled a lexicon of all the recorded names used by the Jews of Palestine between 330 BC and AD 200. She examined the writings of Josephus, the texts of the New Testament, documents from the Judean desert and Masada, and the earliest rabbinic works of the period. She even examined ossuary (funeral-tomb) inscriptions from Jerusalem. Ilan included the New Testament writings in her study as well. She discovered that the most popular men's names in Palestine (in the time span that encompassed the gospel accounts) were Simon and Joseph. The most popular women's names were Mary and Salome. You may recognize these names from the gospel accounts. As it turns out, when Bauckham examined all the names discovered by Ilan, he found that the New Testament narratives reflect nearly the same percentages found in all the documents Ilan examined:

The Corroboration of Language

The gospel writers did more than correctly cite the popular names of first-century Palestinian Jews. They also appear to have written in a style that was similar to those who lived at that time. Nonbiblical scraps of papyrus and pottery from the first century provide us with samples of the form of Greek that was popular in the ancient Middle East. The Greek used by the gospel writers is very similar to the vernacular "common" Greek that was used by others who lived in this region at this time in history. (For more details, refer to *The New Testament Documents: Are They Reliable?* by F. F. Bruce.)

Popularity of Names Cited in Palestinian Literature of the Time

15.6% of the men had the name Simon or Joseph

41.5% of the men had one of the nine most popular names

7.9% of the men had a name no one else had

28.6% of the women had the name Mary or Salome

49.7% of the women had one of the nine most popular names

9.6% of the women had a name no one else had

Popularity of Names Cited by the New Testament Authors

18.2% of the men had the name Simon or Joseph

40.3% of the men had one of the nine most popular names

3.9% of the men had a name no one else had

38.9% of the women had the name Mary or Salome

61.1% of the women had one of the nine most popular names

2.5% of the women had a name no one else had[54]

The most popular names found in the Gospels just happen to be the most popular names found in Palestine in the first century. This is even more striking when you compare the ancient popular Palestinian Jewish names with the ancient popular Egyptian Jewish names:

Top Jewish Men's Names in Palestine	Top Jewish Men's Names in Egypt
Simon	Eleazar
Joseph	Sabbataius
Eleazar	Joseph
Judah	Dositheus
Yohanan	Pappus
Joshua	Ptolemaius

If the gospel writers were simply guessing about the names they were using in their accounts, they happened to guess with remarkable accuracy. Many of the popular Jewish names in Palestine were different from the popular names in Egypt, Syria, or Rome. The use of these names by the gospel writers is consistent with their claim that they were writing on the basis of true eyewitness familiarity.

When names are very common, people find themselves having to make a distinction by adding an extra piece of information. My name is Jim Wallace, but I am often confused with Jim Wallis, the founder and editor of *Sojourners* magazine. For this reason, I will sometimes add the additional descriptor "of ColdCaseChristianity.com" when describing myself. I am Jim

Wallace "of ColdCaseChristianity.com" (as opposed to Jim Wallis "of *Sojourners*"). When you see the addition of a descriptor, you can be sure that the name being amended is probably common to the region or time in history. We see this throughout the gospel accounts. The gospel writers introduce us to Simon "Peter," Simon "the Zealot," Simon "the Tanner," Simon "the Leper," and Simon "of Cyrene." The name Simon was so common to the area of Palestine in the first century that the gospel writers had to add descriptors to differentiate one Simon from another. This is something we would expect to see if the gospel writers were truly present in Palestine in the first century and familiar with the common names of the region (and the need to better describe those who possessed these popular names).

Jesus (Hebrew: Joshua) was one of these popular first-century names in Palestine, ranking sixth among men's names. For this reason, Jesus was one of those names that often required an additional descriptor for clarity's sake. Interestingly, the gospel writers themselves (when acting as narrators) didn't use additional descriptors for Jesus, even though they quoted characters

The Corroboration of Location

The gospel writers were evidently extremely familiar with the locations they wrote about. While late noncanonical forgeries written from outside the area of Palestine seldom mention any city other than Jerusalem (the one famous city that everyone knew was in Israel), the gospel writers alone included the specific names of lesser first-century towns and villages. The gospel writers mentioned or described Aenon, Arimathea, Bethphage, Caesarea Philippi, Cana, Chorazin, Dalmanutha, Emmaus, Ephraim, Magadan, Nain, Salim, and Sychar. Some of these villages are so obscure that only people familiar with the area would even know they existed.

within the narrative who did. Matthew, for example, repeatedly referred to Jesus as simply "Jesus" when describing what Jesus did or said. But when quoting others who used Jesus's name, Matthew quoted them identifying Jesus as "Jesus from Nazareth in Galilee," "Jesus the Galilean," "Jesus of Nazareth," "Jesus who was called Christ," "Jesus who was crucified." Why the difference? Matthew, as the narrator of history, simply called Jesus by His first name over the course of many chapters. His readers were already familiar with the person of Jesus Matthew introduced early in his account. But Matthew accurately recorded the way we would expect people to identify Jesus in the context of the first century. Matthew appears to be acting merely as an eyewitness *recorder of facts*, limiting himself to "Jesus" when he is doing the talking, but accurately reporting the way he heard others refer to Jesus.

The manner in which the gospel writers described details (unintentionally supporting one another) and the approach the gospel writers took when they referred to people (using the names and descriptors we would expect in first-century Palestine) corroborate their testimonies *internally*. The gospel accounts appear authentic from the "inside out." The words of the Gospels themselves are consistent with what we would expect from eyewitnesses.

CORROBORATION FROM THE "OUTSIDE IN"

If the Gospels are true, we should also expect them to be corroborated *externally* as well. Aimee's testimony, for example, was corroborated by two additional pieces of evidence (the discovery of the gas receipt and the testimony of Danny's sister). The Gospels are similarly corroborated from the "outside in" by the testimony of witnesses who reported what they knew to be true, even though they were not Christians and did not necessarily believe the testimony of the gospel writers. These non-Christian eyewitnesses were often hostile to the growing Christian movement and critical of the claims of the Gospels. In spite of this, they affirmed many of the details that were reported by the gospel writers.

As a cold-case detective, I've encountered this sort of thing many times. I once had a case with a victim who was killed in her condominium. The primary suspect in her murder originally denied ever being in her home. I interviewed him a second time and told him that we discovered his DNA was in the house, in the very room where the victim was murdered. He changed his story and told me that he remembered that the victim called him and asked him to come over to the house to help her move some boxes from this room to her garage. The suspect said he came over on the day of the murder and was in the victim's room for a very short time to help her move these boxes. He still denied being involved in her murder, however. Although he continued to deny his involvement in the crime, his new statement included two *reluctant admissions*. The suspect now admitted to the fact that he had been in the room where the murder occurred and on the very day when the victim was killed. While he still denied the fact that he committed the crime, he *reluctantly admitted* important facts that would eventually be assembled with other pieces of circumstantial evidence to form the case against him.

NONBIBLICAL EYEWITNESSES CORROBORATED THE GOSPELS

In a similar way, ancient observers and writers who were hostile to Christianity *reluctantly admitted* several key facts that corroborate the claims of the Christian eyewitnesses, even though they denied that Jesus was who He claimed to be. Let's examine some of these *reluctant admissions* and reconstruct the picture they offer of Jesus.

JOSEPHUS (AD 37–CA. 100) DESCRIBED JESUS

Josephus described the Christians in three separate citations in his *Antiquities of the Jews*. In one of these passages, Josephus described the death of John the Baptist, in another he mentioned the execution of James (the brother of Jesus), and in a third passage he described Jesus as a "wise man." There is controversy about Josephus's writing because early Christians appear to have altered some copies of his work in an effort to *amplify* the references to Jesus. For this reason, as we examine Josephus's passage related to Jesus, we will rely on a text that scholars believe escaped such alteration. In 1971, Shlomo Pines, scholar of ancient languages and distinguished professor at the Hebrew University of Jerusalem, published a long-lost tenth-century Arabic text written by a Melkite bishop of Hierapolis named Agapius. This Arabic leader quoted Josephus and did so in the Arabic language, unlike the Greek used by other authors from antiquity. Overtly Christian references that are seen in other ancient versions of Josephus's account are also missing from Agapius's quote, and as a result, scholars believe that this version best reflects Josephus's original text:

> At this time there was a wise man who was called Jesus. His conduct was good, and [he] was known to be virtuous. And many people from among the Jews and the other nations became his disciples. Pilate condemned him to be crucified and to die. And those who had become his disciples did not abandon his discipleship. They reported that he had appeared to them three days after his crucifixion and that he was alive; accordingly, he was perhaps the Messiah concerning whom the prophets have recounted wonders.[55]

There are many other ancient versions of Josephus's citation that are more explicit about the nature of Jesus's miracles, His life, resurrection, and status as "the Christ," but this brief and conservative version of Josephus's text reluctantly admits a number of key facts about Jesus. From this text, we can conclude that Jesus lived, was a wise and virtuous teacher who reportedly demonstrated wondrous power, was condemned and crucified under Pilate, had followers who reported that He appeared to them after His death on the cross, and was believed to be the Messiah.

THALLUS (CA. AD 5-60) DESCRIBED JESUS

Thallus was a Samaritan historian who wrote an expansive (three-volume) account of the history of the Mediterranean area in the middle of the first century, only twenty years after Jesus's crucifixion. Like the writings of many ancient historians, much of his work is now lost to us. Another historian, Sextus Julius Africanus, wrote a text entitled *History of the World* in AD 221, however, and Africanus quoted an important passage from Thallus's original account. Thallus chronicled the alleged crucifixion of Jesus and offered an explanation for the darkness that was observed at the time of Jesus's death. Africanus briefly described Thallus's explanation:

> On the whole world there pressed a most fearful darkness; and the rocks were rent by an earthquake, and many places in Judea and other districts were thrown down. This darkness Thallus, in the third book of his *History*, calls, as appears to me without reason, an eclipse of the sun.[56]

It's a pity that we don't have the complete account and explanation from Thallus, but in offering an explanation for the darkness, Thallus "reluctantly admitted" important details that corroborated portions of the Gospels. Even though Thallus denied that the darkness at the point of the crucifixion was caused supernaturally, he inadvertently corroborated the claim that Jesus was indeed crucified and that darkness covered the land when He died on the cross.

TACITUS (AD 56-CA. 117) DESCRIBED JESUS

Cornelius Tacitus was known for his analysis and examination of historical documents and is among the most trusted of ancient historians. He was a senator under Emperor Vespasian and was also proconsul of Asia. In his *Annals* of AD 116, he described Emperor Nero's response to the great fire in Rome and Nero's claim that the Christians were to blame:

> Consequently, to get rid of the report, Nero fastened the guilt and inflicted the most exquisite tortures on a class hated for their abominations, called Christians by the populace. Christus, from whom the name had its origin, suffered the extreme penalty during the reign of Tiberius at the hands of one of our procurators, Pontius Pilatus, and a most mischievous superstition, thus checked for the moment, again broke out not only in Judaea, the first source of the evil, but even in Rome, where all things hideous and shameful from every part of the world find their centre and become popular.[57] (*Annals*, 15:44)

Tacitus, in describing Nero's actions and the presence of the Christians in Rome, *reluctantly admitted* several key facts related to the life of Jesus. Tacitus corroborated that Jesus lived in Judea, was crucified under Pontius Pilate, and had followers who were persecuted for their faith in Him.

MARA BAR-SERAPION (AD 70–UNKNOWN) DESCRIBED JESUS

Sometime after AD 70, a Syrian philosopher named Mara Bar-Serapion, writing to encourage his son, compared the life and persecution of Jesus with that of other philosophers who were persecuted for their ideas. The fact that Mara Bar-Serapion described Jesus as a real person with this kind of influence is important:

> What advantage did the Athenians gain from putting Socrates to death? Famine and plague came upon them as a judgment for their crime. What advantage did the men of Samos gain from burning Pythagoras? In a moment their land was covered with sand. What advantage did the Jews gain from executing their wise King? It was just after that that their kingdom was abolished. God justly avenged these three wise men: the Athenians died of hunger; the Samians were overwhelmed by the sea; the Jews, ruined and driven from

their land, live in complete dispersion. But Socrates did not die for good; he lived on in the teaching of Plato. Pythagoras did not die for good; he lived on in the statue of Hera. Nor did the wise King die for good; He lived on in the teaching which He had given.[58]

Although Mara Bar-Serapion does not seem to place Jesus in a position of pre-eminence (he simply lists Him alongside other historic teachers like Socrates and Pythagoras), Mara Bar-Serapion does admit several key facts. At the very least, we can conclude that Jesus was a wise and influential man who died for His beliefs. We can also conclude that the Jews played a role in Jesus's death and that Jesus's followers adopted and lived lives that reflected Jesus's beliefs.

PHLEGON (AD 80–140) DESCRIBED JESUS

In a manner similar to his citation of Thallus, Sextus Julius Africanus also wrote about a historian named Phlegon who penned a record of history in approximately AD 140. In his historical account, Phlegon also mentioned the darkness surrounding the crucifixion:

Ancient Jewish Corroboration

The Jewish Talmud (the writings and discussions of ancient rabbis) dates to the fifth century, but is thought to contain the ancient teachings from the early *Tannaitic* period from the first and second centuries. Many of the Talmudic writings reference Jesus:

"Jesus practiced magic and led Israel astray" (b. Sanhedrin 43a; cf. t. Shabbat 11.15; b. Shabbat 104b).

"Rabbi Hisda (d. 309) said that Rabbi Jeremiah bar Abba said, 'What is that which is written, "No evil will befall you, nor shall any plague come near your house"? (Psalm 91:10).... "No evil will befall you" (means) that evil dreams and evil thoughts will not tempt you; "nor shall any plague come near your house" (means) that you will not have a son or a disciple who burns his food like Jesus of Nazareth'" (b. Sanhedrin 103a; cf. b. Berakhot 17b).

"It was taught: On the day before the Passover they hanged Jesus. A herald went before him for forty days (proclaiming), 'He will be stoned, because he practiced magic and enticed Israel to go astray. Let anyone who knows anything in his favor come forward and plead for him.' But nothing was found in his favor, and they hanged him on the day before the Passover" (b. Sanhedrin 43a).

From just these passages that mention Jesus by name, we can conclude that Jesus had magical powers, led the Jews away from their beliefs, and was executed on the day before the Passover.

Phlegon records that, in the time of Tiberius Caesar, at full moon, there was a full eclipse of the sun from the sixth hour to the ninth.[59]

Origen, the Alexandrian-born, early church theologian and scholar, also cited Phlegon several times in a book he wrote in response to the criticism of a Greek writer named Celsus:

> Now Phlegon, in the thirteenth or fourteenth book, I think, of his Chronicles, not only ascribed to Jesus a knowledge of future events (although falling into confusion about some things which refer to Peter, as if they referred to Jesus), but also testified that the result corresponded to his predictions. So that he also, by these very admissions regarding foreknowledge, as if against his will, expressed his opinion that the doctrines taught by the fathers of our system were not devoid of divine power.
>
> And with regard to the eclipse in the time of Tiberius Caesar, in whose reign Jesus appears to have been crucified, and the great earthquakes which then took place, Phlegon too, I think, has written in the thirteenth or fourteenth book of his Chronicles.
>
> He imagines also that both the earthquake and the darkness were an invention; but regarding these, we have in the preceding pages made our defence [sic], according to our ability, adducing the testimony of Phlegon, who relates that these events took place at the time when our Saviour suffered.[60]

Although Phlegon was not a follower of Jesus and denied many of the claims of the gospel writers, his statements did *reluctantly admit* that Jesus had the ability to accurately predict the future and was crucified under the reign of Tiberius Caesar.

These late first-century and early second-century writers were not friends of Christianity. In fact, they were largely indifferent to the fledgling Christian movement. In spite of this, they all provided important corroborating details of Jesus's life, even if they did so *reluctantly*. If all the Christian documents had been destroyed, we would still be able to reconstruct a modest description of Jesus from these writers.

The ancient (and "reluctant") nonbiblical description of Jesus would include the fact that Jesus was a true historical person and a virtuous, wise man who worked wonders, accurately predicted the future, and taught His disciples. His teaching drew a large following of both Jews and Gentiles; He was identified as the "Christ," believed to be the Messiah, and widely known as the "Wise King" of the Jews. His disciples were eventually called Christians. His devoted followers became a threat to the Jewish leadership, and as a result, these leaders presented accusations to the Roman authorities. Pontius Pilate condemned Jesus to crucifixion during the reign of Tiberius Caesar. A great darkness descended over the land when Jesus was crucified, and an earthquake shook a large region surrounding the execution. Following his execution, a "mischievous superstition" spread about Him from Palestine to Rome.

This description of Jesus, although incomplete, is remarkably similar to the description offered by the gospel writers. Early, external, non-Christian sources corroborate the testimony of the New Testament authors.

ARCHAEOLOGY CONTINUES TO CORROBORATE THE GOSPELS

Because Christianity makes historical claims, archaeology ought to be a tool we can use to see if these claims are, in fact, true. The archaeological efforts of the past two centuries have confirmed several details that skeptics used to highlight as areas of *weakness* in the case for Christianity. There are a large number of biblical passages that are now corroborated by both ancient non-Christian witnesses and archaeological evidence. Here are just a few:

QUIRINIUS HAS BEEN CORROBORATED

Luke wrote that Joseph and Mary returned to Bethlehem because a Syrian governor named Quirinius was conducting a census (Luke 2:1–3). Josephus confirmed the existence of this governor, but Josephus recorded Quirinius's governorship from AD 5 to AD 6.[61] This period of time is too late, however, as Matthew wrote that Jesus was born during the reign of Herod the Great (who died nine years prior to Quirinius's governorship as recorded by Josephus). For many years, skeptics pointed to this discrepancy as evidence that Luke's gospel was written late in history by someone who was unfamiliar with the chronology of leaders. Archaeological discoveries in the nineteenth century have provided additional information to remedy this apparent contradiction, however, revealing that Quirinius (or someone with the same name) was also a proconsul of Syria and Cilicia from 11 BC to the death of Herod.

Quirinius's name has been discovered on a coin from this period of time,[62] and on the base of a statue erected in Pisidian Antioch.[63] Archaeology now corroborates the early existence of Quirinius as a governor at the time of the census recorded by Luke.

LYSANIAS HAS BEEN CORROBORATED

Luke also described a tetrarch named Lysanias and wrote that this man reigned over Abilene when John the Baptist began his ministry (Luke 3:1). Josephus also recorded the existence of a man named Lysanias,[64] but this man was a king who ruled over the region from 40 to 36 BC (long before the birth of John the Baptist). Skeptics once again used

Other Significant Archaeological Corroborations

Erastus

In Romans 16:23, Paul wrote, "Erastus, the city treasurer greets you." A piece of pavement was discovered in Corinth in 1929 confirming his existence.

Iconium

In Acts 13:51, Luke described this city in Phrygia. Some ancient writers (like Cicero) wrote that Iconium was located in Lycaonia, rather than Phrygia, but a monument was discovered in 1910 that confirmed Iconium as a city in Phrygia.

this apparent discrepancy to cast doubt on Luke's account. As before, archaeology appears to have resolved the issue and corroborated Luke's claim. Two inscriptions have been discovered that mention Lysanias by name. One of these, dated from AD 14 to 37, identifies Lysanias as the tetrarch in Abila near Damascus.[65] This inscription confirms the reasonable existence

of two men named Lysanias, one who ruled prior to the birth of Jesus and a tetrarch who reigned in the precise period of time described by Luke.[66]

THE POOL OF BETHESDA HAS BEEN CORROBORATED

John wrote about the existence of a pool of Bethesda (John 5:1–9) and said that it was located in the region of Jerusalem, near the Sheep Gate, surrounded by five porticos. For many years, there was no evidence for such a place outside of John's gospel; skeptics again pointed to this passage of Scripture and argued that John's gospel was written late in history by someone who was unfamiliar with the features of the city. In 1888, however, archaeologists began excavating the area near St. Anne's Church in Jerusalem and discovered the remains of the pool, complete with steps leading down from one side and five shallow porticos on another side.[67, 68] In addition, the twentieth-

The Corroboration of Government

Luke accurately described the government that existed in first-century Palestine under Roman rule. His account demonstrates that he was writing at the time and place he claimed:

He correctly described two paths to Roman citizenship in Acts 22:28.

He correctly described the process by which accused criminals were brought to trial in Acts 24:1–9.

He correctly described the manner in which a man could invoke his Roman citizenship and appeal his case to Caesar in Acts 25:6–12.

He correctly described the manner in which a prisoner could be held by a Roman soldier and the conditions when imprisoned at one's own expense in Acts 28:16 and Acts 28:30–31. (Refer to Norman Geisler's *Baker Encyclopedia of Christian Apologetics*.)

century discovery of the Dead Sea Scrolls also provided us with ancient confirmation of the pool's existence. The Copper Scroll (written between AD 25 and AD 68) described a list of locations in Jerusalem that included a pool called "Beth Eshdathayin" located near a porch.[69] Once again, the claims of a gospel writer were corroborated by archaeology.

THE POOL OF SILOAM HAS BEEN CORROBORATED

John also wrote about the "pool of Siloam" (John 9:1–12) and described it as a place of ceremonial cleansing. Although the pool is also mentioned in the Old Testament (in Isa. 8:6 and 22:9), John was the only other ancient author to describe its existence. Scholars were unable to locate the pool with any certainty until its discovery in the City of David region of Jerusalem in 2004. Archaeologists Ronny Reich and Eli Shukrun excavated the pool and dated it from 100 BC to AD 100 (based on the features of the pool and coins found in the plaster).[70] This discovery corroborated the reliability of Christian Scripture and the testimony of John.

Other Significant Archaeological Corroborations

Politarchs

For many centuries, Luke was the only ancient writer to use the word *politarch* to describe "rulers of the city." Skeptics doubted that it was a legitimate Greek term until nineteen inscriptions were discovered. Five of these were in reference to Thessalonica (the very city in which Luke was claiming to have heard the term).

Sergius Paulus

In Acts 13, Luke identified Sergius Paulus, a proconsul in Paphos. Skeptics doubted the existence of this man and claimed that any leader of this area would be a "propraetor" rather than a proconsul. But an inscription was discovered at Soli in Cyprus that acknowledged Paulus and identified him as a proconsul.

PONTIUS PILATE HAS BEEN CORROBORATED

For many years, the only corroboration we had for the existence of Pontius Pilate (the governor of Judea who authorized the crucifixion of Jesus) was a very brief citation by Tacitus (described in the previous section). In 1961, however, a piece of limestone was discovered bearing an inscription with Pilate's name.[71] The inscription was discovered in Caesarea, a provincial capital during Pilate's term (AD 26–36), and it describes a building dedication from Pilate to Tiberius Caesar. This single discovery corroborates what the gospel writers said about Pilate's existence in history, his position within the government, and his relationship to Tiberius Caesar.

THE CUSTOM OF CRUCIFIXION HAS BEEN CORROBORATED

The gospel writers weren't the only ones who described the Roman custom of crucifixion.

Josephus, in his description of the destruction of Jerusalem, also described the practice.[72] But while thousands of condemned criminals and war prisoners were reportedly executed in this manner, not a single one of them had ever been discovered in any archaeological site. Some skeptical scholars speculated that this was because executed criminals of this sort were not afforded decent burials; they were typically thrown into common graves along with other similarly executed prisoners. The gospel writers, however, wrote that Jesus received a proper burial. Skeptics doubted this was possible because they lacked evidence that a victim of crucifixion had ever been buried in this way. In 1968, however, Vassilios Tzaferis found the first remains of a crucifixion victim, Yohanan Ben Ha'galgol, buried in a proper Jewish "kôkhîm-type" tomb.[73] Yohanan's remains revealed that he had a spike driven into both feet and nails driven between the lower bones of the arms. The discovery of Yohanan's tomb corroborates the fact that some criminals were, in fact, given burials similar to the one described by the gospel writers.

Many other gospel details have been corroborated by archaeology; such discoveries continue to validate the claims of the gospel writers from the "outside in." Even when the written accounts of ancient nonbiblical writers seem to contradict the testimony of the gospel authors, archaeological findings continue to resolve the apparent contradictions by confirming the claims of the New Testament.

BROAD STROKES AND MINOR DETAILS

The *internal* and *external* evidences corroborate the gospel narratives and capture an image of Jesus's life and ministry. The broad and general elements of the Gospels are *imaged* for us by the ancient nonbiblical authors of the first and early second centuries, and they are confirmed by the archaeological record. This part of the picture is minimal and less focused, but the image is clear enough to recognize. It matches (in broad strokes) the testimony of the gospel writers found in the New Testament. Beyond this general corroboration, however, many of the specific details of the gospel accounts are made clear for us from the internal evidence of the Gospels themselves. The more we identify instances of *unintentional support* that occur between the gospel writers (what J. J. Blunt referred to as "undesigned coincidences"), correct identification of proper names and locations, and the appropriate Greek language of the region and time, the more confidence we can have that these accounts are providing details consistent with first-century Palestine.

The Broad Strokes Corroborated by the "External Evidence" of Ancient Nonbiblical Witnesses and Archaeology

The Fine Details Corroborated by the "Internal Evidence" of Names, Locations, Language, and "Unintentional Support"

Our picture of Jesus is made clearer by the corroboration of the *internal* evidence as it authenticates the *external* evidence and validates the claims of the gospel writers themselves.

SO, WHY DO SOME CONTINUE TO DENY IT?

Some critics of the Gospels are unimpressed with the internal and external evidences we've discussed so far, in spite of the fact that these evidences are diverse and consistent with one another. Many skeptics have argued that there are still passages within the Gospels that are yet to be understood or supported by extrabiblical evidence. Let's take a look at the objections of skeptics related to these areas of internal and external evidence to see why some (like Albert Einstein) have described the Gospels as an "expression and product of human weaknesses."

SOME ORIGINAL WRITINGS OF ANCIENT AUTHORS ARE MISSING

Many critics have rejected some of the *external* corroboration we've described from ancient non-Christian authors like Thallus and Phlegon. They've argued that the original texts from these two ancient historians are unavailable to us. Instead we have been examining quotes from these writers as they were cited by Christian authors (Sextus Julius Africanus and Origen) who wrote much later in history. How do we know that these ancient Christian apologists didn't distort or misquote Thallus and Phlegon? Skeptics argue that we cannot trust the quotes we have today because we don't have access to the copies of Thallus's or Phlegon's complete texts.

BUT …

Both Africanus and Origen cite the work of Thallus and Phlegon from a position of skepticism, not agreement. Africanus said that Thallus proposed an eclipse to explain the darkness at Jesus's crucifixion, but Africanus clearly did not agree with this conclusion; he said that Thallus made this claim "without reason." In a similar way, Origen argued that Phlegon was mistaken about many aspects of his account ("falling into confusion about some things which refer to Peter"), even as Phlegon reluctantly admitted that Jesus could predict the future. Neither Africanus nor Origen sterilized the accounts they cited, removing the details that didn't support their case. Instead, Africanus and Origen quoted the work of Thallus and Phlegon even though they didn't always agree with their conclusions. The best inference from the evidence here is that Africanus and Origen were correctly and honestly citing their sources, especially since we have no other competing ancient citations of Thallus and Phlegon that contradict what Africanus and Origen reported.

SOME GOSPEL TERMS ARE STILL "TROUBLESOME"

Some critics have cited a number of terms that appear to be used incorrectly by the gospel writers. They argue that these mistaken references either expose that the gospel writers were unfamiliar with the time and region they were describing, or that the Gospels were written much later than some would claim. As an example, skeptics have pointed to the Sermon on the Mount and argued that Jesus's remarks about praying in public, as the hypocrites did in the synagogues (Matt. 6:5), are out of place. Some Jewish scholars have contended that ancient Jews of Jesus's day did not pray in the synagogues and that this practice began only after the temple was destroyed in AD 70.[74] If this were the case, the gospel of Matthew contains a claim that is curiously out of sequence. There are a handful of other similar examples offered by critics who claim there are terms that are either suspiciously unique to the gospel writers or appear to be used in a way unparalleled in other ancient writings of the time.

BUT ...

Objections like these presume that we have perfect knowledge of the first-century environment in Palestine. In this specific objection, for example, there is no archaeological or ancient-document evidence that contradicts the claims of the gospel writers. Instead, critics have argued against the Gospels because they have not yet found external support for the biblical claims. But we've already seen a number of examples of other gospel claims that were once uncorroborated (the pool of Bethesda, for example) or appeared to be contradictory (the identities of Quirinius or Lysanias, for example) but were ultimately corroborated by archaeology. Much of the skepticism leveled at the biblical historical account is based on the presumption, even without evidential support, that the account is false unless corroborated. In essence, the gospel writers are guilty until proved innocent. There is no presumption of innocence for the authors of the New Testament. Unlike other ancient historical witnesses, the writers of the Gospels are not afforded the luxury of presumed credibility when there is silence on a particular claim from other ancient sources.

Much of this skepticism is due to the presupposition of philosophical naturalism that we talked about in chapter 1. The Gospels contain descriptions of the supernatural: healings, prophetic utterances, and miracles. Because critics deny the possibility of such things, they reject the biblical accounts and look for ways to describe them as fallacious. It is this presupposition that drives many skeptics to claim that the Gospels were written late in history, far from the region where the miraculous events reportedly occurred. How else could the gospel writers have fooled so many people with these stories about the supernatural? Certainly they couldn't have written these accounts at a time or place in which the true eyewitnesses could expose their fabrications, could they? The evidence we have from archaeology and ancient sources does not support the claim for late or distant authorship, however, and Paul argued that there were many eyewitnesses still available to corroborate the miracles of Jesus (particularly His resurrection) at the time of Paul's letter to the Corinthians in AD 53–57 (1 Cor. 15:6). If we can overcome our bias against descriptions of the supernatural, the claims of the gospel accounts are convincingly corroborated.

ARCHAEOLOGY CANNOT CONFIRM EVERY GOSPEL DETAIL

Some skeptics have argued that archaeology simply cannot satisfactorily corroborate the claims of any historical author or ancient eyewitness. There are many portions of the gospel accounts that are not supported by the current finds of archaeology, and (as we've demonstrated) there have been a number of biblical claims that seemed to contradict other ancient accounts and were unanswered by archaeology for many centuries. If archaeology is as limited as it appears to be, how can we trust it to completely corroborate the claims of the gospel writers? In addition, what kind of archaeological evidence could ever corroborate the miracles described in the Bible? Even if we believed that miracles were reasonable, what kind of archaeological evidence could, for example, corroborate Jesus's healing of the blind man? For these skeptics, archaeology, while interesting, seems too limited to be of much assistance.

BUT ...

The archaeological evidences we've discussed in this chapter are only one category of evidence in the cumulative circumstantial case we are presenting for the corroboration of the Gospels. Like all circumstantial cases, each piece of evidence is incapable of proving the case entirely on its own. Circumstantial cases are built on the strength of multiple lines of evidence and the fact that all the individual pieces point to the same conclusion. The archaeological support we have for the gospel accounts (like the archaeological support for any ancient event) is limited and incomplete. That shouldn't surprise us. Dr. Edwin Yamauchi, historian and professor emeritus at Miami University, has rightly noted that archaeological evidence is a matter of "fractions." Only a fraction of the world's archaeological evidence still survives in the ground. In addition, only a fraction of the possible archaeological sites have been discovered. Of these only a fraction have been excavated, and those only partially. To make matters more difficult, only a fraction of those partial excavations have been thoroughly examined and published. Finally, only a fraction of what has been examined and published has anything to do with the claims of the Bible![75] In spite of these limits, we shouldn't hesitate to use what we do know archaeologically in combination with other lines of evidence. Archaeology may not be able to tell us everything, but it can help us *fill in* the circumstantial case as we corroborate the gospel record.

It's also important to remember that many of the objections leveled by skeptics trade on the assumption that the Gospels are written late, well after the lives of anyone who could testify to what really happened. The evidence from chapter 11, however, leaves little doubt that the Gospels emerged within the lifetime of eyewitnesses. If Luke's gospel was written as early as the evidence suggests, any claim that Luke errantly cited a particular governorship or errantly described a sequence of leaders is unreasonable. If this were the case, the early readers of Luke's gospel, reading it in the first century with a memory of what truly happened, would have caught Luke's error from the very beginning. If nothing else, we would expect to see some early scribe try to alter the narrative to correct the mistaken history. No alteration of this sort ever took place, and the early readers of Luke's gospel did not challenge Luke's account. The gospel was delivered to them early, while they still knew the correct order of governors and kings. Thousands of years later, we may initially doubt Luke and then be surprised that archaeology eventually corroborates his account. If the evidence supporting the early dating of Luke's gospel is correct, however, we really shouldn't be surprised that Luke will ultimately be vindicated.

THE CASE FOR CORROBORATION

This circumstantial case can be examined with some *abductive reasoning* as we try to determine if the Gospels have been reasonably corroborated. Let's once again list all the evidence we've examined so far, including the claims of skeptics. Is it reasonable to infer that the Gospels are sufficiently corroborated?

Even when considering the limits of archaeology and the limits of *internal* literary analysis, the most reasonable inference from the evidence is that the Gospels are incredibly reliable, especially considering the nature of such accounts. Few ancient records have been as critically examined as the New Testament Gospels. Few other documents from antiquity have been as heavily challenged and scrutinized. This prolonged scrutiny has given us a robust and detailed set of evidences that we can examine with abductive reasoning.

If we accept the first explanation (that the Gospels are reliable and trustworthy), we can integrate and embrace all the evidence without any contradiction or friction between pieces. The second explanation may exploit the last three claims but cannot account for the first seven truths. The inference that the Gospels are reliable and consistent with other contemporary evidences is the best explanation. The explanation is *feasible, straightforward,* and *logical.* It is *superior* to the alternative explanation. Once again, it meets the criteria we established for abductive reasoning; we can have confidence that we've arrived at the most reasonable explanation.

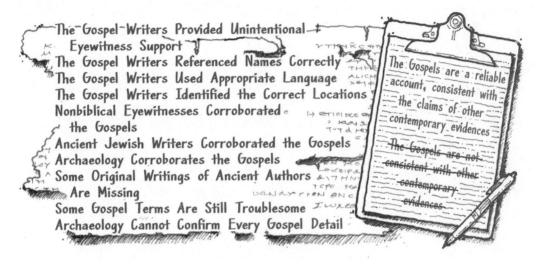

The Gospel Writers Provided Unintentional Eyewitness Support
The Gospel Writers Referenced Names Correctly
The Gospel Writers Used Appropriate Language
The Gospel Writers Identified the Correct Locations
Nonbiblical Eyewitnesses Corroborated the Gospels
Ancient Jewish Writers Corroborated the Gospels
Archaeology Corroborates the Gospels
Some Original Writings of Ancient Authors Are Missing
Some Gospel Terms Are Still Troublesome
Archaeology Cannot Confirm Every Gospel Detail

The Gospels are a reliable account, consistent with the claims of other contemporary evidences

The Gospels are not consistent with other contemporary evidences

THE GOSPELS PASS THE SECOND TEST

So far we've examined two areas that juries consider when evaluating eyewitnesses. The evidence supports the fact that the gospel writers were present in the first century, and their claims are consistent with many pieces of corroborative evidence. Does this mean that they are reliable? Not yet, but we are halfway there. The Gospels have passed the first two tests; their testimony appears early enough in history, and their claims can be corroborated. Now we have to make sure they haven't been corrupted over time. We've got to make sure that the accounts we have today are an accurate reflection of what was originally recorded by the eyewitnesses.

Chapter 13

WERE THEY ACCURATE?

*The characters and events depicted in the … bible are fictitious. Any
similarity to actual persons, living or dead, is purely coincidental.*[76]

—Comedians and magicians "Penn and Teller"

*How do we know that our holy books are free from error?
Because the books themselves say so. Epistemological black holes
of this sort are fast draining the light from our world.*[77]

—Sam Harris, neuroscientist, speaker, and author of *The End
of Faith: Religion, Terror, and the Future of Reason*

TIME, DOCUMENTATION, AND LIES

People who claim that the biblical narratives are mere fiction and filled with error presume
that the authors of the Bible wrote the Gospels long after the reported events allegedly
occurred and far from the locations they described. False, fictional elements can be inserted
into an account if they are inserted well after any living eyewitnesses are alive to identify
them as lies. In addition, if the true historical record has not been preserved well or guarded
to prevent corruption, errors can slip in without much notice. If this occurred with the
Gospels, they are untrustworthy. Even if they are corroborated at several points by archaeology or internal evidences, they may still be inaccurate about any number of episodes they
describe.

Cold-case investigators understand the relationship between time and reliability. We have to evaluate the prior statements of witnesses and suspects and do our best to figure out if these statements are true or fictional. Sometimes the passage of time provides an advantage to cold-case investigators that was not available to the detectives who originally worked the case. Time often exposes the inaccuracy of eyewitnesses and the lies of suspects. I've taken advantage of this over the years.

I once had a case where the suspect (Jassen) provided an alibi at the time he was originally investigated in 1988. Jassen said that he was driving to a friend's house at the time of the murder, although he never made it there because he had a flat tire. When he said this to the original detectives, they wrote it in their notes. They failed, however, to document Jassen's statement in their final report. They never found enough evidence to arrest Jassen, and as a result, they didn't write an arrest report; their closing reports were far less complete than they would have been if anyone had actually been arrested for this crime.

Years later, I reopened the case and examined the original reports and notes of the first detectives. They had been carefully preserved in our department's records division, where they were originally copied and stored on microfiche. I saw Jassen's original statement in the first detective's notes and asked this investigator to meet with me. He told me about his interview with Jassen, and without prompting from his notes, he recalled the details of what Jassen said with great accuracy. When I showed him the copy of his notes, he recognized them without hesitation.

I next arranged an impromptu interview with Jassen. While the original detective was careful to take notes about the interview he conducted in 1988, Jassen made no such record. With the passage of time, Jassen forgot what he first told the detective. The story he now gave to me was completely different from the story he first gave to detectives. Gone was his claim that he was driving to a friend's house. Gone was his claim that he suffered a flat tire. Jassen now said that he was changing the oil in his garage at the time of the murder. When I presented him with the original story, he not only failed to recognize it as his own, but also adamantly denied ever making such a statement. Jassen couldn't remember (or repeat) his original lie. The more I talked to him, the more he exposed the fact that the original story was a piece of fiction. Once he knew he had been caught in a lie, his alibi and confidence began to crumble.

Jassen was ultimately convicted of first-degree murder. The jury was convinced that the original notes from the detective were authentic and well preserved. They were convinced that the notes contained an accurate description of Jassen's first statement. They were also convinced that Jassen's latest statement was untrue.

WHAT DID THEY SAY, AND HOW WELL WAS IT PRESERVED?

How do we know that the biblical documents we have today are accurate and reliable? How do we know that they haven't been corrupted over time and contain little more than fiction? Like our cold-case investigations, we need certainty in two important areas of investigation. First, we need to make sure we know what the Gospels said in the first place. Second, we need to know if there is good reason to believe that these documents were preserved well over time. Jassen's statement in 1988 was well documented and preserved. We were later able to make a case for the accuracy of his statement in front of the jury. Can a case be made for the accuracy of the Gospels? In order to find out if this is possible, we're going to investigate what the gospel writers first said and then study the way these statements were preserved over time.

One way to be certain about the content and nature of the early eyewitness statements is to examine the evidence related to the *transmission* of the New Testament. In chapter 8 we talked about the importance of identifying the original eyewitnesses and their immediate disciples in order to establish a New Testament chain of custody. If we can examine what these first eyewitnesses said to their students, we can reasonably trace the content of the Gospels from their alleged date of creation to the earliest existing copies. The oldest complete, surviving copy of the New Testament we have (Codex Sinaiticus) was discovered in the Monastery of Saint Catherine, Mount Sinai. Constantine Tischendorf observed it and published the discovery in the nineteenth century; scholars believe that it was produced sometime close to AD 350.[78] The text of Codex Sinaiticus provides us with a picture of what the New Testament said in the fourth century, and scholars have used it to inform and confirm the content of Bible translations for many years now. Our examination of the New Testament chain of custody will attempt to link the claims of the original authors to this fourth-century picture of Jesus's life and ministry.

When I first began to examine the "chain," I searched the historical record to identify the first students of the apostles. After all, the apostles claimed to have seen Jesus and experienced life with Him; I wanted to know what, exactly, they said to their students. While the apostles had a number of pupils, not every one of these *second-generation* Christians became a leader in his own right or was identified by history. Not every apostolic student had occasion to lead a group or author a letter revealing what the original disciples taught him. While many of the apostles' students may have written about the content of their teachers' testimony, only a few of these documents have survived. That shouldn't surprise us given the antiquity of the events we are examining. In spite of all this, I was able to identify several *chains of custody* that give us an idea of what the apostles observed and taught. In fact, I bet we could comfortably reconstruct an accurate image of Jesus from just the letters of the students of the apostles, even if all of Scripture was lost to us. Let's take a look at the evidence from the New Testament "chains of custody":

JOHN'S STUDENTS CONFIRMED THE ACCURACY OF THE GOSPELS

The apostle John (ca. AD 6–100) was the youngest of Jesus's disciples. He was the son of Zebedee and Salome and the brother of James. Unlike all the other apostles (who died as martyrs), it appears that John lived to approximately ninety-four years of age and died a natural death. John taught two important students and passed his gospel into their trusted hands.

JOHN TAUGHT IGNATIUS

Ignatius (ca. AD 35–117) also called himself "Theophorus" (which means "God Bearer"). Not much is known about his early life, although early church records describe Ignatius as one of the children Jesus blessed in the gospel accounts. We do know, however, that Ignatius was a student of John and eventually became bishop at Antioch (Turkey), following the apostle Peter. He wrote several important letters to the early church, and seven authentic letters from Ignatius survive to this day (six to local church groups and one to Polycarp).[79] Some of these letters were corrupted in later centuries and amended with additional passages. We do, however, possess copies of the shorter, genuine versions of each epistle, and these brief writings reveal the influence of John (and other apostles) on Ignatius. It's important to remember that it was not Ignatius's desire to retell the gospel narratives; his writings presume that these Gospels were already available to his readers. It was Ignatius's goal to encourage and admonish local church groups. Along the way, he did, however, refer to the New Testament documents and the nature of Jesus, even though this was not his primary goal. It's clear from Ignatius's letters that he knew many of the apostles, as he mentioned them frequently and spoke of them as though many of his older readers also knew them. Scholars have pored over the letters (written in AD 105–115) and have observed that Ignatius quoted (or alluded to) seven to sixteen New Testament books (including the gospels of Matthew, John, and Luke, and several, if not all, of Paul's letters). While this establishes the fact that the New Testament concepts and documents existed very early in history, Ignatius's letters also provide us with a picture of Jesus and a glimpse of how the apostle John (as an eyewitness) described Him. As I read through Ignatius's letters, I found the following portrayal of Jesus:

> The prophets predicted and waited for Jesus.[80]
>
> Jesus was in the line of King David.[81]
>
> He was (and is) the "Son of God."[82]
>
> He was conceived by the Holy Spirit.[83]
>
> A star announced His birth.[84]
>
> He came forth from God the Father.[85]
>
> He was born of the virgin Mary.[86]
>
> He was baptized by John the Baptist.[87]
>
> He was the "perfect" man.[88]
>
> He manifested the will and knowledge of God the Father.[89]
>
> He taught and had a "ministry" on earth.[90]
>
> He was the source of wisdom and taught many commandments.[91]
>
> He spoke the words of God.[92]
>
> Ointment was poured on Jesus's head.[93]
>
> He was unjustly treated and condemned by men.[94]
>
> He suffered and was crucified.[95]
>
> He died on the cross.[96]
>
> Jesus sacrificed Himself for us as an offering to God the Father.[97]
>
> This all took place under the government of Pontius Pilate.[98]
>
> Herod the Tetrarch was king.[99]
>
> Jesus was resurrected.[100]
>
> He had a physical resurrection body.[101]

He appeared to Peter and the others after the resurrection.[102]

He encouraged the disciples to touch Him after the resurrection.[103]

He ate with the disciples after the resurrection.[104]

The disciples were convinced by the resurrection appearances.[105]

The disciples were fearless after seeing the risen Christ.[106]

Jesus returned to God the Father.[107]

Jesus now lives in us.[108]

We live forever as a result of our faith in Christ.[109]

He has the power to transform us.[110]

Jesus is the manifestation of God the Father.[111]

He is united to God the Father.[112]

He is our only Master[113] and the Son of God.[114]

He is the "Door,"[115] the "Bread of Life,"[116] and the "Eternal Word."[117]

He is our High Priest.[118]

Jesus is "Lord."[119]

Jesus is "God."[120]

He is "our Savior"[121] and the way to "true life."[122]

His sacrifice glorifies us.[123]

Faith in Christ's work on the cross saves us.[124]

This salvation and forgiveness are gifts of grace from God.[125]

Jesus loves the church.[126]

We (as the church) celebrate the Lord's Supper in Jesus's honor.[127]

The letters of Ignatius demonstrate that the New Testament's claims and writings existed early in history; Ignatius appears to be very familiar with many passages from the Gospels and the letters of Paul. In addition, Ignatius echoed John's description of Jesus.

JOHN TAUGHT POLYCARP

Polycarp (AD 69–155) was a friend of Ignatius and a fellow student of John. Irenaeus (we'll talk about him more in a moment) later testified that he once heard Polycarp talk about his conversations with John, and Polycarp was known to have been converted to Christianity by the eyewitness apostles themselves. Polycarp eventually became the bishop of Smyrna[128] (now Izmir in Turkey) and wrote a letter to the church in Philippi, in response to its letter to him. The content of Polycarp's letter (an ancient document written from AD 100 to 150 and well attested in history) refers to Ignatius personally and is completely consistent with the content of Ignatius's letters. Polycarp also appears to be familiar with the other living apostles and eyewitnesses to the life of Jesus. He wrote about Paul, recognizing Paul's relationship with the church at Philippi and confirming the nature of Paul's life as an apostle. Polycarp's letter is focused on encouraging the Philippians and reminding them of their duty to live in response to the New Testament teaching with which they were clearly familiar. In fact, Polycarp mentioned that the Philippians were well trained by the "sacred Scriptures" and quoted Paul's letter to the Ephesians as an example of these Scriptures. Polycarp quoted or referenced fourteen to sixteen New Testament books (including Matthew, Luke, John, Acts, Romans, 1 Corinthians, Galatians, Ephesians, Philippians, 1 Thessalonians, 2 Thessalonians, 1 Timothy, 1 Peter, and 1 John, with some scholars observing additional references to 2 Timothy and 2 Corinthians). Along the way, Polycarp also presented the image of Jesus he gleaned from his teacher, the apostle John, describing Jesus in the following ways:

Jesus was sinless.[129]

He taught commandments.[130]

He taught the Sermon on the Mount.[131]

He suffered and died on a cross.[132]

He died for our sins.[133]

His death on the cross saves us.[134]

Our faith in Jesus's work on the cross saves us.[135]

We are saved by grace.[136]

Jesus was raised from the dead.[137]

His resurrection ensures that we will also be raised.[138]

Jesus ascended to heaven and is seated at God's right hand.[139]

All things are subject to Jesus.[140]

He will judge the living and the dead.[141]

Jesus is our "Savior."[142]

Jesus is "Lord."[143]

Like that of Ignatius, Polycarp's writing affirms the early appearance of the New Testament canon and echoes the teachings of John related to the nature and ministry of Jesus. Ignatius and Polycarp are an important link in the New Testament chain of custody, connecting John's eyewitness testimony to the next generation of Christian "evidence custodians." We have a picture from the "crime scene" taken by the apostle John (recorded in his own gospel); this image was carefully handed to Ignatius and Polycarp, who, in turn, treasured it as sacred evidence and transferred it carefully to those who followed them.

IGNATIUS AND POLYCARP TAUGHT IRENAEUS

Irenaeus (AD 120–202) was born in Smyrna, the city where Polycarp served as bishop. He was raised in a Christian family and was a "hearer" (someone who listened to the teaching) of Polycarp; he later recalled that Polycarp talked about his conversations with the apostle John. He eventually became the bishop of Lugdunum in Gaul (now Lyons, France).[144] Irenaeus matured into a theologian and guardian of Christianity and wrote an important work called *Against Heresies*. This refined defense of Christianity provided Irenaeus with the opportunity to address the issue of scriptural authority, and he specifically identified as many as twenty-four New Testament books as Scripture (including Matthew, Mark, Luke, John, Acts, Romans, 1 Corinthians, 2 Corinthians, Galatians, Ephesians, Philippians, Colossians, 1 Thessalonians, 2 Thessalonians, 1 Timothy, 2 Timothy, Titus, 1 Peter, 1 John, 2 John, and Revelation). Irenaeus provided us with another link in the chain of custody, affirming the established eyewitness accounts and faithfully preserving them for the next generation as he connected the students of the apostles to the generations that followed him.

IRENAEUS TAUGHT HIPPOLYTUS

One of these "next-generation" Christians was a courageous man named Hippolytus (AD 170–236). Hippolytus was born in Rome and was a student and disciple of Irenaeus.[145] As he grew into a position of leadership, he opposed Roman bishops who modified their beliefs to accommodate the large number of "pagans" who were coming to faith in the city. In taking a stand for orthodoxy, Hippolytus became known as the first "antipope" or "rival pope" in Christian history. He was an accomplished speaker of great learning, influencing a number of important Christian leaders such as Origen of Alexandria. Hippolytus wrote a huge ten-volume treatise called *Refutation of All Heresies*. In this expansive work, Hippolytus identified as many as twenty-four New Testament books as

Scripture (including Matthew, Mark, Luke, John, Acts, Romans, 1 Corinthians, 2 Corinthians, Galatians, Ephesians, Philippians, Colossians, 1 Thessalonians, 2 Thessalonians, 1 Timothy, 2 Timothy, Titus, Philemon, 1 Peter, 1 John, 2 John, and Revelation). Unfortunately, Hippolytus was persecuted under Emperor Maximus Thrax and exiled to Sardinia, where he most likely died in the mines. The writings of Hippolytus (like the writings of Irenaeus before him) confirm that the New Testament accounts were already well established in the earliest years of the Christian movement.

As a result of Hippolytus's exile and martyrdom, this particular chain of custody ends without a clear *next link*, although it is certain that Hippolytus had many important students who preserved the Scripture with the same passion he had as a student of Irenaeus. While Origen of Alexandria may have considered himself to be a disciple of Hippolytus, we have no concrete evidence that this was the case. To be safe, we simply have to acknowledge that history has not yet revealed the certain identity of Hippolytus's students. One thing we know for sure: the truth about the life and ministry of Jesus (and the *canon of Scripture*) was established in the first century. The eyewitness account of John (along with the other New Testament documents) was recorded and handed down to his disciples.

John's students recorded this teaching and identified the sources for later generations. Long before the Codex Sinaiticus was first penned or the Council of Laodicea formalized the canon, the New Testament was established as a reliable eyewitness account.

PAUL'S STUDENTS CONFIRMED THE ACCURACY OF THE GOSPELS

The apostle Paul (ca. AD 5–67) wrote the largest portion of the New Testament and was closely associated with several key apostles, historians, and eyewitnesses who helped to document and guard the Scripture we have today. Paul's friend Luke, for example, was a meticulous historian with access to the eyewitnesses and a personal involvement in the history of the New Testament church. As described in chapter 11, Paul quoted Luke's version of the gospel in 1 Timothy 5:17–18 and 1 Corinthians 11:23–25. Those who knew Paul were probably familiar with the writings of Luke. Paul had several key students and disciples who protected and transmitted his writings (along with the emerging writings of other eyewitnesses, including Luke) to the next generation of Christian leaders. Paul's chain of custody is much harder to trace than that of John, but we can follow Paul's influence through the early leadership in Rome to places as far away as Syria.

PAUL TAUGHT LINUS AND CLEMENT OF ROME

Paul spent his last years in Rome under house arrest, awaiting trial. During this time he had free access to other believers and taught many men who would eventually lead the church. We know two of these men specifically. Irenaeus described a man named Linus as one of Paul's coworkers (Paul identifies a coworker named Linus specifically in 2 Timothy 4:21 along with Eubulus, Pudens, and Claudia). History tells us that Linus was born in Tuscany to Herculanus and Claudia, and became the pope of Rome following the deaths of Peter and Paul.

History is unclear on the precise order of popes in these first years, and some early records indicate that Clement of Rome may have preceded Linus.[146] Clement was also a coworker of Paul (mentioned specifically in Philippians 4:3), and he became an important assistant to Paul and Peter in the first years in Rome.[147] In fact, Peter appears to have elevated both Linus and Clement to positions of leadership so that he could focus on prayer and preaching. Clement wrote several letters, and one of these letters (*The First Epistle of Clement to the Corinthians*) survives as the earliest Christian document outside the New Testament. Clement's letter (written in AD 80–140) was written to encourage the Corinthian church and call it to holy living. Clement referenced a number of examples from the Old Testament and also referred to the life and teaching of Jesus as it was passed on to him from Paul and Peter. In fact, Clement talked about the chain of custody that existed from the apostolic eyewitnesses to his own *second-generation* readers. Clement told the Corinthian believers that "the Apostles for our sakes received the gospel from the Lord Jesus Christ; Jesus Christ was sent from God. Christ then is from God, and the Apostles from Christ. Both therefore came in due order from the will of God."[148] Clement understood the "appointed order" of the eyewitness "chain of custody." When examining the letter carefully, scholars have observed that Clement quoted or alluded to seven New Testament books (Mark, Matthew or John, Romans, Galatians, Ephesians, and Philippians) as he penned his work. Clement also described the person and work of Jesus, echoing the description of Jesus that was first communicated by the eyewitnesses. Clement's description of Jesus was very similar to the description offered by Ignatius and Polycarp:

> The prophets predicted the life and ministry of Jesus.[149]
>
> Jesus provided His disciples with important instruction.[150]
>
> He taught principles as described by Mark and Luke.[151]
>
> He was humble and unassuming.[152]
>
> He was whipped.[153]
>
> He suffered and died for our salvation.[154]
>
> He died as a payment for our sin.[155]
>
> He was resurrected from the dead.[156]
>
> He is alive and reigning with God.[157]
>
> His resurrection makes our resurrection certain.[158]
>
> We are saved by the "grace" of God[159] through faith in Jesus.[160]
>
> He is "Lord"[161] and the Son of God.[162]
>
> He possesses eternal glory and majesty.[163]
>
> All creation belongs to Him.[164]
>
> He is our "refuge"[165] and our "High Priest."[166]
>
> He is our "defender" and "helper."[167]
>
> The church belongs to Him.[168]

While it is clear that Clement presumed his readers already understood the truth about Jesus from the Gospels he quoted, Clement still referenced many attributes of Jesus that were consistent with the picture painted by Peter, Paul, and the gospel writers. Clement certainly wrote much more than this single letter and may have affirmed an even larger number of texts. His surviving letter to the Corinthians provides us with another link in the chain of custody, acknowledging the delivery of the eyewitness accounts from the original eyewitnesses to the next generation of believers.

CLEMENT PASSED THE TRUTH FROM EVARISTUS TO PIUS

Linus and Clement of Rome established the lineage of bishops who followed Paul (and Peter) at Rome.[169] They taught, discussed, and passed the eyewitness Scripture along to their successors, from Evaristus (AD ?–109) to Alexander I (AD ?–115) to Sixtus I (AD ?–125) to Telesphorus (AD ?–136) to Hyginus (AD ?–140), to Pius I (AD 90–154). The writings of Ignatius, Polycarp, and Clement demonstrate that the second generation of Christian leaders already considered the writings of the eyewitnesses to be precious Scripture. It's reasonable to conclude that the papal leaders who followed Clement were raised to appreciate and honor the primacy of the eyewitness accounts as well; they understood the importance of guarding these accounts for future generations.

PIUS I AND JUSTIN MARTYR GUARDED THE ACCOUNTS

In the early years of the Christian church, the city of Rome was filled with people who either came to faith there (under the preaching of the apostles or their disciples) or traveled there after coming to faith somewhere else in the Roman Empire. One such person, Justin of Caesarea (AD 103–165), became an important philosopher and contributor to the history of Christianity. Justin Martyr, as he came to be known, was one of the earliest Christian apologists.[170] He was born in Flavia Neapolis (now Nablus, Palestine) to Greek parents. He was raised as a pagan and called himself a Samaritan, but he studied philosophy and eventually converted to Christianity. He taught Christian doctrine in Rome when Pius I was leading the Christian community. He wrote several voluminous and important works, including the *First Apology*, *Second Apology*, and the *Dialogue with Trypho*. In these early Christian texts, Justin Martyr quoted or alluded to Matthew, Mark, Luke, John, and Revelation. While we don't have surviving writings from some of the earliest bishops and popes of Rome (including Pius I), Justin Martyr provided us with a contemporary glimpse of how these men viewed the eyewitness accounts and guarded them for the future.

JUSTIN TAUGHT TATIAN

Not everyone who played a role in the scriptural chain of custody had orthodox beliefs. Many recognized (and wrote about) the eyewitness accounts, while misinterpreting them for themselves and their followers. Tatian the Assyrian (AD 120–180) was one such example.[171]

Tatian was born (and probably died) in Assyria. He came to Rome, however, for some period of time and studied the Old Testament. He met and became a student of Justin Martyr and converted to Christianity. He studied in Rome with Justin for many years and eventually opened a Christian school there. Over time, he developed a strict form of Christianity that forbade marriage and the eating of meat. When Justin died, Tatian was driven from the church in Rome. He traveled to Syria and eventually wrote his most famous contribution, the *Diatessaron*, a biblical paraphrase, or *harmony*, which recognized the existence of the four eyewitness accounts of the Gospels, even as it sought to combine them into one document. The earliest church records in Syria (traced back to Tatian) identified an early canon that included the *Diatessaron*, the letters of Paul, and the book of Acts. Tatian's work, combined with this ancient canonical list, acknowledges the early formation of the canon in the chain of custody from Paul to the late second century.

Life of Jesus (AD 1–33) — Apostle Paul AD 60 — Linus 70 — Clement (7 Books) AD 95 — Evaristus 100 — Alexander 110 — Sixtus 120 — Telesphorus 130 — Hyginus 135 — Pius AD 150 — Justin Martyr (5 Books) AD 160 — Tatian (20 Books) AD 175 — Codex Sinaiticus Council of Laodicea (AD 350–363)

History does not provide us with precise information about the next link in this particular chain of custody. In any case, this custodial sequence from Paul acknowledges that the eyewitness accounts existed, were treated as sacred Scripture from a very early time, and were handed down with care from one generation to another. All of this happened many years before any council determined what would officially become the New Testament record.

PETER'S STUDENTS CONFIRMED THE ACCURACY OF THE GOSPELS

The apostle Peter (ca. 1 BC–AD 67) was perhaps the oldest of Jesus's disciples. He was also known as Simon Cephas (from the Aramaic version of his name). He was the son of Jonah (John) and was raised in Bethsaida (in Galilee). He was a fisherman (along with his brother Andrew) when he first met Jesus and quickly became a disciple. His story is well known, replete with human failures and triumphs. After the ascension, Peter established the church in Antioch and served there as its bishop for seven years. He eventually traveled to Rome and became bishop there as well. In chapter 5 we discussed the evidence that supports the claim that Mark authored Peter's eyewitness account in the gospel of Mark. This gospel (like the gospel of John) is a critical piece of evidence from the "crime scene," and Peter carefully handed it (along with other eyewitness texts that were emerging in the first century) to his own students and disciples:

PETER COMMUNICATED THROUGH MARK

John Mark was the cousin of Barnabas, and his childhood home was well known to Peter (Acts 12:12–14). Mark became so close to Peter that the apostle described him as "my son" (1 Pet. 5:13). Peter preserved his eyewitness testimony through his primary disciple and student, who then passed it on to the next generation in what we now recognize as the "gospel of Mark."

MARK TAUGHT ANIANUS, AVILIUS, KEDRON, PRIMUS, AND JUSTUS

Mark established the church in Alexandria and immediately started preaching and baptizing new believers. History records the fact that he had at least five disciples, and these men eventually became church leaders in North Africa.[172] Mark discipled and taught Anianus (AD ?–82), Avilius (AD ? –95), Kedron (AD ? –106), Primus (ca. AD 40–118), and Justus (AD ?–135), passing on his gospel along with the other early New Testament accounts from apostolic eyewitnesses. These five men eventually became bishops of Alexandria (one after the other) following Mark's death. They faithfully preserved the eyewitness accounts and passed them on, one generation to another.

JUSTUS PASSED THE TRUTH TO PANTAENUS

While Mark was still alive, he appointed his disciple Justus as the director of the Catechetical School of Alexandria. This important school became an esteemed place of learning where the eyewitness accounts and Scriptures were collected and guarded. A key figure in the early development of this school was an ex-Stoic philosopher who converted to Christianity. His name was Pantaenus.[173] He became an important teacher and missionary, traveling east of Alexandria (perhaps as far as India) and reporting that believers were already established in the East and were using the gospel of Matthew written in Hebrew letters. In any event, Pantaenus provided another important link in the chain of custody because the writing of one of his students survives to this day, chronicling and identifying the books of the New Testament that were already considered sacred.

PANTAENUS TAUGHT CLEMENT OF ALEXANDRIA

Titus Flavius Clemens (ca. AD 150–215) was also known as Clement of Alexandria.[174] He was a student of Pantaenus and eventually became the leader of the Catechetical School of Alexandria. Clement was very familiar with the pagan literature of his time and wrote extensively. Three important volumes (the *Protrepticus*, the *Paedagogus,* and the *Stromata*) address Christian morality and conduct. Most importantly, Clement discussed the existing Scripture of the time (as it was handed down to him by Pantaenus) and quoted or alluded to all the New Testament books except for Philemon, James, 2 Peter, 2 John, and 3 John. Clement appears to have received and accepted the same New Testament documents that were known to his predecessors in the "chain of custody."

CLEMENT OF ALEXANDRIA TAUGHT ORIGEN

Origen (ca. AD 185–254) carefully preserved and identified those ancient eyewitness accounts used by the Christian church around the Mediterranean. He was an Egyptian who came to faith and eventually taught at the Catechetical School of Alexandria.[175] He wrote prolifically and penned commentaries for nearly every book of the Bible. Along the way, he quoted all of the New Testament books. He did express hesitation about James, 2 Peter, 2 John, and 3 John, but included them in his list of reliable orthodox eyewitness documents. Origen played a pivotal role because he had a number of students who became important links in the New Testament chain of custody.

PAMPHILUS OF CAESAREA ADOPTED ORIGEN'S WORK

In his later life, Origen fled Alexandria (under the persecution of an archbishop who expelled Origen because he had not been ordained with proper permission) and settled in Caesarea Maritima. Pamphilus[176] also settled in Caesarea Maritima after a long stay in Alexandria, where he became devoted to the works of Origen and even wrote a five-volume treatise called *Apology for Origen*. Pamphilus guarded and defended the work of Origen, and he also accepted the eyewitness accounts of Scripture as authoritative, expressing his confidence in these documents to his own pupils.

PAMPHILUS OF CAESAREA TAUGHT EUSEBIUS

One of Pamphilus's students was Eusebius of Caesarea (ca. AD 263–339), a man who later became an important church historian, church father, and devoted student who documented Pamphilus's career in a three-volume work called *Vita.*[177] Eusebius was a prolific writer, and much of his work survives to this day, including his *Church History*. A close survey of Eusebius's work reveals that he recognized and identified twenty-six New Testament books as Scripture. He strongly affirmed Matthew, Mark, Luke, John, Acts, Romans, 1 Corinthians, 2 Corinthians, Galatians, Ephesians, Philippians, Colossians, 1 Thessalonians, 2 Thessalonians, 1 Timothy, 2 Timothy, Titus, Philemon, 1 Peter, 1 John, and Revelation, and less-strongly affirmed James, Jude, 2 Peter, 2 John, and 3 John.

This chain of scriptural custody, from Peter to Eusebius, brings us well into the period of time in which the Codex Sinaiticus was penned and to the doorstep of the Council of Laodicea. It is clear that the eyewitness accounts and writings of the apostles were collected, preserved, and transmitted from generation to generation during this span of time.

The New Testament chain of custody preserved the primacy and sacred importance of the eyewitness documents and delivered them faithfully to those who would later identify them publicly in the councils that established our present canon of Scripture. These councils did not *create* the canon or the current *version* of Jesus we know so well; they simply acknowledged the canon and description of Jesus that had been provided by the eyewitnesses.

THE LEAST WE CAN LEARN

Now let's imagine for a moment that all the alleged Christian *eyewitness* accounts have been destroyed. Imagine that all we have available to us is the written record of a few students of these supposed eyewitnesses. If this were the case, we would have to rely on the writings of

Mark, Ignatius, Polycarp, and Clement. This remaining record would certainly be sufficient for us to learn the truth about Jesus; after all, Mark was tasked with chronicling the memoir of Peter and wrote a thorough account. So let's make it a little more challenging. Let's remove Mark's gospel from consideration and force ourselves to consider only the *nonbiblical* letters of the other three students, even though these students made no conscious effort to record the details of Jesus's life and ministry. What would we learn about Jesus from just these three men? Would their nominal description affirm what our twenty-first-century Bible tells us?

From the earliest *nonbiblical* records, we would learn the following: Jesus had been predicted by the Old Testament prophets; He was a man in the line of David, conceived by the Holy Spirit as the only begotten Son of God, born of the virgin Mary, and announced with a star. He came forth from God and manifested God's will and knowledge. He was baptized by John the Baptist, lived a humble, unassuming, perfect, and sinless life, spoke the words of God, and taught people many important divine truths (including the principles we recognize from the Sermon on the Mount). Although Jesus was anointed with oil, He was unjustly treated and condemned, whipped, and ultimately executed on the cross. This execution took place during the government of Pontius Pilate and the reign of Herod the Tetrarch. Jesus's death was a personal sacrifice He offered to God in our behalf as a payment for the debt of our sin. Jesus proved His divinity by physically resurrecting from the dead, appearing to Peter and the other disciples, eating with them, and encouraging them to touch Him and see for themselves. The disciples were so emboldened by their observations of the risen Jesus that they became fearless, understanding that Jesus's resurrection ensured eternal life and the resurrection for all of those who placed their faith in Him. Jesus returned to God the Father and now reigns in heaven, even as He lives in everyone who has accepted His offer of forgiveness and salvation. Jesus is the "Door," the "Bread of Life," the "Eternal Word," the "Son of God," our "High Priest," "Savior," "Master," "Guardian," "Helper," "Refuge," and "Lord." Jesus and the Father are one; Jesus possesses eternal glory and majesty. All creation belongs to Him and is subject to Him. Jesus will judge the living and the dead. Jesus is "God."

We would learn all of this, not on the basis of what is taught in the gospel accounts, but on the basis of what is taught by the earliest first-century students of the gospel writers (and only three of them, at that)! The letters of Ignatius, Polycarp, and Clement confirm the accuracy of the Gospels. Even if, as skeptics, we had some doubt about the minute details that exist in each eyewitness account, there can be no doubt about the major themes and claims of the Gospels. Jesus was described as God, walked with His disciples, taught the masses, died on a cross, and rose from the dead. This version of Jesus is not a late invention or exaggeration; it is the version of Jesus that existed from the very first telling. This version of Jesus was witnessed and accurately described by the gospel writers and confirmed by their students. Unlike the man I interviewed, Jassen, whose early story *was not* aligned with the version he provided twenty years later, the earliest account of Jesus's story (as given by the eyewitnesses and their students in the first century) *is* aligned with the version we have two thousand years later.

THE JEWISH RECORDS DIVISION

But how do we know if the other gospel details (not specifically mentioned by the students of the apostles) are accurate? How do we know that these portions of the Gospels weren't corrupted in the period of time spanning from the first century to the inking of Codex Sinaiticus? I came to trust the detective's notes in Jassen's case because I had confidence in the record-keeping ability of my records division. I understood the precise and careful manner in which they copied and preserved the case files. Is there any good reason to believe that the primitive, first-century Christians would be equally willing and capable of such preservation?

THE EYEWITNESSES WERE CONSCIENTIOUS AND PROTECTIVE

In chapter 4 we looked at the role the apostles played as eyewitnesses. They clearly understood the gravity and importance of their testimony. The apostles recognized that their role in God's plan was simply to tell others about their experiences with

Jesus and their observations of His resurrection. It's reasonable that people who saw themselves as critical eyewitnesses would be careful to protect the accuracy of their testimony. In the earliest years, their contribution came in the form of verbal testimony. That's reasonable, given the sense of urgency the apostles felt as they eagerly awaited the imminent return of Jesus. But as the months and years passed without the arrival of Christ, the apostles inked their testimony so their observations could be shared with local church congregations. If the Gospels were written early (during the time in which these eyewitnesses actually lived), it is reasonable to expect that the witnesses would *fact-check* the content of their testimony as it was being told to others. If, for example, Mark's gospel was written as early as the circumstantial evidence in chapter 11 suggests, it's reasonable to expect that Peter would have caught (and corrected) any errors.

THE COPYISTS AND SCRIBES WERE METICULOUS

The ancient Jewish religious culture was already well established in the first century, and it was from this culture that the apostles and first believers emerged. It's clear that the Jews guarded Scripture with extreme care and precision. From the postexile time of Ezra (and even before), there were priests (Deut. 31:24–26) and scribes (called *Sopherim*) who were given the responsibility of copying and meticulously caring for the sacred text. The scribes continued to work in Jesus's day and were mentioned throughout the New Testament by the eyewitnesses who observed them alongside the Pharisees and other Jewish religious leaders. The Old Testament Scriptures were revered and protected during this period of time, largely because early believers considered them to be the holy Word of God along with the New Testament documents. Paul described Luke's gospel as Scripture (1 Tim. 5:17–18), and Peter also described Paul's letters as Scripture (2 Pet. 3:15–16). Paul told the local churches to treat his letters accordingly, making them available to other congregations so they could read them during their meetings (Col. 4:16 and 1 Thess. 5:27). It's reasonable to conclude that the New Testament documents were handled in a way that was similar to the manner in which other ancient Scripture was cherished and preserved.

It's difficult to know with complete certainty the exact method in which the first-century Christian scribes copied and cared for their sacred texts, but we do know that they worked within a religious tradition that spanned hundreds of years, both before and after the first century. The Masoretic tradition, for example, gives us a glimpse into the obsessive care that Jewish scribes historically took with their sacred texts. Scribes known as the Masoretes (a group of Jewish copyists living and working primarily in Tiberias and Jerusalem) took over the precise job of copying the ancient Scripture and transmitting it for later generations. They developed something now known as the Masoretic Text.[178] These documents are recognized as an incredibly trustworthy replica of the original Scripture, and we've come to trust these texts because we understand the manner in which they were copied. To ensure the accuracy of the Masoretic copies, the Masoretes developed a number of strict guidelines to guarantee that every fresh copy was an exact reproduction of the original. The rules of the Masoretes were every bit as comprehensive as any set of regulations used in modern-day records divisions; they copied and handled their documents with all the precision available to them.

History has demonstrated the remarkable accuracy of these ancient scribes who worked under the conviction that the documents they were copying were divine in nature. The discovery of the Dead Sea Scrolls in Qumran confirms their amazing ability. In 1947, a Bedouin herdsman found some unusual clay jars in caves near the valley of the Dead Sea. The jars contained a number of scrolls revealing the religious beliefs of monastic farmers who lived in the valley from 150 BC to AD 70. When this group saw the Romans invade the region, it apparently put its cherished scrolls in the jars and hid them in the caves. The Dead Sea Scrolls contain fragments of almost every book in the Old Testament and, most importantly, a complete copy of the

The Meticulous Masoretes

The Masoretes established comprehensive procedures to protect the text against changes:

When they noted an obvious error in the text, they labeled it as a "kethibh" ("to be written") and placed a correction called a "qere" ("to be read") in the margin.

When they considered a word textually, grammatically, or exegetically questionable, they placed dots above the word.

They kept detailed statistics as a means of guarding against error. Leviticus 8:8, for example, was identified as the middle *verse* of the Torah. In Leviticus 10:16, the word "darash" was identified as middle *word* in the Torah, and the "waw" located in the Hebrew word *gachon* in Leviticus 11:42 was identified as the middle *letter* of the Torah.

They also placed statistics at the end of each book, including the total number of verses, the total number of words, and the total number of letters. By assembling statistics such as these, they could measure each book mathematically to see if there was any copyist error. (Refer to Gleason Archer's *A Survey of Old Testament Introduction*.)

book of Isaiah. This scroll was dated to approximately 100 BC; it was incredibly important to historians and textual experts because it was approximately one thousand years older than any Masoretic copy of Isaiah. The Dead Sea Scroll version of Isaiah allowed scholars to compare the text over this period of time to see if copyists had been conscientious. Scholars were amazed by what they discovered.

A comparison of the Qumran manuscripts of Isaiah "proved to be word for word identical with our standard Hebrew Bible in more than 95 percent of the text."[179] Some of the 5 percent differences were simply a matter of spelling (like you might experience when using the word *favor* instead of *favour*). Some were grammatical differences (like the presence of the word *and* to connect two ideas or objects within a sentence). Finally, some were the addition of a word for the sake of clarity (like the addition of the Hebrew word for "light" to the end of 53:11, following "they shall see"). None of these grammatical variations changed the meaning of the text in any way.

What was it that compelled the ancient scribes to treat these documents with such precision and meticulous care? It was clearly their belief that the documents themselves were sacred and given to them by God. When Paul and Peter identified the New Testament documents (such as the gospel of Luke and the letters of Paul) as Scripture, they ensured that the documents would be honored and cared for in a manner befitting the Masoretic tradition. The first-century Christian scribes didn't have access to photocopiers, microfiche, or digital imaging like modern police-department records divisions do, but they understood the importance of divine record keeping, and they used the first-century equivalent in technology (the meticulous tradition of their predecessors) to carefully guarantee the accuracy of the texts.

 ## CONSISTENT AND WELL PRESERVED

Given the evidence from the chain of custody and what we know about the diligence of the first-century copyists, what is the most reasonable inference we can draw about the accuracy of the Gospels? Unlike Jassen's statement in my cold-case investigation, the message of the apostles appears unchanged over the span of time; it is the same in the first and twenty-first centuries. Like the notes from the first detective, the details of the first-century account appear to have been adequately preserved. The Jewish *records division* was capable and efficient; it copied and guarded the eyewitness accounts over time.

SO, WHY DO SOME CONTINUE TO DENY IT?

Some are still skeptical of the accuracy of the Gospels, in spite of the strong circumstantial evidence that supports such a conclusion. Let's see if a little *abductive reasoning* can help us determine if any of the objections of critics are reasonable when they describe the Scriptures as "fictitious."

IGNATIUS, POLYCARP, AND CLEMENT DIDN'T QUOTE SCRIPTURE PRECISELY

Some have argued that the writings of the first-century students of the apostles either cannot be authenticated or fail to precisely quote the Gospels in a way that would vouch for their accuracy. These critics claim that the letters attributed to Ignatius, for example, are not truly from this student of John. Many have also argued that those passages where these *second-generation* students appear to be quoting from a gospel (such as their references to the Sermon on the Mount) are not precise *word-for-word* quotes; they argue that the students were only alluding to vague and unreliable early oral accounts that hadn't yet been inked on papyrus and were corrupted long before they were ever finalized.

BUT ...

While there has been controversy related to some of Ignatius's letters, there is no reason to doubt the authenticity of the seven letters we've isolated in our chain of custody. Yes, there are additional letters that appear late in history and are falsely attributed to Ignatius, but the seven letters we've referenced are listed in the earliest records of Ignatius's work, and they are corroborated by Polycarp's letter (which refers to Ignatius).

It is true that Ignatius, Polycarp, and Clement often referenced passages of Scripture in a way that captured the meaning of the passage without quoting the specific verse *word for word*. But this was not uncommon of authors at this time in history. Paul also paraphrased Scripture (the Old Testament) on occasion (e.g., 1 Cor. 2:9, where Paul is likely paraphrasing both Isa. 64:4 and Isa. 65:17). Polycarp's and Clement's use of paraphrase is not evidence that the New Testament documents didn't exist at the time these second-generation authors wrote their letters any more than Paul's use of a paraphrase is evidence that the Old Testament did not exist when he wrote his letters.

Most importantly, the Jesus described by these letters is identical to the Jesus described by the apostolic eyewitness, even if the students of the apostles paraphrased or used their own words to describe Him.

THERE ARE MANY COPYIST INSERTIONS THAT ARE OBVIOUS CORRUPTIONS

Skeptics have also challenged some of the late insertions we talked about in chapter 6. It does appear that some copyists intentionally corrupted the manuscripts they were duplicating either to fill in a detail or to make some theological point that was missing in the original text. If this is the case, how can we trust that anything we have is reliable or accurate? If some parts of the text have been corrupted, none of the text can be trusted.

BUT ...

The fact that these corruptions are *obvious* should alert us to something. Why are the corruptions and late additions we mentioned in chapter 6 so evident? They stand out to us because we have hundreds of ancient copies of the Gospels to compare to one another. There are no better-attested ancient documents than the New Testament Gospels. By way of comparison, the Greek researcher and historian Herodotus wrote *The Histories* in the fifth century BC. We trust that we have an accurate copy of this text even though we possess only eight ancient copies. By contrast, we possess thousands of ancient copies of the New Testament documents. These copies come to us from all over the ancient world surrounding the Mediterranean. When compared to one another, the diverse manuscripts, coming from a number of different Christian groups located in a number of different regions, reveal the variations immediately. The textual deviations are *obvious* because we have a rich treasure trove of manuscripts to examine and compare. With this many copies at our disposal, we can easily identify and eliminate the variations. As a result, we can remove the late additions and reconstruct the original with a high degree of confidence.

Let me give you an example of how this process of comparison works. Imagine that you are my patrol partner one afternoon as we are working beat 514C. We get a call from dispatch on our MDT (the mobile computer in our police unit) that summons us to a robbery taking place at a local mini-mart. The dispatch operator sends us the call but accidentally types the wrong street name and misspells the weapon. We recognize that there is no street by this name in our city, but we know that a very similar street (with the same hundred block) does exist in our beat. As we head in that direction, we notify dispatch and receive a new communiqué with the corrected street name. In this second dispatch, however, the operator makes an additional error and misspells the word *Markey*. We again notify the dispatcher and receive yet another message, but once again, there is a misspelling. The dispatcher makes two more repeated efforts to correct the misspelling but, in the pressure of the moment (remember a robbery is occurring), is never quite able to do it without some form of error:

Now let me ask you a question: With the robbery in progress and time of the essence, should we stop at the curb and wait for dispatch to type the call correctly, or do we have enough information, given the growing number of duplicated lines the dispatcher is sending, to proceed to the call? The more the dispatcher repeats the call, even with a number of typos and errors, the more confidence we have that we know what kind of call we are handling and where the crime is occurring. The more copies we possess, the more we can compare them to determine the dispatcher's original meaning, and the more confidence we can have in our conclusion.

Something very similar to this occurs when we examine the ancient biblical manuscripts. Yes, we can see the errors and late additions, but that's the beauty of our large manuscript collection: it allows us to remove the inaccuracies with confidence.

THERE ARE MANY BIBLICAL NARRATIVES THAT DIFFER FROM ONE ANOTHER

Skeptics have also observed the different way in which the gospel writers described the same events and have argued that these variations constitute *contradictions* that simply cannot be reconciled. These irreconcilable differences, according to the skeptics, invalidate the accuracy of the biblical account.

BUT ...

We've already discussed the nature of eyewitness accounts in chapter 4, and we now know that we should *expect* variations among true eyewitness accounts. These expected variations are not a problem for those of us who are working as detectives, so long as we can understand the perspective, interests, and locations from which each witness observed the event. It's our duty, as responsible investigators, to understand how eyewitness statements can be harmonized so we can get the most robust view of the event possible.

THE MOST REASONABLE CONCLUSION

Let's return once again to the process we know as *abductive reasoning* to determine which explanation related to gospel accuracy is the most reasonable. Once again we'll list all the evidence that we've looked at in this chapter, including the evidence cited by the skeptics. Alongside these facts, we'll consider the two possible explanations that can account for what we have seen so far.

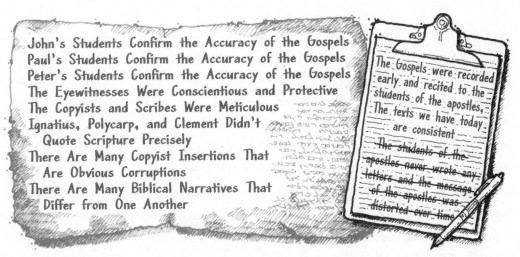

John's Students Confirm the Accuracy of the Gospels
Paul's Students Confirm the Accuracy of the Gospels
Peter's Students Confirm the Accuracy of the Gospels
The Eyewitnesses Were Conscientious and Protective
The Copyists and Scribes Were Meticulous
Ignatius, Polycarp, and Clement Didn't
　　Quote Scripture Precisely
There Are Many Copyist Insertions That
　　Are Obvious Corruptions
There Are Many Biblical Narratives That
　　Differ from One Another

The Gospels were recorded early and recited to the students of the apostles
The texts we have today are consistent

The students of the apostles never wrote any letters and the message of the apostles was distorted over time

Given the record of the second-generation disciples of John, Peter, and Paul, we can have confidence that the essential teachings of the Gospels have remained unchanged for over two thousand years. The first explanation, that the Gospels and other New Testament documents were written early and taught to the students of the apostles, is the most reasonable conclusion, and this explanation is also consistent with the evidence for early dating we examined in chapter 11. The evidence from the chain of custody and the nature of the copyists support the first explanation, and this explanation offers reasonable responses to the challenges offered by skeptics. The second explanation, on the other hand, fails to adequately account for the evidence offered by Ignatius, Polycarp, and Clement. The first explanation is *feasible, straightforward,* and *logical.* It *exhausts* all the evidence we have assembled, and it is *superior* to the alternative explanation. It is, once again, the most reasonable explanation.

THE GOSPELS PASS THE THIRD TEST

We've now evaluated the nature of the gospel eyewitness accounts in three of the four areas in which we evaluate witnesses in criminal trials. The most reasonable inference from the evidence indicates that the gospel writers were *present* and *corroborated.* By studying the chain of custody and the manner in which these records have been preserved over time, we can now draw the reasonable conclusion that they are also *accurate.* Are we ready to say that they are reliable? Almost. There is still one final area we need to examine.

Chapter 14

WERE THEY BIASED?

The one thing we know about the Christians after the death of Jesus
is that they turned to their scriptures to try and make sense of it....
How could Jesus, the Messiah, have been killed as a common criminal?
Christians turned to their scriptures to try and understand it, and they
found passages that refer to the Righteous One of God's suffering death.
But in these passages, such as Isaiah 53 and Psalm 22 and Psalm 61,
the one who is punished or who is killed is also vindicated by God.
Christians came to believe their scriptures that Jesus was the Righteous
One and that God must have vindicated him. And so Christians
came to think of Jesus as one who, even though he had been cruci-
fied, came to be exalted to heaven, much as Elijah and Enoch had in
the Hebrew scriptures.... But if Jesus is exalted, he is no longer dead,
and so Christians started circulating the story of his resurrection.[180]

—Bart Ehrman, New Testament scholar, professor of religious

studies, and author of *Forged: Writing in the Name of God—Why*

the Bible's Authors Are Not Who We Think They Are

THREE MOTIVES

Everyone has a motive. We tend to think of criminals when we hear the word, but jurors must
also consider motive when examining and evaluating eyewitnesses who have testified in a trial.

Jurors learn that they must think about whether or not a witness was "influenced by a factor such as bias or prejudice, a personal relationship with someone involved in the case, or a personal interest in how the case is decided." There are two factors at work in a question like this: *bias* and *motive*. Were the disciples lying about the resurrection, as Bart Ehrman claims? Were their claims based on religious expectation or bias? If so, what was it that they were hoping to gain from this elaborate lie? If the apostles wanted Jesus to be God, an elaborate lie wouldn't actually accomplish this, at least for the apostles. Lies might fool those who weren't there, but they wouldn't fool those who knew better. What did the disciples hope to gain if their stories were false? Let's study the issue of motive and finish our journey with an examination of Christian eyewitness *bias*.

In all my years working homicides, I've come to discover that only three broad motives lie at the heart of any murder. As it turns out, these three motives are also the same driving forces behind other types of misbehavior; they are the reasons why we sometimes think what we shouldn't think, say what we shouldn't say, or do what we shouldn't do.

FINANCIAL GREED

This is often the driving force behind the crimes that I investigate. Some murders, for example, result from a botched robbery. Other murders take place simply because they give the suspect a financial advantage. As an example, I once worked a homicide committed by a husband who didn't want his wife to receive a portion of his retirement.

SEXUAL OR RELATIONAL DESIRE

I've also investigated a number of murders that were sexually (or relationally) motivated. Some sexual attackers murder their victims so they can't testify later. Some murders occur simply because a jealous boyfriend couldn't bear to see his girlfriend dating another man.

PURSUIT OF POWER

Finally, some people commit murders to achieve or maintain a position of power or authority. It might be a rivalry between two people who are trying to get the same promotion. Others have killed simply because the victim dishonored or "disrespected" them in front of a group of peers.

Sex, money, and power are the motives for all the crimes detectives investigate. In fact, these three motives are also behind lesser sins as well. Think about the last time you did something you shouldn't have. If you examine the motivation carefully, you'll probably see that it fits broadly into one of these three categories.

The presence of motive doesn't always mean that a suspect actually committed the crime. Someone might have the motive to do something criminal, yet be able to resist the temptation to act. On the flip side, however, defense attorneys often cite the *lack of motive* when they are making a case for their client's innocence. "Why would my client have done such a thing when it would not benefit him in any way?" That's a fair question and one that we need to ask as we examine the claims of the apostles.

APOSTOLIC MOTIVATION

Did the alleged eyewitnesses of Jesus's life and ministry have an ulterior motive when writing the Gospels? Do we have any good reason to believe that the apostles were driven to lie by one of the three motives we have described? No. There is nothing in history (neither Christian history nor secular history) to suggest that the disciples had anything to gain from their testimony related to Jesus:

THE APOSTLES WERE NOT DRIVEN BY FINANCIAL GAIN

There are many ancient accounts describing the lives of the apostles following the period of time recorded in the book of Acts. Local believers in a variety of ancient communities wrote about the activities of the individual disciples as they preached the gospel across the region. None of these texts describe any of the disciples as men who possessed material wealth. The disciples repeatedly appear as men who were chased from location to location, continually abandoning whatever property they owned and vacating whatever homes they were borrowing. The disciples were accustomed to living in this manner; they decided to leave their homes and families when they first began to follow Jesus. Peter acknowledged as much when he told Jesus, "Behold, we have left our own homes and followed You" (Luke 18:28). The disciples rejected all material wealth, believing that the truth of the gospel provided eternal life, something that was vastly more valuable. Paul described their impoverished financial condition many times, reminding his listeners that the apostles were "both hungry and thirsty, and [were] poorly clothed, and [were] roughly treated, and [were] homeless" (1 Cor. 4:11). The apostles lived "as unknown yet well-known, as dying yet behold, we live; as punished yet not put to death, as sorrowful yet always rejoicing, as poor yet making many rich, as having nothing yet possessing all things" (2 Cor. 6:9–10). If the disciples and apostles were lying for financial gain, their lies didn't seem to be working. Those who watched Paul closely knew that he was dedicated to spiritual life rather than material gain; he "coveted no one's silver or gold or clothes" (Acts 20:33).

The other apostles were in a very similar financial situation. When Peter and John were in Jerusalem in the first half of the first century, they were approached by a poor disabled man who asked them for money. Peter told the man, "I do not possess silver and gold, but what I do have I give to you: In the name of Jesus Christ the Nazarene—walk!" (Acts 3:6). The disciples were consistently described as having chosen a life of material poverty in pursuit of spiritual truth. When James described the rich (as in James 5:1–5), he always did so in the second person. He didn't include himself in their numbers. The apostles never described themselves as wealthy; instead, they warned those who were rich that their wealth could indeed threaten their perspective on eternal matters. Like the other apostolic writers, James described his fellow believers as joyfully impoverished: "Did not God choose the poor of this world to be rich in faith and heirs of the kingdom which He promised to those who love Him?" (James 2:5).

The apostles gained nothing financially from their testimony of Jesus's life and ministry. The New Testament letters of Paul were written very early in history to people who knew Paul personally. If he was lying about his financial situation, his readers would have known it. All the nonbiblical accounts related to the lives of the apostles, whether legitimate or legendary, affirm

Motive

Judges advise juries that they may consider motive as they assess the guilt of defendants:

"The People are not required to prove that the defendant had a motive to commit (any of the crimes/the crime) charged. In reaching your verdict you may, however, consider whether the defendant had a motive."

"Having a motive may be a factor tending to show that the defendant is guilty. Not having a motive may be a factor tending to show the defendant is not guilty" (Section 370, *Judicial Council of California Criminal Jury Instructions*, 2006).

the poverty of the disciples as they traveled the world to proclaim their testimony. The most reasonable inference from the early record of the New Testament documents and the agreement of the nonbiblical record is that the writers of the New Testament were as contentedly penniless as they proclaimed. It is reasonable to conclude that financial greed was not the motive that drove these men to make the claims they made in the Gospels. In fact, they remained impoverished primarily because of their dedication to their testimony.

THE APOSTLES WERE NOT DRIVEN BY SEX OR RELATIONSHIPS

It's equally unreasonable to suggest that the apostles were motivated by lust or relationships. While the New Testament documents say little about the "love lives" of the apostolic eyewitnesses, we do know that Peter was married and had a mother-in-law (Matt. 8:14). Paul confirmed this and suggested that Peter wasn't the only one who was married when, in his letter to the Corinthians, he asked, "Do we not have a right to take along a believing wife, even as the rest of the apostles and the brothers of the Lord and Cephas [Peter]?" (1 Cor. 9:5). The early church fathers also suggested that all of the apostles were married, with the possible exception of the youngest apostle, John. Clement of Alexandria wrote that Peter and Philip had children[181] and that Paul, although married, did not take his wife with him when testifying as an apostle:

> The only reason why he did not take her about with him was that it would have been an inconvenience for his ministry.... [The apostles], in accordance with their particular ministry, devoted themselves to preaching without any distraction, and took their wives with them not as women with whom they had marriage relations, but as sisters, that they might be their fellow-ministers in dealing with housewives.[182]

Clement suggested here that the apostles were not only married, but also denied themselves sexual contact with their wives after the ascension in order to better minister to those they sought to reach with their testimony. Ignatius also referred to the apostles as married men:

For I pray that, being found worthy of God, I may be found at their feet in the kingdom, as at the feet of Abraham, and Isaac, and Jacob; as of Joseph, and Isaiah, and the rest of the prophets; as of Peter, and Paul, and the rest of the apostles, that were married men. For they entered into these marriages not for the sake of appetite, but out of regard for the propagation of mankind.[183]

Like Clement of Alexandria, Ignatius also reported that the apostles held a view of sexuality that placed their testimony ahead of their personal desire. This was affirmed by another early Christian author named Tertullian, who wrote in the early third century:

[The] Apostles, withal, had a "licence" to marry, and lead wives about (with them). They had a "licence," too, to "live by the Gospel."[184]

The apostles had a right to bring their wives with them on their journeys, and some may have done so. In any case, it is clear from both the biblical record and the nonbiblical history that the apostles were careful to live their sexual lives in a manner that was beyond reproach. In fact, while other men within the culture often had more than one wife, the apostles allowed men to rise to leadership only if they limited themselves to one wife (1 Tim. 3:2).

The twelve apostles were not twelve single men in search of a good time. They weren't using their position or testimony to woo the local eligible women. If the apostles were motivated by sexual desire, there is certainly no record of it in the ancient writings of the time and no hint of it in their own texts. They were married men (most likely) who held chastity and sexual purity in high regard. The most reasonable inference, given what we know about the lives of the apostles, is that sexual or relational desire was not the motive that drove these men to make the claims they made in the Gospels.

THE APOSTLES WERE NOT DRIVEN BY THE PURSUIT OF POWER

Some skeptics have argued that the apostles were motivated by a desire to be powerful within their individual religious communities. They will often point to the power that Christian leaders eventually had in Rome when Christianity became the state-sponsored religion in the fourth century. There is no doubt that the popes of the Roman Catholic Church eventually became incredibly powerful both religiously and politically. But when we examine the lives of the first-century apostles, they bear little resemblance to the lives of the Roman Catholic popes.

Power has its perks, not the least of which is the ability to protect oneself. This kind of power was never available to the apostles. The early Christian movement immediately faced hostility from those who actually did possess power in the first century. Rumors quickly spread that the Christians practiced rituals that offended Roman sensibilities and were unwilling to worship Emperor Nero as divine. Tacitus recorded Nero's response:

> Consequently, to get rid of the report, Nero fastened the guilt and inflicted the most exquisite tortures on a class hated for their abominations, called Christians by the populace. Christus, from whom the name had its origin, suffered the extreme penalty during the reign of Tiberius at the hands of one of our procurators, Pontius Pilatus, and a most mischievous superstition, thus checked for the moment, again broke out not only in Judaea, the first source of the evil, but even in Rome, where all things hideous and shameful from every part of the world find their centre and become popular. Accordingly, an arrest was first made of all who pleaded guilty; then, upon their information, an immense multitude was convicted, not so much of the crime of firing the city, as of hatred against mankind. Mockery of every sort was added to their deaths. Covered with the skins of beasts, they were torn by dogs and perished, or were nailed to crosses, or were doomed to the flames and burnt, to serve as a nightly illumination, when daylight had expired.[185]

At this early point in Christian history, leadership within the Christian community was a liability rather than an asset. Prominent believers and leaders who openly admitted their allegiance to Jesus ("pleaded guilty") and refused to recant this allegiance were the first to die. It was during this time in history when Peter and Paul were executed in Rome, but they weren't the only apostles whose prominence as Christian leaders cost them their lives. The nonbiblical histories and writings related to the lives and ministries of the twelve disciples consistently proclaimed that the apostles were persecuted and eventually martyred for their testimony. The apostolic eyewitnesses refused to change their testimony about what they saw, even though they faced unimaginable torture and execution. Only John appears to have escaped martyrdom, but he, too, was exiled and persecuted for his position as an apostle.

Persecution was the uniform experience of the apostles, long before they were finally executed for their faith. Paul's experience, as he told it in his letter to the Corinthians, was sadly normative for the apostles:

> *Five times I received from the Jews thirty-nine lashes. Three times I was beaten with rods, once I was stoned, three times I was shipwrecked, a night and a day I have spent in the deep. I have been on frequent journeys, in dangers from rivers, dangers from robbers, dangers from my countrymen, dangers from the Gentiles, dangers in the city, dangers in the wilderness, dangers on the sea, dangers among false brethren; I have been in labor and hardship, through many sleepless nights, in hunger and thirst, often without food, in cold and exposure. Apart from such external things, there is the daily pressure upon me of concern for all the churches. (2 Cor. 11:24–28)*

Bias and Prejudice

Bias:

"An inclination of temperament or outlook; especially a personal and sometimes unreasoned judgment."

Prejudice:

"(1): Preconceived judgment or opinion (2): An adverse opinion or leaning formed without just grounds or before sufficient knowledge."

(*Merriam-Webster's Collegiate Dictionary*, 11th edition)

As the apostles rose to positions of leadership, they made themselves the target of persecution and abuse. The more prominent they became, the more they risked death at the hands of their adversaries. The most reasonable inference, given what we know about their deaths, is that the pursuit of power and position was not the motive that drove these men to make the claims they made in the Gospels.

If a defense attorney were representing any of the apostles, defending them against the accusation that they lied about their testimony, the attorney could fairly ask the question "Why would my client have done such a thing when it would not benefit him in any way?" Certainly there was no benefit to any of the apostles in the three areas we would expect to motivate such a lie.

FREE FROM ULTERIOR MOTIVE

Motive is a key factor that jurors must assess when evaluating the reliability of witnesses. That's why judges advise jurors to ask questions like "Was the witness promised immunity or leniency in exchange for his or her testimony?" (See chapter 4.) We need to know if something other than the simple desire to report the truth motivated the witnesses to say what they said. As we examine the motives of the gospel writers, it's clear that the forces that typically compel people to lie didn't drive the authors. The apostles were free from ulterior motive.

But what about bias? Even if they didn't possess one of these three self-serving motives, how do we know that the gospel writers weren't simply biased? Judges encourage jurors to find out if the witness was "influenced by a factor such as bias or prejudice, a personal relationship with someone involved in the case, or a personal interest in how the case is decided." If a witness held a *preconception* or *partiality* as he or she watched the event, that bias may have influenced how the witness interpreted what he or she saw. Bias can cause people to see something *incorrectly*. Was this the case with the apostles?

SO, IS THIS WHY SOME CONTINUE TO DENY IT?

Some skeptics base their distrust of the Gospels (and of the nonbiblical accounts of the apostles' lives following Jesus's ascension) on the possible presence of bias. Even though there is no evidence to suggest that the apostles were motivated by greed, lust, or power, critics are still suspicious of the gospel accounts. Let's look at the reasons behind their suspicions and include them in our final evaluation utilizing abductive reasoning.

THE GOSPELS WERE WRITTEN BY CHRISTIANS

Skeptics have argued that the Gospels cannot be trusted because they were not authored by *objective* non-Christians. The New Testament records, according to this view, were written by biased Christians who were trying to convince us of their religious perspective. Critics claim that these Christians observed the events through a charged religious lens and then reported the events from this viewpoint. As a result, the gospel narratives are biased and unreliable.

BUT ...

This is not an accurate description of what occurred in the first century as the gospel eyewitnesses observed the life and ministry of Jesus. Let me give you an example from one of my cases to illustrate the point. Many years ago, when I was working robberies, I had a case in which a local bank was robbed. The suspect (Mark Hill) entered the bank in the afternoon and waited in line to approach the teller. He stood in the lobby for two or three minutes, waiting to walk up to the counter, where he eventually gave the teller a "demand note" and flashed a handgun in his waistband. While he was waiting for the opportunity, a bank employee (Kathy Smalley) saw him standing in line. Kathy was working as an assistant manager and had a desk located in the lobby, adjacent to the teller line. She recognized Mark as he waited for his turn. Kathy had attended high school with Mark and recognized him because he was a talented (and popular) athlete. Even though many years had passed, Kathy still recognized him with certainty. Mark, on the other hand, was focused as he waited to rob the bank. He never even looked up to see Kathy watching him. He eventually approached the teller (Debra Camacho) and completed his robbery. Debra gave Mark the money he demanded and then pushed the silent alarm button as he turned to walk away. She motioned quickly to Kathy, who was sitting within her view.

Kathy recognized the fact that Debra had just been robbed. She couldn't believe it. She never considered Mark to be the kind of person who would commit a robbery. In fact, she thought Mark got an athletic scholarship after high school and assumed he became a successful athlete and college graduate. When she first saw Mark enter the lobby, she never thought he was about to commit a robbery. After the fact, however, she was certain that Mark was the robber. She was now a *true believer* in Mark's guilt. After all, she saw it with her own eyes. You might say that Kathy was now a "Mark Hillian" believer related to the robbery. So let me ask you a question. Should I trust her testimony? Isn't she too biased to be a reliable witness? Kathy is not neutral about what she saw in the bank. She has a perspective and an opinion about the identity of the robber. She's a Mark Hillian believer; she is certain that of all the possible truths related to who committed the robbery, only one is accurate. If she's this biased, how can I trust what she has to say?

Can you see how ridiculous this concern would be? Kathy didn't start off with a bias against Mark or a presupposition that tainted her observations. In fact, she was shocked to find that Mark was capable of committing such a crime. She was not a "Mark Hillian" believer until *after* the fact.

In a similar way, the authors of the Gospels were not "Christian" believers until *after* they observed the life and ministry of Jesus. Much has been written about the fact that Jews in first-century Palestine were looking for a Messiah who would save them from Roman oppression. They were expecting a military liberator, not a spiritual savior. Even Bart Erhman admits that the disciples found themselves asking the question "How could Jesus, the Messiah, have been killed as a common criminal?" They didn't expect Jesus (as the military messiah) to die, and they certainly didn't expect Him to come back to life.

The Gospels are filled with examples of the disciples misunderstanding the predictions and proclamations of Jesus. There are many examples of doubt and hesitancy on the part of those who witnessed Jesus's life. The skeptical disciples continually asked Jesus for clarification, and Thomas, after spending three years with Jesus, still wouldn't believe His prediction of the resurrection until he saw Jesus with his own eyes and touched Jesus with his own hands.

The apostles became convinced of Jesus's deity *after* they observed His life and resurrection. They didn't start off as Christians any more than Kathy started off as a "Mark Hillian." The disciples ended up as Christians (certain that Jesus was God) as a result of their observations, just as Kathy ended up as a "Mark Hillian" (certain that he was the robber) as a result of her observations. The disciples were not prejudicially biased; they were evidentially certain.

THE DEATH NARRATIVES OF THE APOSTLES WERE WRITTEN BY CHRISTIANS

Skeptics have also argued that little or no weight can be given to the fact that the apostles were allegedly martyred for their testimony because the "histories" that describe their martyrdom are largely Christian legends written by believers. How do we even know that these martyrdoms really occurred if the only records we have are biased stories and legends filled with miraculous tales?

BUT ...

As described in chapter 1, we can't allow the description of miraculous occurrences to automatically disqualify the ancient accounts. If we are going to claim that the ancient stories are biased (because they were written by Christians), we cannot reject them with a bias of our own (against supernaturalism). While it is true that some accounts related to the martyrdom of the apostles are more reliable than others, we have no reason to reject all of them as historically inaccurate. The deaths of Peter, Paul, James, and John are very well attested, and the remaining martyrdom accounts of the apostles (with the possible exception of Matthias and Philip) are sufficiently documented to provide us with confidence that we know the truth about their deaths.

Most importantly, there aren't any ancient non-Christian accounts that contradict the claims of the Christian authors who wrote about the deaths of the eyewitness disciples. It's not as though we have competing accounts related to the testimony of these men. We don't have ancient Christians on one side, claiming that the apostles died because they proclaimed the truth about Jesus and refused to recant their testimony, and ancient non-Christians on the other side, claiming that the apostles eventually confessed that it was all a lie. There are no ancient authors claiming anything other than what the Christians described; there are no contradictory accounts that portray the apostles as liars who confessed their lies when pressured. The unanimous testimony of antiquity is that the early Christian eyewitnesses suffered for their testimony but stayed the course. They didn't flinch, and they never changed their story.

THE MOST REASONABLE CONCLUSION

Abductive reasoning can help us decide between two possible conclusions related to the bias or motive that the apostolic eyewitnesses may have had when writing their Gospels or testifying to their observations. Let's list the evidence one final time, alongside the two possible explanations that can account for what we have seen so far:

The Apostles Were Not Driven by Financial Gain

The Apostles Were Not Driven by Sex or Relationship

The Apostles Were Not Driven by the Pursuit of Power

The Gospels Were Written by Christians

The Death Narratives of the Apostles Were Written by Christians

The gospel writers reported what they actually observed

The gospel writers had ulterior motives that drove them to make false claims to accomplish a particular goal

The apostles lacked evil intent. They simply couldn't benefit from lying about what they saw. In fact, they would have been far better off if they had kept their mouths shut. What could they possibly have gained from this elaborate lie? It's clear that the gospel writers appeared to be more concerned about eternal life than material gain. Could a lie about Jesus make His spiritual claims true? Does it make sense that the disciples would forsake everything for spiritual claims they knew were untrue? The evidence from history once again supports the first explanation better than the second. It offers reasonable responses to the challenges offered by skeptics. The second explanation, on the other hand, is simply unable to account adequately for the lack of motive on the part of the apostles. The first explanation is *feasible*, *straightforward*, and *logical*. It *exhausts* all the evidence we have assembled, and it is *superior* to the alternative explanation. It is, once again, the most reasonable explanation.

THE GOSPELS PASS THE LAST TEST

We've examined the four important areas that jurors must consider when determining the reliability of eyewitnesses. The most reasonable inference is that the gospel writers were *present, corroborated, accurate,* and *unbiased.* If this is the case, we can conclude with confidence that their testimony is *reliable.* We've done the *heavy lifting* needed to determine the reliability of these accounts; we've been diligent and faithful as jurors and have considered the evidence. It's time to make a decision.

BECOMING A "TWO DECISION" CHRISTIAN

Santiago Ortega turned the key and started his tired 1975 Triumph Tr6. The engine sputtered and backfired, spouting smoke into the small parking lot adjacent to the cheap hotel Santiago called home. Santiago was addicted to rock cocaine, and his addiction preoccupied much of his day. He was either smoking rock or trying to find a way to pay for it, and he was increasingly desperate.

He hadn't seen his wife in weeks. His family was scattered across the county and wouldn't offer him refuge, especially now. His father and brother were in federal prison for bank robbery, and sadly, Santiago was following in their footsteps. He'd already committed seven bank robberies in Los Angeles County before he did his first one in our city. I was working on our undercover surveillance team at the time, and an informant gave us a tip that led us to Santiago's hotel. We were sitting in the parking lot when Santiago fired up his battered and weary convertible.

While Santiago looked like the man in the bank surveillance photographs, we weren't sure if he was the robber we were looking for. We would find out shortly. Santiago backed out of the parking lot and drove into the city of Long Beach. Our team carefully followed him; five officers and a sergeant trailing our suspect in a series of unremarkable midsized cars. Santiago didn't make it far before he succumbed to his addiction. At the first traffic light Santiago fired up a homemade rock pipe and filled the interior of his small car with smoke. He was nearly invisible in the hazy capsule of the Triumph. Somehow he managed to drive, bathed in smoke, without ever rolling down his windows. He continued for approximately two miles until he came to a Home Savings and Loan.

Santiago parked his car at the edge of the parking lot, just out of view from the bank doors. He exited, smoothed out his shirt, and pressed down his hair. He looked about the parking lot nervously as he walked toward the bank entrance. One of our team members, dressed in jeans and a T-shirt, jumped out of his car and followed Santiago into the business. He communicated to the rest of our team via his portable radio. Like Mark Hill, Santiago was a "demand-note" bank robber. In his past robberies, he never had to show his gun to the tellers; his note was enough to cause them to comply. Today's teller was no exception. She emptied her drawer and gave Santiago the money; he quickly turned and walked from the bank. The customers in the lobby were completely unaware that a robbery had even occurred.

But my partner knew. He quickly radioed from the interior of the bank and told us that Santiago was, in fact, a bank robber. By this time, Santiago had already run to the Triumph and was now fleeing the parking lot. Our team quickly moved in behind him. In situations like these, we would typically conduct a tactical arrest at the nearest red light, maneuvering our cars into position to prevent the suspect's escape. But Santiago now had a heightened awareness of his surroundings, and he became suspicious of one of our surveillance vehicles. The chase was on.

Intoxicated rock-cocaine addicts and aging Triumphs are a recipe for disaster, especially when they are partnered in an effort to run from the police. Santiago crashed the car in the first mile of the pursuit. I was the case agent; it was my responsibility to handcuff Santiago and drive him back to the police station for booking. Along the way I was able to talk to him about his life and his future. I began with a simple observation.

"Santiago, you look terrible," I said.

"I know," he replied, shaking his head. To his credit, Santiago Ortega was a broken man, remorseful and repentant about his life and crime spree.

"How long did you think you could go on like this?" I asked the question as a matter of genuine concern. Santiago's eyes were red and infected; he was gaunt and disheveled. He looked like he hadn't eaten in days.

"I knew it was coming to an end, really I did. I don't even know how it got this crazy. I'm not really a bad person. I know better." He was remarkably talkative and honest.

"So why are you doing this?" I asked.

"I'm a junkie. I want to stop. But I always end up back here. You know, I'm actually married and my wife is a beautiful lady. She left me when I started up again." Santiago began to cry, and his tears caused him to wince in the pain from his infected eyes. "A couple years ago I went with her to a crusade and I got saved. She did too. But here I am, still messed up." Santiago told me about his experience at the large evangelistic stadium event he attended. He told me that he was moved by what the preacher said at that event, and he accepted the invitation to walk down from the stands and become a follower of Jesus. He thought his decision that night would change his life forever.

"So I guess you probably think I'm some kind of hypocrite, right? Just another messed-up Christian." He didn't know that he was talking to a follower of Jesus.

Santiago made a decision to trust Jesus for his salvation, but he never made a decision to examine the life and teaching of Jesus evidentially. Santiago failed to make a second decision to examine what he believed. He was unable to see his faith as anything more than *subjective opinion* as he struggled to live in a world of *objective facts*. As a result, his *beliefs* eventually surrendered to the *facts* of his situation and the pressures of his addiction. He allowed his friends and family situation to influence him, rather than becoming a source of inspiration and truth for his family and neighborhood. Santiago was a one-decision Christian, and that decision was unsupported by a reasonable examination of the evidence.

I wrote back and forth with Santiago in the years that followed. He was ultimately convicted and sentenced to many years in federal prison. He finally found himself in a place where he had the time and opportunity to examine the evidence for Christianity.

DECISIONS, "BELIEF THAT," AND "BELIEF IN"

My journey was just the opposite of Santiago Ortega's. I decided to investigate the claims of Christianity (to see if they could be defended) *before* I ever decided to call myself a Christian. My investigation (some of which I described in section 2) led me to conclude that the Gospels were reliable. But this conclusion presented me with a dilemma. When the jury in chapter 4 established that Jerry Strickland was a reliable witness, they trusted his testimony related to the identity of the robber. I now had to take a similar step with the reliable gospel eyewitnesses. It's one thing, however, to accept the historicity of locations or key characters in the biblical narrative; it's another to accept what the Gospels were telling me about Jesus. Did Jesus really demonstrate His deity as the gospel eyewitnesses claimed? Did He truly rise from the dead? Did He speak the truth about who He was and about the nature of eternal life? I understood that deciding in favor of the most reasonable inference would require me to release my naturalistic presuppositions entirely. C. S. Lewis was correct; the claims about Jesus, if true, were of infinite importance. This decision would likely change my life forever.

I knew I could never take a blind leap of faith. For me, the decision to move beyond "belief that" to "belief in" needed to be a reasonable decision based on the evidence. I ask jurors to do this every time I present a case—to assemble the circumstantial evidence and draw the most reasonable inference from what they have examined. That's what I did as I assembled the cumulative case for the reliability of the Gospels:

I knew that my concerns about the Gospels had always been rooted in the miraculous events the accounts described. Philosophical naturalism prevented me from taking miracles seriously. But the apostles claimed to see miracles, and in every way that we typically evaluate eyewitnesses, the gospel authors passed the test.

I can remember the day that I finally surrendered my naturalistic biases and moved from "belief that" to "belief in." I was sitting in a church service with my wife. I don't remember exactly what the pastor was talking about, but I remember leaning over and telling my wife that I was a believer. Much like Mark Walker, the officer who trusted in his bulletproof vest, in that singular moment I moved from believing *that* the Gospels were reliable eyewitness accounts to trusting *in* what they told me about Jesus.

The gospel eyewitnesses had something very specific to say about Jesus. They did not give their lives sacrificially for personal *opinions* about God; they gave their lives because their claims were an objective matter of life and death. They knew that Jesus offered more than a guideline for personal behavior. They understood that Jesus was "the way, and the truth, and the life" and that "no one comes to the Father but through" Him (John 14:6). The apostolic eyewitnesses gave their lives to help us understand that we, as fallen, imperfect humans, are in desperate need of a Savior. They died as martyrs trying to show us that Jesus was, in fact, the Savior who could provide forgiveness for our imperfection. Peter was clear about this when testifying to others:

> *You know of Jesus of Nazareth, how God anointed Him with the Holy Spirit and with power, and how He went about doing good and healing all who were oppressed by the devil, for God was with Him. We are witnesses of all the things He did both in the land of the Jews and in Jerusalem. They also put Him to death by hanging Him on a cross. God raised Him up on the third day and granted that He become visible, not to all the people, but to witnesses who were chosen beforehand by God, that is, to us who ate and drank with Him after He arose from the dead. And He ordered us to preach to the people, and solemnly to testify that this is the One who has been appointed by God as Judge of the living and the dead. Of Him all the prophets bear witness that through His name everyone who believes in Him receives forgiveness of sins. (Acts 10:38–43)*

The apostles recognized that their message was a life-saving cure for what was (and is) killing all of us; they gave their lives to save ours, so we could save even more. When I recognized the power of this message, I moved from "belief that" to "belief in." People started to notice a change almost immediately. It wasn't as though I was trying hard to behave differently or follow a new set of rules; I didn't even know all the "rules" when I first decided to trust Christ. But I did know this: I was grateful. I began to understand not only the true nature of Jesus, but also the true nature of my own fallen condition. It's hard not to see your own imperfection when you are confronted with the perfect God of the universe. As I came to appreciate my own need for forgiveness and what Jesus did to accomplish this for me, I became truly grateful and optimistic for the first time in my life. I had been a cop for about eight years prior to being a Christian. In that time, I slowly lost my faith in people. I was suspicious; I considered everyone to be a liar and capable of horrific behavior. Nothing surprised me when it came to the depravity of humanity. I trusted no one and thought of myself as superior to the vast majority of people I encountered. I was cocky, cynical, and distant. My wife and kids were my entire world. I had a few acquaintances who were also police officers, but few other friends. My heart was shrinking and growing harder with every case I worked and with every passing year. None of this bothered me in the slightest. In fact, I saw my suspicion as a virtue.

That all changed when I put my faith *in* Jesus. As I began to understand my need and the gift I had been given, my compassion and patience grew. As someone who had been forgiven, I now developed the capacity to forgive. My excitement became contagious. It spilled over into everything I said and did. My partners noticed it, even though I was careful in the early days to hide my conversion from them. My wife was perhaps the most surprised by all of this. She was raised in a Christian environment but patiently accepted my resistance and growing cynicism for the first seventeen years of our relationship. She was about to see my life (and hers) change dramatically. Looking back at it sixteen years later, she is still amazed at the transformation. The truth about Jesus impacted every aspect of our lives as I became consumed by the desire to learn more about Him. I slept less, studied more, worked with more urgency, and loved others in a way that I had never loved before. I wanted to share what I had discovered with the people in my world. Everyone I came in contact with eventually heard about the gospel. I became known as a vocal Christian. I entered seminary, became a pastor, and even planted a small church. Over the past sixteen years, as I have studied the eyewitness accounts, I have become more and more confident in their reliability and message. This confidence has motivated me to defend and share the truth.

THE IMPORTANCE OF BECOMING A *TWO-DECISION* CHRISTIAN

In televised criminal cases, the jurors are sometimes interviewed following their decision. Some make a second decision when approached by reporters. They choose to make a case for why they voted the way they did. Not every juror decides to defend his or her decision, but those who do find that they are far more likely to persuade others and grow in their own personal confidence related to their decision. Had Santiago Ortega made the decision to investigate and defend what he believed, I can't help but wonder if he would also have been able to persuade those around him or at least grow in his own personal confidence and ability to resist the influence of others.

When I decided to believe what the gospel writers were telling me, I also decided to become a Christian case maker. The second decision was just as important as the first. I began modestly; I started an inexpensive website (ColdCaseChristianity.com) and posted my own investigations in a variety of areas. When I was a youth pastor, I also posted the lessons and messages I presented to my students. Eventually, I started a podcast. Now I've written a book. At first, like many Christians, I was uncomfortable defending the claims of Christianity. How would I ever learn enough (or know enough) to be an effective case maker? Don't I need a doctorate in philosophy or Christian apologetics? Shouldn't I be an "expert" of some sort before trying to defend what I believe?

Jurors aren't experts, yet they are required to make the most important decision in the courtroom. In fact, the experts introduced by the prosecution or the defense never cast a single vote. Our justice system trusts that folks like you and me can examine the testimony of experts and come to a reasonable conclusion about the truth. One of the jurors will even become a leader in the jury room. As the "foreperson," chosen by the other jurors, this man or woman will shepherd the deliberations and eventually present the decision to the judge. You don't have to be an expert to serve on a jury or lead the jury as a foreperson. Jurors need to be able to listen to the experts, carefully evaluate the evidence, and draw the most reasonable inference. Jurors don't need to be experts in the field under consideration; they simply need to be attentive, conscientious, and willing to get in the game.

And that's all we need to be effective Christian case makers: attentive, conscientious, and willing to get in the game. As it turns out, each of us is already an expert of one kind or another. We've got life experiences we can draw upon for the expertise we'll need to answer the challenges of skeptics, and we can make the conscious decision to become better Christian *case makers*. It's time well spent and an important part of our identity as Christians.

THE DANGER OF BECOMING AN *ABBREVIATED* CHRISTIAN

Many of us have neglected our duty in this area. In fact, we've been unable to see our duty in the first place. We've become *abbreviated* Christians. Let me explain. Most of us understand the importance of evangelism in the life of Christians. Jesus told the apostles to "make disciples of all the nations" and to instruct these disciples to obey everything that He taught (Matt. 28:16–20). We've come to call this the "Great Commission." We are clearly commanded to make disciples, just as the apostles did in their own generation. As a result, Christians typically feel that they have been called to evangelism of some sort, even though many of us feel ill equipped to share our faith.

Paul seemed to recognize this and discussed evangelism as a matter of gifting. When describing all of us as members of the church, Paul said that God gave "*some* as apostles, and *some* as prophets, and *some* as evangelists, and *some* as pastors and teachers, for the equipping of the saints for the work of service, to the building up of the body of Christ" (Eph. 4:11–12). Not everyone is a pastor or a prophet. Some of us are gifted in this area and some are not. In a similar way, only some of us are gifted as evangelists; not everyone has the ability to share his or her faith like Billy Graham. I've often been comforted by these words from Paul when struggling to begin a conversation about Christianity.

But the New Testament authors, while recognizing that not all of us are gifted to be evangelists, described a responsibility that does apply to each and every one of us as Christians. Peter said that no one is allowed to relegate his or her duty as a Christian case maker. According to Peter, *all* of us need to "be prepared to give an answer to everyone who asks [us] to give the reason for the hope that [we] have" (1 Pet. 3:15 NIV). While only some of us are gifted and called to be evangelists, all of us are called to be *case makers*. It's our duty as Christians. We need to stop thinking of ourselves in an abbreviated manner. As biblical, New Testament believers, we aren't just "Christians"; we are "case-making Christians." We can't allow ourselves to get comfortable and relegate the hard work of defending the faith to those who write books on the topic.

Some of us prepare meals for a living. The world is filled with popular and proficient chefs who make a living preparing meals for restaurants or television programs. We recognize these chefs, and we can learn something from their recipes and experiences. But even if you aren't a professional chef, I bet you know how to prepare a meal. Meal preparation is an important part of living. Yes, some of us are professional chefs; but the rest of us need to be able to cook if we want to survive. In a similar way, some of us make a living preparing a defense for Christianity. The rest of us can learn a lot from the arguments and presentations of professional "Christian apologists." But that doesn't get us off the hook. All of us, as Christians, need to be able to prepare a defense for what we believe. It's just as important as preparing our daily meals. Our meals may not be as creative or flamboyant as those prepared by professional chefs, but they are typically sufficient and satisfying. Our personal defense of Christianity may not be as robust as what can be offered by a professional apologist, but it can be just as powerful and persuasive.

Each of us has to answer God's call on our lives as *two-decision* Christians. If you've already decided to believe the Gospels, take a second step and decide to defend them. Become a *case-making* Christian; work in your profession, live your life faithfully, devote yourself to the truth, and steadily prepare yourself to make a defense for what you believe. I want to encourage you to make that second decision. Start small. Read and study. Engage your friends. Start a blog or host a website. Volunteer to teach a class at your church. *Get in the game.*

My life as a Christian took flight the minute I decided to become a *case maker*. God cleverly used all my experiences as a detective to give me a perspective that I've tried to share with you in the pages of this book. It's my hope that the skeptics who read this might at least lay down their presuppositions long enough to recognize that there is a substantive circumstantial case supporting the reliability of the gospel writers. It's also my hope that Christians who read this book will be encouraged to know that God can use you right now, in this very moment, to make a case for the truth.

WITNESSES AND RESOURCES

Compiling the resources necessary to make the case

Case Files

EXPERT WITNESSES

I've yet to bring an investigation to trial without the assistance of expert witnesses who testified about specific and detailed aspects of the evidence. The following expert witnesses may be called to the stand as you make a case for the claims of Christianity.

Chapter 1:
DON'T BE A "KNOW-IT-ALL"

J. P. Moreland and William Lane Craig

Will testify to the philosophical biases and presuppositions that impact issues of faith and reason in their book, *Philosophical Foundations for a Christian Worldview* (InterVarsity Press, 2003).

Chapter 2:
LEARN HOW TO "INFER"

Gary Habermas and Michael Licona

Will testify to the *minimal facts* and evidences related to the resurrection in their book, *The Case for the Resurrection of Jesus* (Kregel, 2004).

Chapter 3:
THINK "CIRCUMSTANTIALLY"

William Lane Craig

Will testify to the causal evidence related to the cosmological argument in his book *The Kalām Cosmological Argument* (Wipf & Stock, 2000).

John Leslie

Will testify to the fine-tuning evidence related to the anthropic principle in his book *Universes* (Taylor & Francis, 2002).

Neil Manson

Will testify to the design evidence related to the teleological argument in his book *God and Design: The Teleological Argument and Modern Science* (Routledge, 2003).

Paul Copan and Mark Linville

Will testify to the moral evidence related to the axiological argument in their book *The Moral Argument* (Continuum Publishers, 2013).

Chapter 4:
TEST YOUR WITNESSES

Richard Bauckham

Will testify to the nature of the New Testament Gospels as eyewitness accounts of the life of Jesus in his book *Jesus and the Eyewitnesses: The Gospels as Eyewitness Testimony* (Eerdmans, 2006).

Bruce Metzger

Will testify to the early collection of the eyewitness accounts and their formation into the New Testament in his book *The Canon of the New Testament: Its Origin, Development, and Significance* (Oxford University Press, 1997).

Chapter 5:
HANG ON EVERY WORD

Craig Blomberg

Will testify to the "forensic" methods of "textual criticism" that can be employed to study the Gospels and discuss some of the conclusions that can be drawn from this effort in his book *The Historical Reliability of the Gospels* (InterVarsity Press, 2007).

Daniel B. Wallace

Will testify to what can be learned "forensically" about the early transmission of the New Testament documents in the compilation *Revisiting the Corruption of the New Testament: Manuscript, Patristic, and Apocryphal Evidence* (Kregel, 2011).

Chapter 6:
SEPARATE ARTIFACTS FROM EVIDENCE

Michelle Brown

Will testify to the early formation of the biblical text, while exhibiting a number of ancient biblical manuscripts in her book *In the Beginning: Bibles before the Year 1000* (Smithsonian, 2006).

Philip Comfort

Will testify to the nature of the early New Testament papyrus manuscripts and the methodology used to re-create the original accounts in his book *Early Manuscripts & Modern Translations of the New Testament* (Wipf & Stock, 2001).

Chapter 7:
RESIST CONSPIRACY THEORIES

William McBirnie

Will testify to the nature of the lives and deaths of the apostles who claimed to see the resurrection of Jesus in his book *The Search for the Twelve Apostles* (Tyndale, 2008).

Chapter 8:
RESPECT THE "CHAIN OF CUSTODY"

Mark D. Roberts

Will testify to the historical manuscript evidence and early appearance of the biblical record in his book *Can We Trust the Gospels? Investigating the Reliability of Matthew, Mark, Luke, and John* (Crossway, 2007).

Mike Aquilina

Will testify to the writings and teachings of the early church fathers in his book *The Fathers of the Church, Expanded Edition* (Our Sunday Visitor, November 2006).

Chapter 9:
KNOW WHEN "ENOUGH IS ENOUGH"

David Wolfe

Will testify to how we come to "know" something is true in his book, *Epistemology: The Justification of Belief* (InterVarsity Press, 1983).

William Rowe

Will testify to the classic atheist presentations of the "problem of evil" and the classic defenses (theodicies) that have been offered by theists in his book *God and the Problem of Evil* (Wiley-Blackwell, 2001).

Chapter 10:
PREPARE FOR AN ATTACK

Craig Evans

Will testify to the assumptions and dubious sources that account for some of the theories and tactics that have been employed by skeptics in *Fabricating Jesus: How Modern Scholars Distort the Gospels* (InterVarsity Press, 2006).

Gregory Koukl

Will testify to successful and reasoned approaches that can be employed by those who seek to defend the Christian worldview in *Tactics: A Game Plan for Discussing Your Christian Convictions* (Zondervan, 2009).

Chapter 11:
WERE THEY PRESENT?

Jean Carmignac

Will testify to the Semitic origin of the synoptic gospels and how they were formed amid the Jewish culture of the first half of the first century in his book, *Birth of the Synoptic Gospels* (Franciscan Herald Press, October 1987).

John Wenham

Will testify to an alternate theory about the early dating of the Gospels (that places Matthew ahead of Mark) by comparing the Gospels to one another and to the writings and records of the church fathers in his book *Redating Matthew, Mark and Luke: A Fresh Assault on the Synoptic Problem* (InterVarsity Press, March 1992).

Chapter 12:
WERE THEY CORROBORATED?

Peter Schafer

Will testify to the ancient Jewish references to Jesus that are scattered throughout the Talmud in his book *Jesus in the Talmud* (Princeton University Press, 2009).

R. T. France

Will testify to the nonbiblical ancient sources that corroborate the existence of Jesus in his book *The Evidence for Jesus* (Regent College, 2006).

John McRay

Will testify to the archaeological corroboration of the New Testament in his book *Archaeology and the New Testament* (Baker, 2008).

Shimon Gibson

Will testify (as an archaeologist) to the archaeological evidence that corroborates the final days of Jesus's life in his book *The Final Days of Jesus: The Archaeological Evidence* (HarperCollins, 2009).

Chapter 13:
WERE THEY ACCURATE?

Michael Holmes

Will testify to the writings of the students of the apostles in his book *The Apostolic Fathers: Greek Texts and English Translations* (Baker, 2007).

Justo González

Will testify to the early history of Christianity and many of the characters who played a part in the "chain of custody" in his book *Story of Christianity: Volume 1, The Early Church to the Dawn of the Reformation* (HarperOne, 2010).

Nicholas Perrin

Will testify to the transmission (and copying) of the gospel accounts in his book *Lost in Transmission? What We Can Know About the Words of Jesus* (Thomas Nelson, 2007).

Chapter 14:
WERE THEY BIASED?

C. Bernard Ruffin

Will testify to the lives and martyrdoms of the apostles in his book *The Twelve: The Lives of the Apostles after Calvary* (Our Sunday Visitor, 1998).

Josh and Sean McDowell

Will testify to the reasonable conclusions that can be drawn about the testimony of the apostles in their book *Evidence for the Resurrection* (Regal, 2009).

Case Files

ASSISTING OFFICERS

I'm not the first police officer or detective to investigate the evidence related to the gospel eyewitnesses and conclude that that they are reliable. Many detectives have used their expertise in evidence to come to the same conclusion. The following detectives are among the many who have assisted the cause of Christianity over the years by contributing their expertise.

Sir Robert Anderson

Assistant Commissioner (Deceased), London Metropolitan Police

Sir Robert Anderson was a theologian and author of numerous books, including *The Coming Prince, The Bible and Modern Criticism,* and *A Doubter's Doubts about Science and Religion.*

Gregory Allen Doyle

Police Sergeant (Retired), Upland Police Department (California)

Gregory Doyle is a writer, worship leader, and the author of *The Sting of the Gadfly, God Is Not an Option,* and *The Stinging Salve: A Hearty Concoction of Essays, Short Stories, Songs, Poems, and Thoughts Mostly about God, Faith, and Eternal Life.*

Michael Dye

Deputy Sheriff, Volusa County Sheriff's Office (Florida), and Marshal with the United States Marshals Service in Los Angeles

Michael Dye is a speaker and the author of *The PeaceKeepers: A Bible Study for Law Enforcement Officers* (www.christianlawenforcement.com). Michael also serves on the Board of Directors for the Fellowship of Christian Peace Officers (www.fcpo.org), a ministry that provides support and accountability to Christian officers to help them become more effective witnesses for Christ as they disciple and train others to carry out the Great Commission.

Conrad Jensen

Deputy Inspector (Deceased), New York City Police Department

Conrad Jensen was a speaker and author. He served as a captain in the twenty-third precinct and founded an evangelical organization working with the youth gangs in east Harlem. After his retirement in 1964, the American Tract Society asked him to write a book, *26 Years on the Losing Side*, in an effort to "stimulate concerted prayer that our nation under God might return to the Scriptural foundations upon which it was built."

Mark Kroeker

Deputy Chief (Retired), Los Angeles Police Department, Chief of Police (Retired), Portland Police Department), United Nations Deputy Police Commissioner (Operations) in Bosnia and Herzegovina (Reassigned), Civilian Police Commissioner for the United Nations' Peacekeeping Mission in Liberia (Reassigned)

Mark Kroeker is a speaker and writer. He founded and continues to serve as the chairman of the World Children's Transplant Fund (wctf.org), a nonprofit organization dedicated to the development of pediatric organ transplantation around the world.

Tony Miano
Investigator and Officer (Retired), Los Angeles County Sheriff's Department
Tony Miano is a sheriff's chaplain and was the founder and director of Ten-Four Ministries (tenfourministries.org), providing practical and spiritual support to the law enforcement community. He is presently the director of the Ambassador's Alliance, an outreach of Living Waters Ministry (www.livingwaters.com). He authored *Take Up the Shield: Comparing the Uniform of the Police Officer and the Armor of God.*

John Moreno
Police Lieutenant (Retired), New York City Police Department
John Moreno is a lay minister, speaker, author, and founder of Catholic Lay Preachers (www.catholiclaypreachers.com), a small group of experienced lay speakers offering their talents to religious organizations. He is the author of *A Spirituality for Police Officers.*

Randy Myers
Police Officer, Oak Ridge Police Department (Tennessee)
Randy Myers is a speaker and founder of International COPS Ministries (www.copsministry.org), a ministry dedicated to praying for the safety and well-being of all law enforcement officers.

Sir Robin Oake
Chief Constable (Retired), Isle of Man, Chief Inspector to the Metropolitan Police and Superintendent to the Assistant Chief Constable in the Greater Manchester Police (England)
Robin Oake, a recipient of the Queen's Police Medal, is a speaker and author of *Father Forgive: The Forgotten "F" Word* and *With God on the Streets.*

Randal (Randy) Simmons

SWAT Officer (Killed in the line of duty), Los Angeles Police Department

Randal Simmons was a minister for Carson's Glory Christian Fellowship International Church (California). His legacy of service to troubled youth in his community inspired the formation of the Randal D. Simmons Outreach Foundation (www.randysimmonsswat.com/foundation), a nonprofit organization designed to serve, empower, and encourage families and individuals in underserved areas.

Robert L. Vernon

Assistant Chief of Police (Retired), Los Angeles Police Department

Bob Vernon is a speaker, writer, founder of Pointman Leadership Institute (www.pliglobal.com), offering leadership training to police forces globally, and author of *L.A. Justice: Lessons from the Firestorm* and *Character: The Foundation of Leadership*.

Larry Warner

Deputy Sheriff (Retired), Los Angeles County Sheriff's Department

Larry Warner is a speaker, author, pastor, and executive director of "b" ministry (www.b-ing.org), formed to provide spiritual direction, contemplative retreats, and holistic leadership development for pastors, ministry leaders, and church staffs. He is also an adjunct professor at Bethel Seminary in San Diego, the coauthor of *Imaginative Prayer for Youth Ministry: A Guide to Transforming Your Students' Spiritual Lives into Journey, Adventure, and Encounter*, and the author of *Journey with Jesus*.

Dave Williams
Assistant Chief of Police (Retired), Portland

Dave Williams is a speaker and the founder and chairman of Responder Life (www.responderlife.com), formed to support and strengthen the families of all first responders.

Michael "MC" Williams
Detective Sergeant, Colorado State Criminal Investigator

Michael Williams is an instructor, speaker, and national vice president of the Fellowship of Christian Peace Officers (www.fcpo.org). He is also the director of the Centurion Law Enforcement Ministry (www.thecenturionlawenforcementministry.org), a ministry created to bring officers to a saving knowledge of Christ and to equip Christian officers to grow in their faith.

Travis Yates
Police Captain, Tulsa Police Department (Oklahoma) and Team Leader with the Tulsa Police Precision Driver Training Unit

Travis Yates is a teacher, speaker, and director of Ten-Four Ministries (tenfourministries.org), and he oversees the Armor of God Project (www.vestforlife.com), a ministry that provides unequipped law enforcement officers with free ballistic vests. Travis also moderates www.policedriving.com, a website dedicated to law enforcement driving issues.

Case Files

CASE NOTES

Detectives become copious note takers, collecting information and documenting their progress along the way. The following notes refer to materials cited in our previous discussions of the evidence.

1. C. S. Lewis, *God in the Dock: Essays on Theology and Ethics* (Grand Rapids, MI: Eerdmans, 1970), 101.

2. Richard Lewontin, "Billions and Billions of Demons," review of *The Demon-Haunted World: Science as a Candle in the Dark,* by Carl Sagan, *New York Review*, January 9, 1997, 31.

3. Bart Ehrman and Mike Licona, "Biblical Evidence for the Resurrection" debate hosted by Justin Brierly, *Unbelievable?* radio program, April 16, 2011, accessed April 17, 2012, www.premierradio.org.uk/listen/ondemand.aspx?mediaid={32EC8B32-035E-4C2D-AB44-38C0210FD9FD}.

4. Judicial Council of California, *Judicial Council of California Criminal Jury Instructions*, LexisNexis Matthew Bender (official publisher of the Judicial Council Jury Instructions), CalCrim Section 101, accessed April 17, 2012, www.courts.ca.gov/partners/documents/calcrim_juryins.pdf.

5. Judicial Council of California, *Judicial Council of California Criminal Jury Instructions*, CalCrim Section 104, accessed May 16, 2012, www.courts.ca.gov/partners/documents/calcrim_juryins.pdf.

6. For more information, see www.garyhabermas.com.

7. For more information, see www.risenjesus.com.

8. Gary Habermas and Mike Licona, *The Case for the Resurrection of Jesus* (Grand Rapids, MI: Kregel, 2004), 47.

9. Judicial Council of California, *Judicial Council of California Criminal Jury Instructions*, CalCrim Section 223.

10. Judicial Council of California, *Judicial Council of California Criminal Jury Instructions*, CalCrim Section 223.

11. Judicial Council of California, *Judicial Council of California Criminal Jury Instructions*, CalCrim Section 223.

12. Gottfried Leibniz, *Philosophical Writings*, trans. and ed. G. H. R. Parkinson (London: Dent, 1973), 199.

13. Stephen Hawking, *Black Holes and Baby Universes and Other Essays* (New York: Bantam, 1993), Google eBook, chapter 7.

14. Richard Dawkins, *The God Delusion* (Boston: Houghton Mifflin, 2006), 188.

15. For more information on design inferences, refer to William A. Dembski, *The Design Inference: Eliminating Chance through Small Probabilities* (Cambridge: Cambridge University Press, 1998).

16. Stephen C. Meyer, *Signature in the Cell: DNA and the Evidence for Intelligent Design* (New York: HarperOne, 2009), 346.

17. Meyer, *Signature in the Cell*, 346.

18. Judicial Council of California, *Judicial Council of California Criminal Jury Instructions*, CalCrim Section 105.

19. Judicial Council of California, *Judicial Council of California Criminal Jury Instructions*, CalCrim Section 105.

20. Benjamin Weiser, "In New Jersey, Rules Are Changed on Witness IDs," *New York Times,* August 24, 2011, accessed April 18, 2012, www.nytimes.com/2011/08/25/nyregion/in-new-jersey-rules-changed-on-witness-ids.html.

21. Papias, quoted in Eusebius, "Church History," *Nicene and Post-Nicene Fathers*, eds. Philip Schaff and Henry Wallace (New York: Cosimo, 2007), 172.

22. Irenaeus, quoted in *The Ante-Nicene Fathers: Translations of the Writings of the Fathers down to A.D. 325,* eds. Alexander Roberts and James Donaldson, vol. 1, *The Apostolic Fathers—Justin Martyr—Irenaeus* (Buffalo: Christian Literature, 1885), 414.

23. Justin Martyr, *Dialogue with Trypho* (Wyatt North, 2012), Kindle edition, Kindle locations 2349–2351.

24. Clement of Alexandria, quoted in Eusebius, "Ecclesiastical History," *The Fathers of the Church: Eusebius Pamphili, Ecclesiastical History Books 1–5,* trans. Roy J. Deferrari (Washington, DC: Catholic University of America, 1953), 110.

25. Tal Ilan, *Lexicon of Jewish Names in Late Antiquity: Palestine 330 BCE – 200 CE* (Philadelphia: Coronet Books, 2002), 91.

26. Richard Bauckham, *Jesus and the Eyewitnesses: The Gospels as Eyewitness Testimony* (Grand Rapids, MI: Eerdmans, 2008), Kindle edition, Kindle location 1938.

27. *The God Who Wasn't There*, directed by Brian Flemming (Hollywood: Beyond Belief Media, 2005).

28. *Zeitgeist, the Movie,* directed by Peter Joseph (GMP LLC, 2007).

29. Ochoa v. Evans, 2009 U.S. Dist. LEXIS 112693 (C.D. Cal. Oct. 1, 2009).

30. William Blackstone, *Commentaries on the Laws of England,* quoted in Frederick Schauer, *Thinking Like a Lawyer: A New Introduction to Legal Reasoning* (Cambridge, MA: Harvard University, 2009), 221.

31. Bart Ehrman, *Jesus Interrupted* (New York: HarperOne, 2010), 177.

32. Geza Vermes, *The Changing Faces of Jesus* (New York: Penguin, 2002), 8.

33. Charles Burlingame Waite, *History of the Christian Religion to the Year Two Hundred* (San Diego: Book Tree, 2011), Kindle edition, Kindle locations 5080–5082.

34. Flavius Josephus, *Complete Works of Flavius Josephus: Wars of the Jews, Antiquities of the Jews, Against Apion, Autobiography,* trans. William Whiston (Boston: MobileReference), Kindle edition, Kindle locations 7243–7249.

35. Barbara Levick, *Vespasian,* Roman Imperial Biographies (New York: Routledge, 1999).

36. Adam Clarke, *Adam Clarke's Commentary on the Bible* (Grand Rapids, MI: Baker, 1983), commenting on Acts 28:31.

37. Josephus, *Complete Works of Flavius Josephus*, Kindle locations 28589–28592.

38. Kenneth Berding, *Polycarp of Smyrna's View of the Authorship of 1 and 2 Timothy, Vigiliae Christianae* 54, no. 4 (1999), 349–360.

39. F. F. Bruce, *The New Testament Documents: Are They Reliable?* (Downers Grove, IL: InterVarsity Press, 1984), Kindle edition, Kindle location 409.

40. Papias, quoted in Eusebius, "Church History," *Nicene and Post-Nicene Fathers*, eds. Philip Schaff and Henry Wallace (New York: Cosimo, 2007), 172–73.

41. Eusebius, *Ecclesiastical History*, 3.39.16, as translated by Bauckham in *Jesus and the Eyewitnesses*, 222.

42. Bauckham, *Jesus and the Eyewitnesses,* Kindle location 3072.

43. Howard I. Marshall, ed., *New Testament Interpretation: Essays on Principles and Methods* (Eugene, OR: Wipf and Stock, 2006), 155.

44. David Alan Black and David S. Dockery, *New Testament Criticism and Interpretation* (Grand Rapids, MI: Zondervan, 1991), 184.

45. Marshall, *New Testament Interpretation*, 156.

46. Black and Dockery, *New Testament Criticism and Interpretation*, 184.

47. Mentioned by Josephus, *Antiquities of the Jews* (Unabridged Books, 2011), bk. 17, chap. 5, sec. 3.

48. Albert Einstein, as quoted from his Gutkind Letter (January 3, 1954) in James Randerson, "Childish superstition: Einstein's letter makes view of religion relatively clear," *Guardian*, May 12, 2008, accessed April 25, 2012, www.guardian.co.uk/science/2008/may/12/peopleinscience.religion.

49. Robert Green Ingersoll, *Lectures of Col. R. G. Ingersoll, Latest* (Valde Books, 2009), Kindle edition, Kindle location 1319.

50. For more information, refer to Oded Borowski, *Agriculture in Iron Age Israel: The Evidence from Archaeology and the Bible* (Boston: American Schools of Oriental Research, May 1987), 7.

51. For more information about the locations where the Gospels were written, refer to Eusebius, *The History of the Church* (Neeland Media LLC, 2009), chap. VIII.

52. For more information, refer to Bauckham, *Jesus and the Eyewitnesses*, Kindle location 1113.

53. For more information, refer to Tal Ilan, *Lexicon of Jewish Names in Late Antiquity: Palestine 330 BCE–200 CE* (Philadelphia: Coronet Books, 2002).

54. Bauckham, *Jesus and the Eyewitnesses*, Kindle location 1189.

55. Shlomo Pines, *An Arabic Version of the Testimonium Flavianum and Its Implications* (Israel Academy of Sciences and Humanities: Jerusalem, 1971), Kindle edition, Kindle locations 9–10, 16.

56. Quoted in *Ante-Nicene Christian Library: Translations of the Writings of the Fathers Down to A.D. 325*, eds. Alexander Roberts and James Donaldson, vol. 9, *Irenaeus, Vol. II—Hippolytus, Vol. II—Fragments of Third Century* (Edinburgh: T & T Clark, 1870), 188.

57. Cornelius Tacitus, *Works of Cornelius Tacitus. Includes Agricola, The Annals, A Dialogue concerning Oratory, Germania and The Histories* (Boston: MobileReference, 2009), Kindle edition, Kindle locations 6393–6397.

58. "Letter from Mara Bar-Serapion to His Son," quoted in Bruce, *New Testament Documents*, Kindle locations 1684–1688.

59. Quoted in *Ante-Nicene Christian Library*, eds. Roberts and Donaldson, vol. 9, 188.

60. Origen, "Origen Against Celsus," *The Ante-Nicene Fathers*, eds. Alexander Roberts and James Donaldson, vol. 4, *Tertullian, Part Fourth; Minucius Felix; Commodian; Origen, Parts First and Second*

(Buffalo: Christian Literature, 1885), 437, 445, 455. For more information related to Origen's quotations of Phlegon, refer to www.newadvent.org/fathers/04162.htm or William Hansen, *Phlegon of Tralles' Book of Marvels,* University of Exeter Press: Exeter Studies in History (Exeter, UK: University of Exeter Press, 1997).

61. Josephus, *Antiquities of the Jews* (Unabridged Books, 2011), bk. 17, chap. 18, sec. 2, v. 1.

62. Jerry Vardaman, from an unpublished manuscript (*The Year of the Nativity: Was Jesus Born in 12 B.C.? A New Examination of Quirinius [Luke 2:2] and Related Problems of New Testament Chronology*) as cited in John McRay, *Archaeology and the New Testament* (Grand Rapids, MI: Baker Academic, 2009), Kindle edition, Kindle locations 6332–6334.

63. Sir William Ramsay, *The Bearing of Recent Discovery on the Trustworthiness of the New Testament* (Primedia eLaunch, 2011), Kindle edition, Kindle locations 3446–3448.

64. Josephus, *Complete Works of Flavius Josephus*, Kindle edition, Kindle locations 1292–1295.

65. John McRay, *Archaeology and the New Testament* (Grand Rapids, MI: Baker Academic, 2009), Kindle edition, Kindle locations 2091–2095.

66. Sir William Ramsay, *The Bearing of Recent Discovery on the Trustworthiness of the New Testament* (Primedia eLaunch, 2011), Kindle edition, Kindle locations 3630–3658.

67. Bruce, *New Testament Documents*, Kindle locations 1393–1400.

68. Shimon Gibson, *The Final Days of Jesus: The Archaeological Evidence* (New York: HarperCollins e-books, 2009), Kindle edition, Kindle location 73.

69. John McRay, *Archaeology and the New Testament* (Grand Rapids, MI: Baker Academic, 2009), Kindle edition, Kindle locations 2537–2543.

70. Gibson, *The Final Days of Jesus*, Kindle location 71.

71. McRay, *Archaeology and the New Testament*, Kindle location 1922.

72. Josephus, *Complete Works of Flavius Josephus*, Kindle edition, Kindle locations 31292–31294.

73. McRay, *Archaeology and the New Testament*, Kindle location 2820.

74. Gerald Friedlander, *The Jewish Sources of the Sermon on the Mount,* Elibron Classics (Whitefish, MT: Kessinger Publishing, LLC, 2011), 266.

75. For more information related to the "fraction" limitations of biblical archaeology, refer to Edwin Yamauchi, *The Stones and the Scripture* (Grand Rapids, MI: Baker Book House, 1981), 146–62.

76. Penn Jillette and Raymond Joseph Teller, *Penn and Teller: Bullshit!,* Season 2, Episode 11, Showtime Network (2005).

77. Sam Harris, *The End of Faith: Religion, Terror, and the Future of Reason* (New York: W.W. Norton & Company, 2005), 35.

78. "Date," Codex Sinaiticus, accessed April 12, 2012, http://codexsinaiticus.org/en/codex/date.aspx.

79. For more information about Ignatius, refer to *Early Christian Writings: The Apostolic Fathers* (London: Penguin, 1968). Kindle edition.

80. Ignatius of Antioch, *The Epistle of Ignatius to the Magnesians* (OrthodoxEbooks), Google eBook, 126.

81. Ignatius of Antioch, *The Epistle of Ignatius to the Ephesians* (OrthodoxEbooks), Google eBook, 114.

82. Ignatius of Antioch, *The Epistle of Ignatius to the Romans* (OrthodoxEbooks), Google eBook, 154.

83. Ignatius, *The Epistle of Ignatius to the Ephesians*, 114.

84. Ignatius, *The Epistle of Ignatius to the Ephesians*, 114.

85. Ignatius, *The Epistle of Ignatius to the Magnesians*, 124.

86. Ignatius, *The Epistle of Ignatius to the Ephesians*, 114.

87. Ignatius, *The Epistle of Ignatius to the Ephesians*, 114.

88. Ignatius of Antioch, "The Epistle of Ignatius to the Smyrneans," *A Collection of Gospels, Epistles, and Other Pieces Extant from the Early Christian Centuries but Not Included in the Commonly Received Canon of Scripture* (Glasgow: Thomson, 1884), 85.

89. Ignatius, *The Epistle of Ignatius to the Ephesians*, 100.

90. Ignatius, *The Epistle of Ignatius to the Magnesians*, 123.

91. Ignatius, *The Epistle of Ignatius to the Ephesians*, 105.

92. Ignatius, *The Epistle of Ignatius to the Romans*, 154.

93. Ignatius, *The Epistle of Ignatius to the Ephesians*, 113.

94. Ignatius, *The Epistle of Ignatius to the Ephesians*, 107.

95. Ignatius, *The Epistle of Ignatius to the Ephesians*, 112.

96. Ignatius of Antioch, *The Epistle of Ignatius to the Philadelphians* (OrthodoxEbooks), Google eBook, 166.

97. Ignatius, *The Epistle of Ignatius to the Ephesians*, 98.

98. Ignatius, *The Epistle of Ignatius to the Magnesians*, 128.

99. Ignatius, "The Epistle of Ignatius to the Smyrneans," 85.

100. Ignatius, *The Epistle of Ignatius to the Ephesians*, 116.

101. Ignatius, "The Epistle of Ignatius to the Smyrneans," 85.

102. Ignatius, "The Epistle of Ignatius to the Smyrneans," 85.

103. Ignatius, "The Epistle of Ignatius to the Smyrneans," 85.

104. Ignatius, "The Epistle of Ignatius to the Smyrneans," 85.

105. Ignatius, "The Epistle of Ignatius to the Smyrneans," 85.

106. Ignatius, "The Epistle of Ignatius to the Smyrneans," 85.

107. Ignatius, *The Epistle of Ignatius to the Magnesians*, 124.

108. Ignatius, *The Epistle of Ignatius to the Magnesians*, 129.

109. Ignatius, *The Epistle of Ignatius to the Ephesians*, 116.

110. Ignatius, "The Epistle of Ignatius to the Smyrneans," 85.

111. Ignatius, *The Epistle of Ignatius to the Magnesians*, 124.

112. Ignatius, *The Epistle of Ignatius to the Magnesians*, 124.

113. Ignatius, *The Epistle of Ignatius to the Magnesians*, 125.

114. Ignatius, *The Epistle of Ignatius to the Magnesians*, 125.

115. Ignatius, *The Epistle of Ignatius to the Philadelphians*, 167.

116. Ignatius, *The Epistle of Ignatius to the Romans*, 154.

117. Ignatius, *The Epistle of Ignatius to the Magnesians*, 125.

118. Ignatius, *The Epistle of Ignatius to the Philadelphians*, 167.

119. Ignatius, *The Epistle of Ignatius to the Ephesians*, 99.

120. Ignatius, *The Epistle of Ignatius to the Ephesians*, 114.

121. Ignatius, *The Epistle of Ignatius to the Ephesians*, 97.

122. Ignatius, *The Epistle of Ignatius to the Ephesians*, 108.

123. Ignatius, *The Epistle of Ignatius to the Ephesians*, 98.

124. Ignatius of Antioch, *The Epistle of Ignatius to the Trallians* (OrthodoxEbooks), Google eBook, 139.

125. Ignatius, *The Epistle of Ignatius to the Ephesians*, 116.

126. Ignatius, "Epistle of Ignatius to Polycarp," quoted in *The Ante-Nicene Fathers: Translations of the Writings of the Fathers down to A.D. 325*, eds. Alexander Roberts and James Donaldson, vol. 1, *The Apostolic Fathers—Justin Martyr—Irenaeus* (Buffalo: Christian Literature, 1885), 95.

127. Ignatius, "The Epistle of Ignatius to the Smyrneans," 86.

128. For more information about Polycarp, refer to *Early Christian Writings: The Apostolic Fathers* (London: Penguin, 1968), Kindle edition.

129. Polycarp, "The Epistle of Polycarp to the Philippians," *The Epistle to the Philippians*, ed. J. J. S. Perowne (Cambridge University Press, 1895), 26.

130. Polycarp, "The Epistle of Polycarp to the Philippians," 25.

131. Polycarp, "The Epistle of Polycarp to the Philippians," 25.

132. Polycarp, "The Epistle of Polycarp to the Philippians," 26.

133. Polycarp, "The Epistle of Polycarp to the Philippians," 25.

134. Polycarp, "The Epistle of Polycarp to the Philippians," 27.

135. Polycarp, "The Epistle of Polycarp to the Philippians," 25.

136. Polycarp, "The Epistle of Polycarp to the Philippians," 25.

137. Polycarp, "The Epistle of Polycarp to the Philippians," 26.

138. Polycarp, "The Epistle of Polycarp to the Philippians," 25.

139. Polycarp, "The Epistle of S. Polycarp," quoted in *Apostolic Fathers*, eds. J. B. Lightfoot and J. R. Harmer (Whitefish, MT: Kessinger), 95.

140. Polycarp, "The Epistle of Polycarp to the Philippians," 25.

141. Polycarp, "The Epistle of Polycarp to the Philippians," 25.

142. Polycarp, "The Epistle of Polycarp to the Philippians," 24.

143. Polycarp, "The Epistle of Polycarp to the Philippians," 24.

144. For more information about Irenaeus, see Robert M. Grant, *Irenaeus of Lyons,* The Early Church Fathers (London: Routledge, 1996).

145. For more information about Hippolytus, see Christopher Wordsworth, *St. Hippolytus and the Church of Rome in the earlier part of the third century. From the newly-discovered Philosophumena* (Charleston: Nabu Press, 2010).

146. For more information about Linus and Clement, see George Edmundson, *The Church in Rome in the First Century* (Charleston: BiblioBazaar, 2009).

147. For more information about Clement, refer to *Early Christian Writings: The Apostolic Fathers* (London: Penguin, 1968), Kindle edition.

148. Clement of Rome, "Epistle to the Corinthians," *Documents of the Christian Church*, eds. Henry Bettenson and Chris Maunder (Oxford University Press, 2011), 67.

149. Clement of Rome, *The First Epistle of Clement to the Corinthians* (Whitefish, MT: Kessinger), 12.

150. Clement, *The First Epistle of Clement to the Corinthians*, 10.

151. Clement, *The First Epistle of Clement to the Corinthians*, 27.

152. Clement, *The First Epistle of Clement to the Corinthians*, 11.

153. Clement, *The First Epistle of Clement to the Corinthians*, 11.

154. Clement, *The First Epistle of Clement to the Corinthians*, 11.

155. Clement, *The First Epistle of Clement to the Corinthians*, 11.

156. Clement, *The First Epistle of Clement to the Corinthians*, 16.

157. Clement, *The First Epistle of Clement to the Corinthians*, 22.

158. Clement, *The First Epistle of Clement to the Corinthians*, 16.

159. Clement, *The First Epistle of Clement to the Corinthians*, 7.

160. Clement, *The First Epistle of Clement to the Corinthians*, 15.

161. Clement, *The First Epistle of Clement to the Corinthians*, 10.

162. Clement, *The First Epistle of Clement to the Corinthians*, 22.

163. Clement, *The First Epistle of Clement to the Corinthians*, 14.

164. Clement, *The First Epistle of Clement to the Corinthians*, 22.

165. Clement, *The First Epistle of Clement to the Corinthians*, 14.

166. Clement, *The First Epistle of Clement to the Corinthians*, 22.

167. Clement, *The First Epistle of Clement to the Corinthians*, 22.

168. Clement, *The First Epistle of Clement to the Corinthians*, 27.

169. For more information about the first popes, see Thomas Meyrick, *Lives of the Early Popes. St. Peter to St. Silvester* (BiblioBazaar, 2009).

170. For more information about Justin Martyr, see *The Writings of Justin Martyr,* eds. Alexander Roberts and James Donaldson (Berkeley: Apocryphile Press, 2007).

171. For more information about Tatian, see Emily J. Hunt, *Christianity in the Second Century: The Case of Tatian,* Routledge Early Church Monographs (London: Routledge, 2003).

172. For more information about the early popes in North Africa, see Stephen J. Davis, *The Early Coptic Papacy: The Egyptian Church and Its Leadership in Late Antiquity,* Popes of Egypt (The American University in Cairo Press, 2005).

173. For more information about Pantaenus, see Vincent J. O'Malley, *Saints of Africa* (Huntington, IN: Our Sunday Visitor 2001).

174. For more information about Clement of Alexandria, see Philip Schaff, *Fathers of the Second Century: Hermas, Tatian, Athenagoras, Theophilus, and Clement of Alexandria,* Kindle edition.

175. For more information about Origen, see Joseph W. Trigg, *Origen,* The Early Church Fathers (London: Routledge, 1998).

176. For more information about Pamphilus, see *History of the Martyrs in Palestine: Discovered in a Very Ancient Syriac Manuscript* (Charleston: Nabu Press, 2010).

177. For more information about Eusebius of Caesarea, see Robert Van De Weyer, *Eusebius: The First Christian Historian,* Early Christian Writings (Berkhamsted, UK: Arthur James Ltd, 1997).

178. For more information about the role of the Masoretes in the transmission of the Bible, see Norman Geisler and William Nix, *General Introduction to the Bible* (Chicago: Moody, 1986).

179. Gleason Archer, *A Survey of Old Testament Introduction* (Chicago: Moody, 2011), Kindle edition, Kindle locations 473–75.

180. Bart Ehrman, from his closing statement at a debate with William Lane Craig, "Is There Historical Evidence for the Resurrection of Jesus?" held at College of the Holy Cross in Worcester, Massachusetts, on March 28, 2006, accessed April 13, 2012, www.philvaz.com/apologetics/p96.htm.

181. Clement, quoted in Eusebius, *The Ecclesiastical History* (Cambridge, MA: Harvard University, 1980), 269.

182. Clement, quoted in *Women in Religion: The Original Sourcebook of Women in Christian Thought,* eds. Elizabeth A. Clark and Herbert Richardson (New York: HarperCollins, 1996), 29. For more information related to Clement's writings, refer to Alexander Roberts, *Ante-Nicene Fathers, vol. 2, Early Church Fathers* (Grand Rapids, MI: Eerdmans, 1988).

183. Ignatius, *The Epistle of Ignatius to the Philadelphians,* 162. For more information related to Ignatius's writings, refer to Alexander Roberts, James Donaldson, and A. Cleveland Coxe, eds., *Ante-Nicene Fathers,* vol. 1, *Apostolic Fathers, Justin Martyr, Irenaeus* (Grand Rapids, MI: Eerdmans, 1950).

184. Tertullian, quoted in *The Ante-Nicene Fathers,* eds. Alexander Roberts and James Donaldson, vol. 4, *Tertullian, Part Fourth; Minucius Felix; Commodian; Origen, Parts First and Second* (Buffalo: Christian Literature, 1885), 55.

185. Cornelius Tacitus, *Works of Cornelius Tacitus. Includes Agricola, The Annals, A Dialogue concerning Oratory, Germania and The Histories* (MobileReference, 2009), Kindle edition, Kindle locations 6393–6400.